A
Philip E. Lilienthal
BOOK

The Philip E. Lilienthal imprint
honors special books
in commemoration of a man whose work
at University of California Press from 1954 to 1979
was marked by dedication to young authors
and to high standards in the field of Asian Studies.
Friends, family, authors, and foundations have together
endowed the Lilienthal Fund, which enables UC Press
to publish under this imprint selected books
in a way that reflects the taste and judgment
of a great and beloved editor.

The publisher gratefully acknowledges the generous support of the Philip E. Lilienthal Asian Studies Endowment Fund of the University of California Press Foundation, which was established by a major gift from Sally Lilienthal.

It's Madness

It's Madness

THE POLITICS OF MENTAL HEALTH IN COLONIAL KOREA

Theodore Jun Yoo

UNIVERSITY OF CALIFORNIA PRESS

University of California Press, one of the most distinguished university presses in the United States, enriches lives around the world by advancing scholarship in the humanities, social sciences, and natural sciences. Its activities are supported by the UC Press Foundation and by philanthropic contributions from individuals and institutions. For more information, visit www.ucpress.edu.

University of California Press
Oakland, California

© 2016 by The Regents of the University of California

Library of Congress Cataloging-in-Publication Data

Yoo, Theodore Jun, 1972–.
  It's madness : the politics of mental health in colonial Korea / Theodore Jun Yoo.
    p. cm.
  Includes bibliographical references and index.
  ISBN 978-0-520-28930-7 (cloth : alk. paper)—ISBN 0-520-28930-7 (cloth : alk. paper)—ISBN 978-0-520-96404-4 (ebook)—ISBN 0-520-96404-7 (ebook)
  1. Mental illness—Political aspects—Korea. 2. Mental illness—Social aspects—Korea. 3. Mental illness—Treatment—History—20th century. 4. Traditional medicine—Korea. 5. Medicine, Chinese. 6. Korea—History—Japanese occupation, 1910–1945. I. Title.
  RC451.K6Y66 2016
  362.19689009519—dc23   2015029797

Manufactured in the United States of America

25 24 23 22 21 20 19 18 17 16
10 9 8 7 6 5 4 3 2 1

In keeping with a commitment to support environmentally responsible and sustainable printing practices, UC Press has printed this book on Natures Natural, a fiber that contains 30% post-consumer waste and meets the minimum requirements of ANSI/NISO Z39.48–1992 (R 1997) (*Permanence of Paper*).

To My Parents,
Min Chul Yoo and Suk Za Yoo

CONTENTS

Acknowledgments ix

Introduction 1

1 · Forms of Madness 14

2 · Madness Is... 45

3 · A Touch of Madness: The Cultural Politics of Emotion 77

4 · Madness as a Social Epidemic 109

Conclusion: A Method to the Madness 142

Notes 155
Glossary 185
Bibliography 197
Index 213

Photographs follow page 76.

ACKNOWLEDGMENTS

In writing this book, I have benefited enormously from the help of many people and institutions. To be able to finally thank family, friends, colleagues, mentors, and students who have contributed in one way or another to the life of this book is truly gratifying.

My first and deepest thanks must go to my sister, ChaeRan Yoo Freeze, for her guidance and friendship. She read countless drafts of the entire manuscript and offered numerous suggestions.

I express my deepest gratitude to my mentors Nancy Abelmann, Bruce Cumings, Takashi Fujitani, John Lie, and Tetsuo Najita for their advice, intellectual generosity, and professional support over the years.

There is a long list of friends who assisted me in this work or inspired me with their work over many years. I am especially indebted to Taeyoon Ahn, Tomoko Akami, Jinsoo An, Noelani Arista, David Armiak, Charles Armstrong, Moon-im Baek, Charles Bergquist, Michael Berry, Antoinette Burton, Peter Carroll, Grace Chae, Hsin-Chieh Chang, Paul Chang, Sarah Chee, John Cho, Hee Jung Choi, Hyaeweol Choi, Kyeonghee Choi, Kyung-ho Choi, Kelly Chong, Hae Yeon Choo, Jennifer Chun, Jinjoo Chung, Rakkoo Chung, Steven Chung, Nicole Constable, Patricia Crosby, Lisa Kim Davis, Dan Devitt, Prasenjit Duara, Alexis Dudden, Henry Em, Sujin Eom, Stephen Epstein, Olga Fedorenko, John Feffer, Paul Fischer, Magnus Fiskesjo, James Flowers, Gregory Freeze, Sabine Frühstück, Jonathan Glade, Kathryn Goldfarb, Judy Han, Nicholas Harkness, Martin Hart-Landsberg, Margot Henriksen, Todd Henry, Heather Hindman, Ji Hyung Hong, Theodore Hughes, Jang Wook Huh, Merose Hwang, Susan Hwang, Myungho Hyun, Chong-myong Im, Kelly Jeong, Jungwon Jin, Jin Su Joo, EuyRyung Jun, Jiyeon Kang, Yoonjung Kang, Bohyeong Kim, Changwook Kim, Charles

Kim, Chi-Hoon Kim, Kim Chul, Chung-kang Kim, Kim Dongno, Eleana Kim, Eunshil Kim, Hyo Shin Kim, Hyunjoo Kim, Jaeeun Kim, Jin Gong Kim, Jinwon Kim, Jisoo Kim, Joy Kim, Jungwon Kim, Kwang Il Kim, Kyu Hyun Kim, Monica Kim, Nan Kim, Kim Puja, Stephanie Kim, Suk-Young Kim, Suzy Kim, Taeyoun Kim, Geun Koh, Sho Konishi, James Kraft, Toshihide Kuroke, Jong Bum Kwon, June Hee Kwon, Tong Lam, Euna Lee, Helen Lee, Hyoduk Lee, Hyun-jeong Lee, Jinhee Lee, Jin-kyung Lee, Katherine Lee, Kathleen Lee, Kwang-cheol Lee, Jae-kyung Lee, Lee Kyounghoon, Namhee Lee, Se Hwa Lee, Sharon Lee, Shirley Lee, Sinwoo Lee, Sohl Lee, Taeku Lee, Yoonkyung Lee, Yu Jung Lee, Nicole Restrick-Levit, Tingting Li, Jie-Hyun Lim, Juncheol Lim, Sung Sook Lim, Sungyun Lim, Hsiang-Kwang Liu, Roald Maliangkay, Kimberly McKee, Mark McNally, Louise McReynolds, Jenny Medina, Marcie Middlebrooks, Jeewon Min, Seungsook Moon, Tessa Morris-Suzuki, Elinor Najita, Hwasook Nam, Laura Nelson, Soung-suk Noh, Arissa Oh, Hye-ri Oh, Se-Mi Oh, Youjeong Oh, Robert Oppenheim, Hyung-il Pai, Young-Gyung Paik, Albert Park, Chunwoong Park, Eugene Park, Euna Park, Eunhee Park, Hye Gyong Park, Joowon Park, Kwang-Hyung Park, Saeyoung Park, Seoyoung Park, Sunyoung Park, Young-a Park, Young Shin Park, Jooyeon Rhee, Fernando Rojas, Seung Yeon Sang, Cedarbough Saeji, Andre Schmid, Mi-Ryong Shim, Shin Hyeon-gi, Jaran Shin, Jeongsoo Shin, Josie Sohn, Deborah Solomon, Felix Song, Jee Eun Song, Jesook Song, Nianshen Song, Song Younok, Michael Sprunger, Jae-Jung Suh, Serkbae Suh, Stefan Tanaka, Bonnie Tilland, Yuma Totani, Jun Uchida, Ji-heum Uh, Seong Gee Um, Aniko Varga, Erica Vogel, Anne Walthall, Wensheng Wang, Aida Wong, Hyo Kyung Woo, Meredith Woo, Myungji Yang, Sunyoung Yang, Christine Yano, Lisa Yoneyama, Hyunkyung Yu, Chong-ae Yu, Herbert Ziegler, and Dafna Zur.

My heartfelt thanks to all those who participated in the Social Science Research Council Korean Studies Dissertation and Book Manuscript workshops, my colleagues and students at the University of Hawaii at Manoa, and Susan Carlson for helping me out with administrative duties.

My thanks to an extraordinary group of colleagues in the history of East Asian medicine and the Institute of Science, Technology, and Society (STS) who have provided many years of encouragement and stimulation. Above all, I would like to thank Susan Burns, Kevin Chang, Hsui-fen Chen, Howard Chiang, Eun Kyung Choi, John DiMoia, Akira Hashimoto, Sang-ik Hwang, Hoi-eun Kim, Ock-joo Kim, Sang-Hyun Kim, Sonja Kim, Tae Ho Kim, Junko Kitanaka, Jen-der Lee, Jieun Lee, Shangjen Li, Izumi Nakayama,

Jinkyung Park, Yunjae Park, Gyu-hwan Sin, Soyoung Suh, Akihito Suzuki, Wen-ji Wang, Yuchuan Wu, Jui-Sung Yang, In-seok Yeo, and Naofumi Yoshida.

I also appreciate the feedback I received at conferences and seminars where I presented parts of this research in various iterations. For their suggestions, I thank the participants at the Association of Asian Studies Conference, the Fifth World Congress of Asian Psychiatry, the Sixth East Asia History of Medicine Conference, Academia Sinica, the STS Institute at National Yangming University, the History Department at National Chengchi University, the East Asian Studies Colloquium at Brandeis University, Underwood College at Yonsei University, the Comparative Society and Culture Workshop at Yonsei University, the Center for Korean Studies at Columbia University, the Center for Asian Studies at the University of California, Santa Barbara, the Center for Korean Studies at Australian National University, the Center for Korean Studies at the University of California, Berkeley, and the Intersections with Science, Medicine, and Technology in Korea Workshop at State University of New York, Binghamton. I am particularly grateful to the faculty at the Korean Languages and Literature Department at Yonsei University for pushing me to write a chapter on emotions. I am grateful to Hyunhwa Kang and Ji-yeon Yang for looking over my romanization.

I am happy to acknowledge the generous support by the CIES-Fulbright for a Senior Research Scholar Award, which financed one year of fieldwork in Korea (2009–10), and the University Research Council at the University of Hawaii at Manoa for funding shorter trips to Korea and Japan as well as academic conferences. I want to also thank Lee Jae-kyung, the former director at the Korean Women's Institute at Ewha Womans University, for providing me office space and a congenial environment to conduct my research in Seoul during my sabbatical leave. Librarians and archivists at Ewha Womans University Library, Yonsei University Library, Seoul National University Library, the National Library of Korea, the National Digital Library of Korea, the Library of Congress, and Hamilton Library at the University of Hawaii at Manoa were very accommodating and helpful.

Portions of chapter 4 will appear in an edited volume provisionally titled *Intersections with Science, Medicine, and Technology in Korea*. I thank the coeditors, Sonja M. Kim and Michael Pettid, for granting me permission to reuse this material.

I owe my editor Reed Malcolm for his guidance and enthusiasm for this project. I want to thank Stacy Eisenstark and Jessica Moll at the University of

California Press for shepherding the manuscript into print. Elisabeth Magnus merits special recognition for skillfully editing the manuscript.

The anonymous readers for the University of California Press and an editorial board member for the University of California Press provided me with detailed and incisive comments to make this a much stronger book. Any flaws and interpretations in my work are of own doing.

I would also like to thank my extended family in Seoul and Boston for their years of support and encouragement. In particular, I want to thank my in-laws Eung Sil Lee and Sung Bum Hong for taking good care of me whenever I visit Seoul. I want to express my gratitude to my partner Juyeon, who was a patient listener and thoughtful adviser throughout the writing of this book. She certainly had to put up with my "mad" work habits.

Finally, to my dear parents Min Chul Yoo and Suk Za Yoo, who worked for thirty years in Ethiopia and continue to lovingly support my work and me, this book is dedicated to you.

Korean names and terms have been transliterated according to the Revised Romanization of Korean system, except for words with commonly accepted alternative spellings (e.g., *chaebol*, Seoul, Kim). I have kept the last name first in referring to Korean and Japanese names, unless they have their own romanized names. All translations are mine unless otherwise indicated. As always, any errors or shortcomings in this study are entirely my own.

Introduction

> Illness is the night-side of life, a more onerous citizenship. Everyone who is born holds dual citizenship, in the kingdom of the well and in the kingdom of the sick. Although we all prefer to use only the good passport, sooner or later each of us is obliged, at least for a spell, to identify ourselves as citizens of that other place.
>
> SUSAN SONTAG, *Illness as Metaphor*

> While a stranger is present before us, evidence can arise of his possessing an attribute that makes him different from others in the category of persons available for him to be, and of a less desirable kind—in the extreme, a person who is quite thoroughly bad, or dangerous, or weak. He is thus reduced in our minds from a whole and usual person to a tainted, discounted one. Such an attribute is a *stigma*, especially when its discrediting effect is very extensive.
>
> ERVING GOFFMAN, *Stigma*

ON FEBRUARY 11, 2008, a fifty-nine-year-old arsonist set ablaze the Sungnyemun (Namdaemun, Gate of Exalted Ceremonies), a six-hundred-year-old gate and National Treasure Number 1 in Seoul. Reactions ranged from sadness to anger; some even compared the incident to the infamous 9/11 attacks on the United States.[1] Official reports suggested that the arsonist, an elderly former fortune-teller, suffered from *hwabyeong* (fire illness), which had reached its boiling point after the government refused to respond to his complaints over a land dispute. Rather than investigating his mental state, the media focused primarily on the social factors that led to his *bunno* (rage) and "misguided eruption." Only a small dissenting minority urged fellow Koreans to consider mental illness as the root cause of not only this tragedy but also other social ills plaguing contemporary Korean society. The public, however, expressed little interest in medical or psychological explanations; rather, it treated the arsonist's alleged *hwabyeong* with shame and disgust. Within days the public discourse shifted to a national debate about how to preserve and protect cultural heritage sites.[2]

Mental illness remains one of the most elusive and neglected topics in Korean history. As in most Asian countries, severe social ostracism, shame, and fear of jeopardizing marriage prospects induce families to conceal the mentally ill behind closed doors. Although the fledging South Korean government passed the Mental Practice Act in 1951, in the middle of an epic civil war, in an effort to create community-based rehabilitation programs and reduce stigmatization, it was only in 1995 that policies to this end were more fully and specifically developed in the form of the Mental Health Act, which went into force as Law No. 5133 in 1996.[3] However, a report on the mental health system in South Korea conducted by the World Health Organization in 2006 specifically noted that "social stigma against mental illness and a strong attitude of 'not in my backyard' [held by] by many of the people in Korea makes it difficult to reintegrate people with mental disorders into the community."[4]

The practice of controlling "deviant behavior" by sequestering in mental institutions and prisons those individuals deemed a "threat to society" is a relatively recent phenomenon in Korea, first introduced during the Japanese colonial period (1910–45). These practices became considerably more prevalent in the 1980s, when nuclear families could no longer provide sufficient care for their mentally ill. In South Korea, as opposed to other Organisation for Economic Co-operation and Development (OECD) nations, where an individual's "free will is strongly protected," the Mental Health Act of 1995 stipulates that the patient must relinquish his or her rights to family members or state agencies. This clause has contributed to a large percentage of "involuntary admissions" to mental health facilities.[5] For example, in a high-profile immigration case in Canada in 2009, the Immigration and Refugee Board legally granted the defendant Oh Mi-sook (O Mi-suk), a South Korean native diagnosed with paranoid schizophrenia, and her daughter refugee status on the grounds that the former was "persecuted not by a church representative [as she claimed], but by a South Korean health care system that mistreats mentally ill patients." The *Vancouver Sun* also reported that a federal judge ruled in favor of Oh because South Korea "illegally and forcefully hospitalizes mentally ill patients, refuses to discharge patients, forges medical records, and unreasonably limits patients' correspondence" as well as resorting to "frequent violence."[6]

Because of the stigma and the negative perceptions of mental illness, the Mental Health Act, which aimed to promote early discharge from hospitals and to expand rehabilitative services, has turned out to be fraught with controversy. Though the trend among OECD nations has been to shorten hospital stays for mentally ill patients, South Korea has bucked that trend, ranking highest in the number of days a patient is hospitalized for psychiatric care—that is, 116 days in 2011, compared to the average of 27.6 days in other member nations.[7] Because there is neither a recovery model of care in South Korea nor a desire among Koreans to integrate the chronically ill back into society, the afflicted tend to hide their disorders out of fear of being hospitalized, abused, or stigmatized.

The facts on the ground are sobering. According to the "Mental Disorder Status Epidemiological Investigation" conducted by the Ministry of Health and Welfare in 2011, mental illness is a staggering national problem, not simply a shameful family secret: one in six Koreans experienced mental illness in 2011. On the basis of a face-to-face in-depth survey of 6,022 participants nationwide aged eighteen years old and older, the study concluded that roughly 5.7 million Koreans were currently experiencing some form of mental illness. Moreover 27.6 percent of the "entire population experienced mental health problems more than once in their lives."[8] Professor Jo Maeng-je, who oversaw this research project, suggested that this mental health crisis was precipitated by "modern society's hectic schedule, fierce competition, economic difficulties, and other causes of extreme stress." The problem, the ministry added, was compounded by inadequate legal protections and privacy rights for such patients: in the absence of legislation against discrimination (especially in the workplace), only 15.3 percent of those with a formal diagnosis sought mental health treatment. Koreans preferred to conceal their symptoms rather than risk ruining their careers with a record of psychiatric treatment.[9]

The report also disclosed that South Korea had the highest suicide rate among the thirty OECD countries in 2012, outpacing Hungary and Japan.[10] In the most recent survey completed in 2014, South Korea still has the highest suicide rate of 29.1 per 100,000 people among member nations of the OECD, eclipsing Hungary and Japan. This rate is also more than twice the OECD average of 12.5 per 100,000 suicides.[11] Sociologists and psychiatrists have described this sudden spate of suicides since the late 1990s as a by-product of South Korea's breakneck industrialization, which has created enormous expectations and pressures to succeed in this hypercompetitive society but at the same time has "left an especially large crack that the poor and disabled populations slip through even more often."[12]

In recent years, a string of high-profile suicides have captured national headlines, prompting harsh criticism of the South Korean government. The list of public figures who have taken their lives includes Bak Yong-o (the former chairman of the Doosan *chaebol* or conglomerate); Roh Moo-Hyun (the former president of South Korea, who killed himself by jumping off a cliff in 2009); celebrities such as the affable Choe Jin-sil and the talented Bak Yong-ha; and a number of faculty and students at the elite Korea Advanced Institute of Science and Technology (KAIST). Critics charge that the authorities have failed to fund and implement effective prevention programs or enact specific mental health acts to assist those with psychological disorders, which have been cited as the most common cause for deaths by suicide.

In response to public criticism, Seoul City partnered with Samsung Life Insurance and the advertising agency Cheil Worldwide in September 2012 to create an "interactive bridge"—complete with high-tech installed sensors and LCD-lit panels—on the guardrails of the Mapo Bridge, one of the most notorious suicide spots in Seoul. The panels would illuminate short inspirational messages and pictures compiled by psychologists and social workers to encourage pedestrians to think twice before hurling themselves off the bridge. Despite garnering the Grand CLIO Award at the 2013 CLIO Awards, as well as a Gold in the Public Relations category and a Silver in the Engagement category, the "Bridge of Life" campaign has failed as an effective deterrent: indeed, suicide rates have quadrupled since the installment of the interactive features.[13] In fact, critics complain that the trite sayings that flash on the panels, like "The most shining moment of your life is yet to come," only aggravate the situation, intensifying an individual's sense of shame or anger. More important, the campaign neglects to address the core problem—the profound social stigma of seeking help from mental health professionals, which leaves suicide as the only conceivable escape from one's problems.

Shocked by the rising suicide rates, the novelist Young-Ha Kim recently penned an op-ed piece in the *New York Times* claiming that he would never write another suicide-filled novel like *Naneun nareul pagoehal gwolliga itda* (I have the right to destroy myself), which had won him critical acclaim in

1995, because he was "too afraid of inspiring others to kill themselves." Kim also highlights another problem besides the stigma of seeking psychiatric help and contending with rumors about medical records: some 60 percent of people who attempt suicide in Korea suffer from depression.[14] He points out that, despite the medical discourse, many South Koreans still hold outdated views of psychological illness and believe that "when someone is suicidal he simply lacks a strong will to live" and is weak. Equally troubling, in his view, is that there is "little sympathy or interest in probing below the surface."[15]

Despite the alarming suicide statistics, the South Korean government has spent only 10 billion *won* (US$1 = W 1,062, approximately $9,416,195) on suicide prevention programs compared with the over 1.8 trillion *won* (approximately $1,694,915,254) it has poured into campaigns to prevent traffic accidents in the past five years. The state has also paid little attention to social and demographic patterns, often neglecting campaigns in rural areas and especially among the elderly, who are considered a "high-risk" group.[16] While party members at the National Assembly have demanded more aggressive policies such as increasing health insurance benefits, the state has yet to fund significant studies to "identify key stressors and supports in the individual's social environment." These would include "the role of religion, family, and other social networks in providing emotional, instrumental, and informational support," a key framework outlined by the recently revised fifth edition of the *Diagnostic and Statistical Manual of Mental Disorders (DSM-5)* for "accessing information about cultural features of an individual's mental health problem and how it relates to a social and cultural content and history."[17] For example, when the father of Yi Teuk (aka Bak Jeong-su), a member of the popular K-pop band Super Junior, murdered his own parents (both of whom were suffering from dementia) and then committed suicide, the public only later learned about the stresses that may have contributed to his actions: he was a primary caretaker for his parents, divorced, financially strapped, and suffering from major depression. In addition, some argued that the pressures of conforming to the Confucian principle of filial piety—still the bedrock of Korean society—could have triggered Yi Teuk's father to commit such a gruesome act of murder and suicide.[18]

A recent article in the *New York Times* echoed similar observations about the specific nature of Korean mental illness: "Koreans—while almost obsessively embracing Western innovations ranging from smartphones to the Internet to cosmetic surgery—have largely resisted Western psychotherapy for their growing anxieties, depression and stress."[19] This stiff resistance to

Western medicalized approaches to mental illness and preference for traditional, "folk" interpretations (such as "fire illness") is embedded in a long history that, as this book will demonstrate, is entwined with the legacy of Japanese colonialism and Korea's dramatic encounter with modernity.

THE HISTORY OF MADNESS, MENTAL ILLNESS, AND PSYCHIATRY

The history of madness, mental illness, and psychiatry has developed into a vibrant field of inquiry, but one that lacks a consensus about the most basic terms and approaches. As one recent article has inquired, "Is madness [a] medical disease, problems in living, or social labeling of deviance?"[20] Are *mad* and *mentally ill* simply catch-all terms for a broad swath of people whose "manner of behavior [is] peculiar enough to be publicly disturbing at any given time"?[21] How should historians approach a topic that is so highly subjective and contentious, often eliciting radically different interpretations and narratives?[22]

To legitimize the field with some semblance of historical "objectivity," one dominant approach has been to treat "madness" as a brain disease or illness, relying on a biomedical model of psychiatry. This model offers biologically derived explanations for specific mental disorders, which are allegedly organic and present in all societies. Accepting the scientific authority of the American Psychiatric Association, for instance, some rely on its now famous *DSM*, first published in 1952, which delineates, categorizes and quantifies four hundred mental disorders. Already in its fifth edition (published in 2013), the *DSM* is nearly universally employed by clinicians and researchers in North American and European psychiatry.

Historians of psychiatry who accept the fundamental premises of the biomedical model have shaped their narratives around notions of disease and illness. In his study *The Mentally Ill in America: A History of Their Care and Treatment from Colonial Times* (first published in 1937), Albert Deutsch insisted that mental illness had "always existed among mankind" but had only recently been understood as a disease. His teleological account traced the "long road upward" from "primitive" understandings of madness as demoniacal possession and witchcraft to modern conceptions of mental illness as a medical disease.[23] Deutsch's journalistic exposé of the "evils of institutional care" contended that the march toward progress was not yet complete.[24]

In recent years, Edward Shorter has become the most vocal proponent of the biomedical model, firmly asserting the fundamental "truth" that mental disorders are organic and "real."[25] Dismissive of older "biopsychosocial models of illness" (i.e., Freudian psychoanalysis) as outdated "dinosaur ideologies" of the past, he exuberantly asserts that only "the biological approach to psychiatry—treating mental illness as a genetically influenced disorder of brain chemistry—has been a smashing success."[26] Thus his history of Western psychiatry highlights specific milestones in biological psychiatry. He focuses on what he deems "real psychotic disorders," such as schizophrenia and bipolar psychosis (manic depression), and on the achievements of scientists and physicians such as Wilhelm Griesinger, Emil Kraepelin, Heinz Lehman, and Robert Spitzer—all of whom practiced "authentic science."[27] For Shorter, culture has proven to be a pitfall for science: "fashionable trends" such as psychoanalysis and therapeutic thinking have been especially costly detours. To emphasize his views, he invokes Hans Eysenck's observation in 1985: "All sciences have to pass through an ordeal by quackery. Chemistry had to slough off the fetters of alchemy. The brain sciences had to disengage themselves from the tenets of phrenology.... Psychology and psychiatry, too will have to abandon the pseudo-science of psychoanalysis ... and undertake the arduous task of transforming their discipline into a genuine science."[28]

Critics of a biological approach to psychiatry not only challenge its claim to scientific objectivity but also reject the purported "benignity of psychiatric enterprises." In an effort to "demedicalize" mental illness, Michel Foucault, Erving Goffman, R. D. Laing, and Thomas Szasz, whose writings galvanized the antipsychiatry movement in the 1960s, began to explore the social, cultural, and economic contexts of mental illness rather than isolating it as purely a "biological fact." Each began to expose the pernicious ways in which psychiatry has functioned as an extension of the state.[29] In contrast to Deutsch, Thomas Szasz, an outspoken critic of modern psychiatry, rejected the very notion of mental illness in his controversial work *The Myth of Mental Illness: Foundations of a Theory of Personal Conduct*: "Strictly speaking ... disease or illness can affect only the body. Hence there can be no such thing as mental illness. The term 'mental illness' is a metaphor."[30] According to Eric J. Dammann, Szasz defined *disease* in purely pathological terms—that is, as "a structural or functional abnormality of the cells, tissues, organs, or body." Disease was something that one had. In the absence of such bodily abnormalities, Szasz argued, psychiatric diagnoses were in fact social constructs, depending on the prevailing currents of the day.[31] While a physical disease could exist independently from society, psychiatric diagnoses, according to Szasz, "depend upon and vary with the educational, economic, religious, social, and political character of the individual and the society in which it occurs."[32] Some critics of the biomedical model have pointed to the history of homosexuality and its erroneous diagnosis as a "disease," or gendered views of mental illness, as evidence of importance of the social context.[33] Szasz also suggested that "what people now call mental illnesses are for the most part *communications* expressing unacceptable ideas, often framed, moreover in an unusual idiom."[34] The refusal to grant agency to the mentally ill, Szasz argued, has led to coercive treatments (from incarceration to mandatory hospital visits) that grant psychiatrists unjustified state-sanctioned power.[35]

The history of psychiatry as a policing profession found its sharpest articulation in Foucault's *Madness and Civilization: A History of Insanity in the Age of Reason* (1964). According to Foucault, the genesis of psychiatry marked an unwelcome intervention in the "undifferentiated experiences" of the mad, who before that could roam the countryside with liberty. Relegated to institutions such as the hospital or asylum (like lepers of the past) starting in the seventeenth century, the mad were now doubly "confined" in these new spaces and in their labels as "insane." In his words, "Confinement, that massive phenomenon, the signs of which are found all across eighteenth-century Europe, is a police matter."[36] It provided the perfect cover to discipline any challenge to the conventional bourgeois order. The hospital and the asylum were similar to other modern "total" institutions, such as prisons, factories, and schools, which Foucault viewed as hardly therapeutic and as deliberately designed to confine those who were economically unproductive or deviant. Underscoring the difficulties in standardizing psychiatric diagnoses of bizarre and incomprehensible behaviors and the creation of arbitrary labels, Foucault, Szasz, and others have emphasized the "moral normalizing function" of institutionalized psychiatry and its pernicious effects.

Drawing on the framework of social control, a wave of sociologists and social historians such as Robert Castel, Klaus Doerner, Andrew Scull, and David Rothman began to reexamine the causes and manifestations of distress and mental disorder.[37] Their important studies continued to raise troubling questions about the connivance of the psychiatric profession with the state, the social utility of incarceration, the quick adoption of untested therapies (e.g., shock treatment), and the social labeling of abnormal behavior. More recently, scholars such as German Berrios and Allan Horowitz have carefully analyzed the very categories of psychopathology used in Continental, British, and American psychiatry and the biomedical biases embedded in the *DSM,* which reduces mental disorders to discrete "biological markers" and clinical diagnoses, ignoring social and cultural contexts as important variables.[38]

These studies have stressed the need for recognizing the cultural specificity of psychiatric categories and what Karen Nakamura has described as the "complex interactions among individuals, their illnesses, and the larger social contexts in which these are all embedded." Nakamura's study of mental illness in Japan demonstrates how behaviors and ideas that "might have been tolerated in rural environments where the predominant form of social existence was the extended family or clan" were distilled through a biomedical filter and relabeled "as aberrant and dangerous."[39] Roy Porter, in his *Madness: A Brief History,* also explores how diagnoses of insanity, while they may have some basis in psychological abnormality, are always filtered through the cultural context of the times.[40] Likewise, studies conducted by Frantz Fanon and then later historians of colonial psychiatry such as Richard Keller, Waltraud Ernst, and Jonathan Sadowsky have shown the limits to a single approach to mental illness, given cross-cultural differences. They have highlighted how institutionalized sanctioned discourses and biopolitical agendas in colonial medicine could profoundly "overdetermine" many symptoms and diagnoses, depriving patients of the authorship of their own illness experience.[41]

The lens of culture has also provided a framework for cultural anthropologists to explore the diversity of mental illness in different societies, in stark contrast to the aforementioned biomedical model, which automatically assumes mental disturbance to be a biological given and constant cross-culturally. In her important study on schizophrenia in rural Ireland, Nancy Scheper-Hughes examined madness among bachelor farmers as a social process—"a manifestation of a disease between an individual and his milieu"—which resulted from the disintegration of rural Irish family life after the collapse of the agrarian economy.[42] Anthropologists have also questioned the diagnostic categories of the *DSM,* which were derived from data gathered almost exclusively from North American and European populations rather than incorporating other cultural groups in non-Western societies. According to Arthur Kleinman, this diagnostic classification system is a "category fallacy" that reifies the diagnostic categories of the West and projects them "onto patients in another culture, where those categories lack coherence and their validity has not been established."[43] In other words, the mechanistic understandings of mental illness in Western societies differ remarkably from the meaning-laden analysis of culture-bound syndromes in non-Western societies. These observations have prompted anthropologists like Kleinman to advocate for a more reflexive cross-cultural psychiatry that is multidisciplinary in its approach and that views culture as a core feature of human biology. This approach recognizes traditional culture-bound understandings of mental illness that privilege somatic rather than psychological symptoms, such as emotionally induced madness in traditional Chinese medicine, as well as causation by demons and spirits in folk culture.

In contrast to this rich literature—as contentious as it may be—there is a dearth of studies on the history of psychiatry in Korea. The works of three prominent and respected South Korean psychiatrists, Yi Bu-yeong, Kim Gwang-il, and Min Seong-gil, were some of the first to address the subject, providing foundational knowledge about the field.[44] Their research inspired a cohort of doctoral students at Seoul National University and Yonsei University respectively to write several important dissertations and articles on the history of mental illness and psychiatric care in Korea.[45] In particular, Yeo In-seok's institutional history of psychiatry at Severance Hospital and Min Seong-gil's biography of Charles McLaren have shed light on missionary psychiatry and their humanistic approaches.[46] Only recently, however, have cultural historians and literary scholars such as Yi Su-yeong and Jeong Chang-gwon begun to undertake research on this neglected topic. Their works have focused on madness in literature, local perceptions of disability, and the social origins of psychiatric disorders.[47] Over the years, a number of scholars have expressed reservations about writing a history of psychiatry in colonial Korea because of the paucity of sources. Unlike the Hôpital de la Salpêtrière in France or various hospitals and municipal archives in Japan, which house detailed patient records, the relative dearth of materials (even court records or police documents) in Korea has often led to frustrating dead ends.

This study attempts to trace the "genealogy of madness" by analyzing how Korean society sought to make sense of behaviors that were unusual, frightening, or bizarre. It imagines different encounters with "madness" as a process of layering that created a palimpsest of memory: inscriptions of new understandings, which partially effaced yet never fully erased older ones. Traditional views of "madness," which remained tenacious, disruptive, and conflictive, constantly bled through the more modern layers even as medicalized language, systems, and ideologies began to take hold. By the end of the Japanese colonial period, an amalgam of ideas from traditional Korean folk culture, Chinese traditional medicine, and modern psychiatry emerged. Thus it is no surprise that even today one can find "fire illness" (*hwabyeong*) as a "cultural syndrome"—specific to Koreans and Korean Americans—in the list of psychological disorders in the *DSM-5*.[48] The inclusion of this term, as will be discussed later, reveals the many layers of the palimpsest: a folk understanding of anger fused with the Chinese medical concept of fire as a pathogenic agent and conceptualized within both a biomedical framework (modern psychiatric categories of anger, anxiety, and major depressive disorders) and a psychosocial context (especially gendered life problems). "Treatments" also reflect the multiple layers of history: shamanistic rites, Chinese medicines, and modern psychotropic medicines. Even if one cannot write the kind of history undertaken by Western scholars because of the paucity of sources, available resources (such as government surveys, hospital records, autobiographies, newspaper articles, and novels) provide glimpses of how the multilayered narratives of the palimpsest were formed.

To trace this genealogy, chapter 1 examines the impact of Chinese traditional medicine and its holistic approach to treating madness as well as the resilient history of folk illness and its explanations for inappropriate and dangerous behaviors. The persistent tendency in Korean society to somatize symptoms as culture-bound maladies or to explain disturbing behavior as spiritual and moral failings reflects the resilience of traditional understandings of mental illness.

Chapter 2 addresses the emergence of clinical psychiatry as a discipline, the establishment of the first mental ward under Japanese colonial rule in 1913, and the institutional treatment of mental illness. In particular, it examines how the Japanese approach to patients changed from treating them as subjects of care to treating them as objects of study. As custodial aspirations for patients diminished, medical staff increasingly focused solely on diagnosis (according to an adopted Krapelinian nosology) and research with the creation of a university psychiatric clinic. The chapter also examines how Christian missionaries sought to combine religion and medicine to treat mentally ill patients under their care, especially at the new Severance Hospital in Seoul.

Chapter 3 shifts the focus from medical discourses to interpretations of culture-bound emotional states that Koreans have viewed as specific to their interpersonal relationships, social experiences, and local contexts. It will examine how Korean society has attributed anomalous behaviors to emotional states gone awry: for instance, one's lack of *jeong* (emotional attachment), pent-up *han* (resentment), or absence of *nunchi* (tact) that provoked excessive *hwa* (anger) or *suchi* (shame). Even as new medical language began to creep into cultural explanations, traditional idioms remained resilient. Thus new categories began to emerge, such as *u-ul* (depression) + *jeung* (syndrome). This phenomenon will be illustrated in contemporary cultural productions such as literature, film, and performances during court hearings.

Chapter 4 explores the discourse of mental illness as social pathology under Japanese colonial rule. In contrast to earlier periods, colonial authorities resorted to modern forms of surveillance (what Michel Foucault terms "bio-power") as they sought to regulate public health. In part, they utilized researchers (from folklorists to psychiatrists, demographers to medical doctors) to conduct studies about the life processes of the Korean people. For the first time, surveys and studies of Korean mental health, crime, genetic illnesses, and other topics proliferated in both the private and state sectors. Chapter 4 examines a wide range of social and institutional discourses featuring new nosological and gendered labels such as "hysteric" and "neurotic" and applying psychiatric diagnoses to bizarre, disturbing, or abnormal behaviors. It explores ways in which the popular press linked mental illness with violent crime. It also examines reactions to suicide, especially the cultural, political-legal, medical, and socioeconomic reasons offered by assorted discourses to explain why people killed themselves. Many of these discourses sought to explain how mental and emotional distress caused by physical, environmental, social, and moral factors could drive a person to suicide, challenging traditional views of suicide as a voluntary act. The chapter explores how depictions and explanations of madness varied with gender and how social stressors such as early marriage, male infidelity, financial losses, unrequited love, and physical illness were alleged to trigger suicidal tendencies. It also shows how the pathologization of deviant behaviors as neurological disorders contributed to a broader discourse on suicide as a measure of social health, the regulation of which was placing people's lives under increasing scrutiny.

The epilogue analyzes a sensational murder case in the 1930s to shed light on the intersection between scientific knowledge and the social imperatives of a colonized state that sought to control unruly elements of the population. It illustrates the impact of new psychiatric discourses on everyday social relations as well as the difficulties of supplanting indigenous beliefs and practices.

By examining the critical years when mental health became defined as a medical and social problem, this study investigates a new "rhetoric of care" and the processes by which standards of normality operated. It provides a broader historical perspective for what contemporaries considered to be a crisis: an epidemic of madness in modernizing Korean society under Japanese colonial rule.

ONE

Forms of Madness

[Huang] Di: Someone suffers from anger and craziness; how does this disease emerge?
Qi Bo: It emerges from the yang.
[Huang] Di: The yang? How can it let a person become crazy?
Qi Bo: As for the yang qi, because [its flow] was suddenly cut off and because [this blockage] is difficult to open, one tends to become angry. The disease is called "yang recession."
Huangdi Neijing Suwen (Inner canon of the Yellow Emperor, basic questions)

Treating mental illness: Hire a blind person ... [to] strike the patient with a peach tree branch.
MURAYAMA CHIJUN, *Chōsen no kishin* (Ghosts of Korea)

IN THE FIRST CHAPTER of the *Dong-ui bogam* (A treasury of Eastern medicine), one of the first encyclopedias on Korean traditional medicine, printed during the Joseon period (1392–1910), the author, Heo Jun (1539–1615), describes a case diagnosed by the famous Chinese physician Master Zhang Congzheng (1156–1228), the founder of the Gong Xie Pai (Attack and Drain School). The patient, who was the wife of a certain Xiang Guanling, reportedly experienced two serious problems: she refused to eat anything despite feeling hungry, and she expressed uncontrollable rage (*bunno*). The wife cursed furiously at the people around her and even threatened to kill them. Her erratic behavior persisted despite the remedies offered by various doctors. After examining her symptoms, Master Zhang decided to eschew the ineffective herbal treatment and recommend a novel approach. On his order, the family hired two courtesans with "rouged faces" to perform an opera, "which made Xiang's wife laugh a lot." The next day, the wife viewed a wrestling match, which inspired more laughter. Master Zhang then suggested that the family invite several women with healthy appetites to eat with gusto by her side during the meals and rave about the delectable cuisine "until she begged for a taste." After a few days, the patient's anger started to diminish, her appetite returned, and she was cured without any medication. Sometime later, the family joyfully reported that she had given birth to a son.[1] In his commentary on Zhang's treatment of his patient, Heo explained how an excess of any of the seven emotions (e.g., joy, anger, anxiety, worry, grief, fear, and fright [shock]) could cause acute damage to the internal organs, namely the liver, heart, and spleen. He observed that Zhang, in order to cure the uncontrollable rage of Xiang's wife, employed laughter to unclog the qi (vital energy) trapped in her meridians; this in turn rebalanced her yin and yang, allowing the blood to circulate equally to all parts of her vital organs and returned her body to its normal state.[2]

Popular remedies such as Heo's based on traditional Chinese medicine began to make inroads into Korea starting in the seventeenth century but confronted resistance from a society steeped in traditional folk beliefs and practices. Koreans continued to resort to influential shamans, seeking their advice, rituals, and healing. As this chapter will show, the resilience of shamanism lay in its intimate, emotional connection to the personal, everyday experience of clients: it was a social practice that offered empathy for the suffering and performed rituals to expel pent-up feelings of *han* (resentment and regret), which, if left unresolved, could lead to violent manifestations such as *hwabyeong* (fire illness).[3] One scholar has observed that shamanistic "prayers to obtain personal and private advantage were anathema" to the rigid cosmic world order of Confucianism, the official ideology of the Joseon dynasty.[4] Supplications for individuals were antithetical to the Confucian goal of accepting "unquestioningly whatever fate Heaven . . . had in store for them"—namely a fate "directed toward public benefit rather than personal interests."[5] Shamanism's association of erratic behaviors with spiritual and moral failings and with disturbances in relationships with the spirit world also came under harsh criticism and ridicule from the modernizing medical world and Western missionaries, who viewed it as backward and irrational. The missionaries, however, would find a place for shamanism's view of madness as possession in their own "discourse on demonology."[6]

In contrast to shamanism, traditional Chinese medicine and the Korean traditional medicine that sprang from it tended to somatize symptoms as manifestations of an organic physical disorder. This holistic approach did not differentiate the mind from the body; as one scholar observed, it claimed to be a "rational, empirical, and systematically synthesized healing tradition largely devoid of supernatural components."[7] Recent studies have shown that

Koreans, even from the lower classes, turned into more avid consumers of naturalistic medicine as both physicians and medical supplies became more accessible to the public.[8] Clearly, the Neo-Confucian government contributed to this trend when it occasionally expelled shamans from the capital and tried to ban shamanistic healing, efforts lauded by the burgeoning medical mutual aid associations.[9] While there was a gradual "popularization of medicine" starting in the early modern period, Koreans did not completely abandon shamanism for relief from problems of the spirit.[10] This was especially true for marginalized groups like women in an increasingly rigid Confucian society. For instance, the diary of Yu Hui-chun (*Miam ilgi*), a high-ranking Confucian scholar and official at the end of the sixteenth century, reveals that out of the 570 entries on medicine there were two entries about a shaman's ritual initiated by "the female members of the family."[11] Shamanistic interpretations of "spirit possession" bled through the naturalistic medical layer of the palimpsest as people sought to cope with their suffering through familiar rituals, music, and dance and to escape the constrictions of Confucian life that left little space for the unconventional.[12] To understand these different layers of understanding, this chapter will explore traditional beliefs of shamanism, the impact of Chinese medicine, and finally the emergence of Korean natural medicine, which drew on understandings of folk illnesses and Chinese medicine to formulate its own syncretistic view of "madness."

TRADITIONAL BELIEFS OF SHAMANISM

According to the late Roy Porter, the discovery of unearthed trepanned skulls by archaeologists in Spain indicates that early humans may have believed in spirit possession and that they bored holes in the skulls of the afflicted with flint tools to allow the demons to escape.[13] In Korea, the oldest belief system and healing tradition, which antedates all historical records, was *musok* (shamanism), which also involved a belief in the supernatural. This "lived religion" was an integral part of everyday life and culture. In the words of one missionary, shamanism was "a religion of the Korean home."[14] Sung-Deuk Oak observes that while official ceremonies and domestic ancestral veneration lay "under Confucian liturgical hegemony," *gut* rituals to appease household spirits remained under the control of the *mudang* (shaman, usually female) and occasionally a *baksu* (male shaman).[15] As healers, shamans offered an outlet (if only temporarily) for the pent-up anger, regret, frustration, and other emotions that pervaded daily existence. In shamanism, inexplicable "illnesses" (perhaps what some would have described as "madness" in the West) were considered a natural consequence of humans' interactions with the spirit world. In fact, shamans themselves had to suffer and overcome an "initiation sickness" (*sinbyeong*) accompanied by hallucinations, dreams, hearing voices, and more to be able to heal others. Only then could they identify and heal the ruptures "in the relationship between the living and the dead."[16] The intimate connection of shamanism to the everyday lives of Koreans made it difficult for the Neo-Confucian order to root it out completely, even as shamanistic practices confronted greater prohibitions and stigma.

Sources on Shamanism

In the absence of sources written by shamans themselves, one must rely on accounts by contemporary observers, being mindful of their specific political agendas. One source is the writings of the Neo-Confucian patriarchal state, which sought not only to repress shaman practitioners, who posed a threat to its core ideologies and authority, but also to decry shamanistic practices as corrupt and superstitious and to contrast them to the Neo-Confucian social and political reforms and virtues that they wished to promote. As Merose Hwang has shown, this critical "*mudang* (shaman) discourse" represented a form of elitist control.[17] American missionaries in the late nineteenth century also provided critical assessments, routinely describing shamans as depraved charlatans and devil worshippers who represented the ills of backward Korea as opposed to the rational and superior belief system of Christianity.[18] According to J. Robert Moose, for example, Korean shamans were "in a league with evil spirits" and had the ability to attract "even the highest and best educated classes."[19] Homer Hulbert likewise dismissed shamanistic practices as "idiotic" performances.[20] Yet as the historian Andrew Scull has pointed out, similar practices are part of the Christian tradition as well: from Christianity's earliest years, missionaries used the casting of demons and healing of the possessed "as proof of the world of Christ over the invisible enemies faced by humans," and in the Byzantine Empire "the existence of demons and the power of religious healing" were beliefs widely held not only among "ordinary folk" but even among "the powerful and the relatively well-educated."[21]

Unlike the missionaries, who relegated shamanism to the category of useless, primitive superstitions, the Japanese Government-General's Office expressed a keen interest in Korean customs and beliefs and commissioned ethnographers such as Akamatsu Chijō (1886–1969), Murayama Chijun (1891–1968), and Akiba Takashi (1888–1954) to direct large-scale studies on these subjects. Their ethnographic surveys both elucidated the similarities between Korean and Japanese culture to facilitate Koreans' assimilation and provided useful information on local laws, land records and transactions, and general customary practices to prepare the population for large-scale social and political engineering. A pervasive Korean police force assisted Japanese investigators of Korean life and customs by rounding up subjects for studies. As E. Taylor Atkins suggests, however, these surveys "did not always need to be immediately applicable to practical administration," so social investigators could "follow their interests to a certain extent" and develop a "special interest in Koreana that exceeded their mandated ethnographic agenda."[22] Indeed, Japanese researchers often prefaced their works "with remarks on the importance of cultural understanding to good inter-cultural relations and enlightened governance."[23]

The sociologist Akiba Takashi and the religious studies scholar Akamatsu Chijō both pioneered the investigation of Korean *musok*. The former had studied functionalism with prominent scholars in Europe such as Émile Durkheim, Marcel Mauss, Bronislaw Malinowski, and Alfred Radcliffe-Brown, and the latter had also spent several years abroad. As professors of Gyeongseong (Keijō) Imperial University, both devoted their time to extensive field research on Korean shamanism, and in 1937 they would coauthor *Chōsen fuzoku no kenkyū* (A study of Korean shamanism), one of the most comprehensive studies to date on shamanism in ninety locations nationwide. While their methodologies differed, both averred that shamanism was perhaps the most "representative cultural aspect" of colonial Korea; its primitive or primordial elements were indicative of Korea's backwardness but offered a clue to understanding Japan's own past and constructing in contrast an identity for Japan that was both "modern" and "Asian."[24]

Another Japanese scholar who became interested in the study of traditional culture and was employed by the Government-General's Central Council (Chūsūin) for several decades was the sociologist Murayama Chijun, a graduate of Tokyo Imperial University and a contemporary of Akiba and Akamatsu. In 1928 he published *Chōsen no kishin* (Ghosts of Korea), a pioneering work on Korean ghosts and spirits. This would be one of several important books he authored on Korean folk culture and religion. Murayama coordinated extensive field surveys and pored over local surveys and reports that Korean police and provincial administrators made available to him. While his works undoubtedly contributed to colonial policies to eliminate shamanistic practices and promote cultural assimilation, they represent an invaluable resource. Murayama was the first to systematically classify local ghosts as well as to document specific folk remedies used to expel diabolic spirits that were known to cause mental disorders. Further, as E. Taylor Atkins observes, Murayama's reports represented much more than just "rich data, classification schemes, and surface description": they also sought to analyze "the indigenous meanings of folk beliefs and practices."[25] In 1932, Murayama authored *Chōsen no fugeki* (Shamans of Korea), an extensive survey of shamans in South Jeolla Province, which had the highest population density of shamans in Korea. In this particular study, he highlighted the importance of a *gut* or sacrificial ritual offered to the spirits by the shaman through ritualized song and dance, entreating the gods for peace and a bountiful harvest (*byeolsin gut*) or for recovery of an ill person afflicted by misfortune (*byeong gut*).[26]

By the mid-1920s, a number of Korean intellectuals like Choe Nam-seon, Seon Jin-tae, and Yi Neung-hwa were aware of these comprehensive ethnographic studies commissioned by the Government-General Office and were beginning to pay serious attention to shamanism and folk beliefs and practices. Nationalistic in their aims and empirical in their methods, these studies sought to differentiate Korean culture from Japanese culture by focusing on what made it unique, contradicting the negative views held by the *yangban* (literati class) and the colonial government. For example, Choe Nam-seon described Dangun, the legendary progenitor of the Korean people and founder of Gojoseon (Old Joseon), as a shaman ruler, mirroring other nationalist writings that presented shamanism and other folk practices and folklore as uniquely Korean spiritual resources.[27] Contrary to these approaches to shamanism, which upheld it as part of a "usable past" in constructing national culture, Korean print media criticized female reliance on shamanistic rites as old-fashioned and promoted in contrast a new vision of modern womanhood that would rely on scientifically approved hygienic practices and consumption choices to maintain the health of the family.[28]

Missionaries such as George Heber Jones (1867–1919), Eli Bar Landis (1865–98), Homer B. Hulbert (1863–1949), and Horace G. Underwood (1859–1916) began to write their own descriptions of shamanism starting in the late nineteenth century.[29] Filtered through their Christian lens, their narratives cast shamanism as a folk religion steeped in supernatural entities, demonic possession, and witchcraft. Sung Deuk Oak posits that shamanism served as the "significant other" of Christianity in missionary discourse. It routinely cast the former as a primitive form of "demonism" that could be vanquished if Koreans could only replace their fraudulent healers (especially *mudang*) with Jesus, and their "household fetishes" of "devil worship" with images of the "the Lord's Prayer, Apostles' Creed, and Ten Commandments."[30] Though missionaries' accounts were fueled by an iconoclastic zeal to destroy what they considered devilish, they recorded detailed descriptions of spirit possessions, *gut* and exorcism rituals, and other aspects of shamanism that can shed light on indigenous understandings of these phenomena.

Despite such differing and competing images of Korean shamanism, one can tease out common descriptions about general shamanistic beliefs and practice (with local variations) from the sources described above and from comparative studies. But seductive as it is to imagine shamanism as pristinely and primordial, it was infused with other traditions, especially Buddhist influences, and as scholars such as Boudewijn Walraven have pointed out, it borrowed from vernacular Korean literature, musical traditions, and even rhetorical devices, infusing popular religious culture with elements of elite genres.[31]

Korean Shamanistic Practices

In Korea, as elsewhere in East Asia, shamanistic practices have existed since antiquity. Koreans who resorted to shamans viewed them as intermediaries between the human and the divine worlds. The underlying dynamics of Korean shamanism revolved around maintaining harmony and balance between these two worlds through sacrificial rites, often large communal happenings, to ensure a good harvest or to ward off epidemics like cholera. These mediators were reputed to have the ability to "lure gods into dwellings, exorcise malevolent beings, and cajole and bargain with a variety of spirits."[32] Acquiring their status either through spontaneous vocation or *ppuri* ("root," or hereditary transmission), shamans received their "calling" in several ways. Misfortunes and the deaths of loved ones (*indari,* literally a human bridge) could be signs of election by the spirits. The most common way, however, was through illness, especially *sinbyeong* (possession sickness), a special feature of Korean shamanism.[33] The characteristics of this illness resembled what might have been identified as "madness" in early modern Europe: physical ailments of weakness, fatigue, and dizziness; ecstatic trances, hallucinations, visions, and dreams of spirits who wanted to enter the body; and the domination of the body by the spirit, accompanied by wild behaviors, falling unconscious, seizures, and even violence.[34] Mircea Eliade has observed a similar phenomenon in a comparative Siberian context: "The disorder provoked in the future shaman by the agonizing news that he has been chosen by the gods or the spirits is by that very fact valuated as an initiatory sickness. The precariousness of life, the solitude and suffering revealed by any sickness, is, in this particular case, aggravated by the symbolism of initiatory death; for accepting the supernatural election finds expression in the feeling that one has delivered oneself over to the divine or demonic powers, hence that one is destined to imminent death."[35]

After experiencing close encounters with death, those who responded to their calling had to endure the *naerim gut* (initiation rite) to accept the "descended" spirits, be cured of their illness, and be "reborn" as fully-fledged shamans who were "prepared to cure others suffering from similar or other ailments."[36] The *mudang*, having transcended her own affliction as well as overcoming various prejudices as a lower-class woman, was highly regarded in traditional Korean society for her empathy toward the afflicted. It was customary for shamans to perform the ritual of *gut* (exorcism) and to treat the afflicted after consulting a fortune-teller first to draw up a *jeom* (reading). The shaman then told the patient what she had gathered through visions and divinations about the patient's family and history of illnesses, and this encouraged the patient to confide more about his circumstances to the shaman.[37] In contrast to modern medicine, with its focus on physical etiologies, however, shamans described "disturbances" in terms of malevolent spirits that had "entered the body of the patient."[38] In other words, their attention was directed at the ill-treatment or neglect of an angry spirit that had caused the sickness and needed to be placated or, in more serious cases, driven away. More importantly, the emphasis was on resolving the human problems caused by disturbances in the cosmic world. In mild cases, shamans would provide an approximate date of recovery and offer supplication to a host of spirits. They sought to win the favor of the spirit through music, dance, and tributes.[39] In these ritualistic performances, the shaman's voice served as the vehicle through which the human and spirit world could communicate. Severe cases required more drastic measures such as the *salpuri* (a series of acts to drive out or strike an evil spirit), a *byeong gut* (illness exorcism) to deal with a wandering or malevolent spirit or ghost, or the *hwajeon* (fire ritual) to drive away the spirits.[40]

Though shamans were marginalized by the Neo-Confucian state, they were "readily available" during the premodern period, and during the Joseon period they were patronized by a large number of female clients who sought to unload their "unbearable existential problems" outside the constraints of the Confucian system of gender and family, which had become increasingly rigid over time.[41] The ideals of the *hyeonmo yangcheo* (wise mother, good wife), which were incumbent on all women regardless of their influence, wealth, and power, began to dictate the practice of everyday life, restraining female roles outside the paradigm. Some women chafed under the practice of *samjong jido* (three rules for women), which demanded a woman's obedience to her father before marriage, to her husband while married, and to her son after the death of the husband. These patriarchal injunctions, which had severely inhibited "open and direct communication" across gender, class, and generational lines, triggered significant social anxieties, compelling desperate women to turn to shamanism as a "pathway out of impasse." Moreover, they could vicariously find solace in the cathartic dramatization of a *gut*: accompanied by frenzied dancing, lively music, and food, the ceremony helped release their pent-up emotions, ill-feeling, suffering, or frustrations.[42]

Koreans also resorted to shamans to deal with others' "bizarre" behavior, which they attributed to the work of malevolent spirits who were believed to inflict illnesses of every type. The shaman invoked the angry spirit into his or her body, providing a vehicle for the spirit to express its suffering (*hanpuri*) or to "disentangle the knot" (*gopuri*) or grudge before letting it depart the world in peace. Only the shaman could placate the spirit and transform its *han* (resentment) that was triggered by an untimely death into a healing force.[43] As the renowned Jungian psychologist and neuropsychiatrist Bou-Yong Rhi (Yi Bu-yeong) observes, the shaman, "Once possessed by the spirit," can articulate the grudges of the deceased and communicate them to bereaved family members.[44] In less severe cases, shamans resorted to what Kim Gwang-il has called the "scapegoat concept," through a ceremony called *pudakgeori*: in front of a spread of prepared food, the shaman offered prayers to the twelve gods, sang chants of supplication to the spirit that was causing the illness, and then killed a rooster by twisting its neck and placed it in a wicker basket in an open shed. The shaman assured the patient and the family that the rooster had taken the illness on itself had died in place of the patient.[45]

When reconciling with the malevolent spirits causing mental illness was not possible, tricking them into leaving was an option. For example, according to Murayama, the shaman might attempt to "charm away the illness" (*jusuljeok chiryo*) using a magic wand made from a peach tree branch to drive the spirit to a huge crock and then close the lid and throw it into a small creek.[46] And when even trickery failed, shamans commonly escalated to more cruel and harsh methods. Customarily, these included threatening the spirits verbally and then overpowering them by binding, beating, stabbing, cutting, or starving the afflicted person.[47] In the most extreme cases, shamans resorted to fire, burning pine needles and driving the smoke into the nostrils of the patient or even suspending the patient with hands and feet tied over burning pine needles or dry pine bark.[48] One article in the *Joseon ilbo* in 1935 recounted such cruel treatments in order to highlight the primitive and superstitious nature of shamanism and alleged that these customs were still being practiced widely in the countryside.[49]

Shamans' methods differed by geographic region. In North Chungcheon Province, Murayama observed that the method for treating mental disorders involved locking up the afflicted in a traditional *ondol* (heated-floor) room for two or three days while a shaman chanted continuously outside. Then the family members or the shaman beat the patient violently with branches of a mulberry or peach tree to drive the spirit away. According to Murayama, while the Chinese recommended five different types of trees to drive away malevolent spirits, Koreans preferred the peach tree because it symbolized the warmth and vitality of spring *yang*, a lethal "poison" to ward off evil spirits. Before the beatings took place, the afflicted would be tied and would face the east where the "*yang* is most abundant." Citing the work of Jan Jacob Maria de Groot, the Dutch sinologist and historian of religion who wrote in *The Religious System of China* (1892), Murayama noted that the Chinese regarded the peach tree as a "powerful demon expeller" and as "a symbol of the vernal sun" that had more vitality than all other trees; its branches were lethally toxic even before "a single leaf unfold[ed]" on them.[50] Likewise, the famous *silhak* (practical studies) scholar Hong Man-seon (1643–1715) described the miraculous power of the peach tree branch and its domination over one hundred different spirits in his book *Sallim gyeongje* (Farm management).[51]

In Korea, the peach branch garnered the appellation of *mugu* (shaman's tool); it was reputed to be most effective when striking patients who suffered from various contagious diseases such as typhoid fever. However, it was most commonly used to expel evil spirits attached to those afflicted with spirit possession. In mild cases, the shaman would stroke the patient's face and head with the branches, urging the spirit to leave the patient's body without any harm. In more extreme cases, the shaman would make the peach tree branch into a sword or an arrow to threaten the evil spirit. For example, in

Yongjae chonghwa (A collection of Yongjae's writings), Seong Hyeon (1439–1504), a renowned scholar and official during the reign of King Seonjong who authored many entertaining stories where he observed ordinary people of his time, writes about a young man who became possessed by a spirit and wandered around town night and day like a crazy person, compelling his father-in-law to cut a branch from a peach tree and make it into the shape of a long sword to threaten the evil spirit by pretending to slash his son-in-law's neck. The evil spirit was successfully driven out: the young man immediately collapsed on the ground and remained unconscious for four days. When he regained his consciousness, his *gwangtae* (lunatic behavior) had disappeared and he was normal again.[52]

The predominance of the blind in performing these exorcisms captured the attention of Homer B. Hulbert, a missionary in Korea. He observed: "If an inmate of a house is sick, someone will run for a blind exorcist who will come and drive out the evil spirit which causes the disease. But men are not the only ones who ply this curious trade. Any Korean blind woman, no matter what her rank, can become an exorcist. A lady exorcist, as might be expected, is in demand among the upper classes most exclusively."[53] Koreans believed that blind female shamans were better suited to approach the evil spirit because they could draw on the feminine *yin* (*eom*) and strength from the "dark world" to attack the spirits. In a comparative context, the *itako* (blind shaman) in Japan was also revered as one who could engage in *kuchiyose* (spirit talk) and transmit the words of the dead while in a trance. Visual impairment was believed to give blind shamans in Korea and Japan a hyper-alert focus and awareness that enabled them to derive power from chanting sacred mantras.[54] According to one study conducted in 1921, out of the 8,792 blind persons in colonial Korea, roughly 20 percent (1,737) were involved in the business of divination, prayer, sutra chanting, or shamanism.[55]

In some of the other provinces, such as Gyeonggi and Pyeongan, Murayama noted that the family of the afflicted would hire a female *mudang* (shaman), a *sulga* (conjurer), and a blind person to strike the patient. Following the offering of some grains, money, and cloth to the gods, the three of them would pray earnestly before banging the drums and then striking all parts of the naked body of the afflicted with a peach tree branch. According to Murayama, this exorcism could last for one to three weeks, depriving the patient of any sleep as a means to induce the evil spirit to surrender; practitioners halted the beatings only after the patient shrieked or lost consciousness, which signaled that the malevolent spirit had left the body.[56]

Japanese ethnographers reported that some towns had the "possessed" bound and pricked with needles all over the hands and feet; sometimes, the needles would be inserted in key acupuncture points in the head before the patient was beaten with a peach tree branch. There were instances when the shaman would suspend the patient, with hands and feet tied, from a rafter or a tree, then spin the patient around and whip him or her with a peach tree branch or shoot at him or her with arrows made of peach tree branches. Murayama also observed villages where the possessed were hoisted on their stomach on a horse saddle, bound, and then beaten on their buttocks with a peach tree branch. After offering prayers to the gods, the shaman would chastise the spirit and then beat the possessed person continuously until he or she promised never to act in a bizarre manner again. In North Gyeongsang Province, when someone experienced *baljak* (suddenly going crazy), several people would be recruited to restrain the afflicted as a shaman struck him or her continuously with branches of a willow tree. And in North Pyeongan Province, villagers faced the afflicted toward the east before beating him or her with a peach branch. Exorcisms in this province were always accompanied by loud drum and gong sounds as well as readings of the *Okchugyeong* (a Daoist text) recited by a blind shaman.[57] Even though shamans were considered to be powerful enough to hold successful exorcisms, they were often at risk of being physically attacked by the afflicted during these rituals.[58]

Shamanistic customs began to receive much scrutiny in the press during the Japanese colonial period (1910–45). According to the various newspapers, the practice of beating mentally ill people with peach tree branches was still a common and even preferred method of treatment in rural areas as late as the 1930s.[59] Newspapers exposed numerous instances of such brutal beatings ending in tragic deaths to highlight their "primitive" nature. For example, when Yi Sam-jae, the wife of Kim Oek-jin, became mentally ill, family members deprived her of sleep for twelve continuous days before two exorcists beat her continuously, inflicting injuries to her entire body that resulted in her death.[60] In another case, the *Joseon ilbo* reported that a man named Kim Hyeon-pil had killed his brother Kim Sang-pil by beating him with a peach branch for two straight days, on the belief that he was suffering from some kind of spiritual affliction. He was arrested by the district military police for murder and was awaiting his sentence by the court.[61] One editorial in the *Joseon ilbo* in 1921 claimed that the *munyeo* (female shamans), unlike the *uiwon-in* (doctors), were illiterate and had "very little knowledge and no techniques to see the master diseases [properly] and to guide people clearly."[62] But social investigators like Murayama, who had spent years studying Korean culture, felt that the colonial state could not fully implement a modern medical system similar to Japan's, which would include building hospitals, sanitariums, and improving the sanitation in the countryside, because of its budgetary constraints and lack of manpower. Likewise, Murayama was convinced that neither he nor the colonial state could transform the consciousness of the Korean people or simply eradicate superstitious practices overnight because "people would have nothing to depend on to cope with illnesses and natural calamities."[63]

The interaction of Christian missionaries and shamanism in the sphere of spirit possession yielded surprising results. According to Sung Deuk Oak, Protestant missionaries were initially uncomfortable with the similarities between shamanistic spirit possession and exorcism stories in the New Testament.[64] Upon witnessing several cases of "possession," however, some reluctantly began to accept the idea that "insanity" (manifested by violent behaviors similar to those described in the Bible) stemmed from demon possession as described by the Bible "in the days of Christ."[65] Charles A. Clark of the Central Presbyterian Church in Seoul, who witnessed a disturbed man tear apart his clothes and room, admitted: "Finally I became convinced that it was a devil's manifestation."[66] In their writings, missionaries used the terms *insane* and *demonic possession* simultaneously as related phenomena. For example, one triumphant report in the *Christian Advocate* related the miraculous "healing" of a Yi Kunson [sic] of Incheon in 1899. After she had suffered from her afflictions for ten years with no relief, even from shamanistic rituals, her husband turned to the church. "Believers visited his house and found the insane woman broke the wall frantically and was hiding and shivering in the bed. After they sang a hymn and prayed, they removed the blanket. She drank three bowls of cold water, and prayed together with them. In less than two weeks her insanity disappeared. Now she is a sincere believer."[67]

Paradoxically, the acceptance of demon possession prompted Christians to resort to the same "remedy" as the shamanistic healers—namely, exorcism. In fact, some of the very *mudang* who had converted to Christianity conducted the "healing ceremonies." This not only challenged the gender dynamics of spiritual leadership but also introduced certain elements of shamanism into the church, including "fetishism, spirit reductionism, fortune-centered fatalism, and earthly blessing-oriented materialism."[68] Such "shamanization" of Christianity ensured the continued survival of some folk beliefs, cast in different language and religious frameworks.

As shown above, descriptions of traditional Korean approaches to "spirit possession" were influenced by the agendas of the Neo-Confucian state, missionary writers, and Korean nationalists. Healing methods such as beatings, for example, gained notoriety and sensational coverage in the press and government reports as signs of Korean backwardness. Behind all the rhetoric, however, it is possible to discern common belief patterns, especially in the power of the shaman not only to heal the afflicted but also to provide an emotional outlet for individuals who chafed under strict gender structures and norms. These beliefs would be both bolstered and challenged by traditional Chinese medicine's new taxonomies of illness, which became popular among intellectuals and health practitioners in particular.

TRADITIONAL CHINESE MEDICINE

According to the *Samguk sagi* (History of the Three Kingdoms), the oldest extant historical record written by Koreans, traditional Chinese medicine, which originated more than three thousand years ago, was introduced to the Korean peninsula along with Buddhism sometime during the Three Kingdoms Period (57 BCE-668 CE). Largely devoid of the supernatural, this holistic healing tradition drew on the multifaceted traditions of Chinese philosophy, which emphasized the balancing of the *yin* and *yang*, or the two opposite forces that shape the cosmos and all life. From this point of view, the health of the body depended on the function of the five elements (metal, wood, water, fire, and earth), the five viscera (liver, heart, spleen, lung, and kidney), the six *fu* organs (gall bladder, stomach, small and large intestines, urinary bladder, and the *sanjiao* or body cavities), the *jinglo* (a system of pathways called meridians), and the circulation of qi (vital energy or life force) with its five cardinal functions (actuation, warming, defense, containment, and transformation). In this complex network of internal and external forces, the five viscera had to be in constant balance with the five intents (spiritual-soul, corporeal-soul, spirit, will, and intent), the seven pathogenic emotions (joy, anger, worry, anxiety, sadness, fear, and fright), and the six atmospheric forces (wind, coldness, hotness, dampness, dryness, and fire). Disease and dysfunction were caused by these forces, which hindered the movement of qi throughout the body. For example, if any of the seven emotions became agitated, it could trigger an excess of yin or yang, qi, or blood and could seriously impair one of the vital organs. Damage to the viscera could manifest externally as depression (dysfunction of the liver or kidney), anxiety (a bad heart), or mental confusion (bad heart or spleen). Taken literally, the Chinese characters for psychiatry (*jingshen* or *jeongsin*) means the study of the "vitality" of the heart and kidney.[69]

As canonical texts of traditional Chinese medicine became more available during the Goryeo dynasty (918–1392) and the Joseon dynasty (1392–1910), Korean physicians started to use the Chinese medical categories of *diankuang* (*jeongwang*), *fengdian* (*pungjeon*), and *fengkuang* (*punggwang*) to describe madness. The character *kuang* (*gwang*) represented disorders of yang excess, while *dian* (*jeon*) represented disorders of yin excess. These labels were accompanied with the characters *byeong* or *jeung*, which meant disease or illness. The *Huangdi neijing* (*Hwangje naegyeong,* Yellow Emperor's inner canon), the earliest medical text authored by several writers, compiled sometime during the Spring and Autumn and Warring States periods (770–221 BCE), became the most influential and cited medical text from China. The *Suwen* (Basic questions) laid the theoretical and diagnostic framework for traditional Chinese medicine, and the *Linshu* (Spiritual pivot) offered a basic primer on acupuncture focusing on needle techniques and key meridian points. Taken together, these two volumes offered a holistic picture of human life, focusing on an individual's relationship with nature (*jayeon suneung*) through a functional rather than a structural approach, identifying the imbalances in the human body and offering treatment to restore it to its normal state.

These texts were written in a question-and-answer format, as a conversation between the mythical Huangdi (Yellow Emperor) and one of his several ministers or physicians, most notably Qi Bo. The *Huangdi neijing* did not classify mental syndromes separately from physical syndromes. In one section, the Yellow Emperor asks Qi Bo why those who become delirious run around naked and "talk loudly while performing great feats." Qi Bo explains that it is because "the four extremities contain an abundance of *yangqi* [yang inversion]," which can cause a surge of adrenaline. As for running around naked, Qi Bo attributes this to fever and aggravation by the heat. Excessive cursing and loud talk, he explains, represent an excess of *yangqi*, "which harasses the spirit and muddles the senses" and can make people appear crazy and unreasonable.[70] In another section of the *Suwen,* the etiology of madness is discussed more clearly as Qi Bo explains to the Yellow Emperor that the manifestation of this disease stems from the flow of the *yangqi* being "suddenly cut off" and that "because this blockage is difficult to open" anger can result.[71] Some of the common symptoms of *kuang* (madness) include restlessness, a loss of appetite, feelings of grandeur, "believing oneself to be wise," "presenting oneself as noble," "laughing in a crazy manner," "wanting to play music and sing," and "walking around madly with no rest."[72] The *Huangdi neijing* also identifies several other mental syndromes such as *yangming* (yang brilliance) and *ganfeng* (liver-wind) and offers specific remedies for such disorders such as fasting, a concoction of iron flakes, or moxibustion.[73]

While the *Huangdi neijing* lays out the overall conceptual foundations of Chinese traditional medicine, Korean physicians consulted a wide variety of medical texts for treating diseases, including mental disorders. Several books were especially influential in shaping the nascent field of Korean medicine. One was *Shang Han Lun* (On cold damage), in which Zhang Zongjin advocated purgative therapies (*xiaofa*) to treat all diseases, which he claimed were caused by external pathogens that had infiltrated the human body. He recommended using the peach seed purgative decoction method to drain the heat to treat the febrile *yangming* syndrome.[74] Interestingly, the use of the peach as a healing agent is reminiscent of folk remedies that included this vital fruit. Another influential text was Chau Yuanfang's *Zhubing yanhou Zonglun* (Treatise on the etiology and symptoms of disease), a fifty-volume encyclopedia that described a variety of pathogenic factors such as *feng* (wind) that could trigger *kuang* (madness).[75]

Three other important medical manuals from China were frequently cited by Korean physicians because they offered deeper insights into the etiology of madness. Li Dongyuan's *Piwei lun* (Treatise of the spleen and stomach) elucidated how problems in two vital organs (spleen and stomach), which were primarily caused by improper food intake, overstrain, and mental irritation, could create an imbalance of qi or yang and trigger mental disorders. Likewise, another medical text by Zhu Danxi, *Danxi xinfa* (The essential methods of Danxi), addressed the importance of keeping these two organs healthy because they nourished the kidney yin and protected it from the dire mental consequences of the ravages of fire.[76] Li Chan's *Yixue rumen* (Introduction to medical learning) provided not only thematic essays on traditional medicine and biographies of well-known physicians and their works but also vivid descriptions of the symptoms of *kuang*: "In a light form one feels superior, and loves to sing and dance; when it is serious, one undresses and walks around, does not avoid water or fire, and furthermore desires to kill people. . . . That which one sees, hears, says, does, is all mad: in a very serious case one talks of things never seen or heard in normal life and of five colored *shengui* or spirits [e.g., hallucinations]."[77]

The aforementioned texts all suggested that imbalances could occur in any individual because of certain behaviors such as improper food intake or attacks on important organs by opposing forces, which had the potential to affect the mind as well. None of the texts claimed that certain people were more prone to these problems; rather, issues arose when an individual was not careful to maintain some form of equilibrium of psyche and soma. Likewise, human emotions such as anger or sadness, which biomedicine considered more psychological and linked to the mind, were linked in Chinese medicine to specific organs, revealing a cultural disposition to somatization. These contending medical theories and prescriptions of Chinese traditional medicine had a tremendous influence on Korean doctors as they developed their own system of diagnosis and treatment.

KOREAN TRADITIONAL MEDICINE

As more medical texts from China became accessible on the Korean peninsula during the Unified Silla period (668–936) and the Goryeo period (918–1392), Korean physicians aligned themselves with certain schools in China and their treatment regimes. By the Goryeo period, the state formally instituted an examination system to test physicians on their knowledge of Chinese medicine and pharmaceutical herbs. During this period the state sponsored the publication of several important medical manuals such as the *Hyangyak gugeupbang* (First aid prescriptions using native ingredients) and the *Eoui chwaryobang* (Concise prescriptions of royal doctors). Korean physicians also adopted the four-step diagnosis method advocated by Bian Que, one of the earliest known Chinese physicians, and relied on Chinese acupuncture, moxibustion (e.g., use of mugwort), cupping, herbal medicines, and manual therapies to treat various ailments.[78] By the Joseon period (1392–1910), Korean traditional medicine began to assume its own identity as physicians started to synthesize the various approaches of the aforementioned texts of Chinese medicine. King Sejong (1418–50) oversaw the publication of the *Hyangyak jipseonbang* (Great collection of native Korean prescriptions), an eighty-five-volume compendium with more than 950 entries of diseases and prescriptions, in 1433, and the *Uibang yuchwi* (Classified collection of medical prescriptions), a 365-volume encyclopedia of material medica, disease classification, and prescriptions, in 1445.[79]

First compiled by royal decree under King Seonjo, the *Dong-ui bogam* (A treasury of Eastern medicine), a twenty-five volume encyclopedia, was completed by the royal physician Heo Jun (1539–1615) during the second year of Gwanghae-gun's reign in 1613. It would be regarded as one of the most important texts of Korean traditional medicine. Heo sought to resolve the differences between the northern and southern schools of Chinese medicine, synthesizing the contents of the *Huangdi neijing* (Yellow Emperor's inner canon) and other early classics with the writings of Zhu Zhenheng, Liu Wansu, Li Gao, and Zhang Congzheng, the four masters of the Jin and Yuan dynasties respectively.[80] Divided into five thematic parts—"Naegyeongpyeon" (Internal landscape of the human body), "Oehyeongpyeon" (External appearances), "Japbyeongpyeon" (Miscellaneous diseases), "Tangaekpyeon" (Herbal decoctions), and "Chimgupyeon" (Acupuncture and moxibustion)—the book explained the dynamic relationship of three vital energies, represented by *jeong* (essence), *sin* (ethereal spirit), and *gi* (qi), that were fundamental to the body's well-being, in addition to cataloging more than two thousand symptoms, each under the different human organs affected rather than the disease itself, and a variety of herbal remedies.

In "Naegyeongpyeon," Heo categorized a variety of mental disorders under a section entitled "*Jeong, gi, sin,* and *mong*" (essence, *qi*, ethereal spirit, and dreams). Here he described different types of sexual psychological disorders such as nocturnal emissions, premature ejaculation, erectile dysfunction, and impotency. Heo also identified seven symptoms of ataxia or neurological dysfunction caused by an excess or loss of life energy and listed a variety of disorders linked to the spirit, the control mechanism of mental activities, such as a variety of nervous and anxiety disorders, memory loss, *jeongwang* (madness), epilepsy, *taryeong* (depression caused by demotion to a lower status), *siljeong* (depression caused by losing one's wealth), and sleep disorders, including excessive dreaming, dyssomnia, and insomnia.[81] In other words, Heo did not separate mental health from physical well-being; instead he prescribed a more holistic approach, linking emotions (e.g., anxiety or depression) and desire with physical health. An abrupt change in emotions, often triggered either by straining male reproductive organs (e.g., excessive sexual activity) or by poor emotional health, could block the nerves and prevent the movement of semen and other fluids, thereby giving rise to impotence or other sexual dysfunction such as premature ejaculation. For Heo, good health began with mental clarity, or calming the mind first, which in turn would manifest in a "sound mental state."[82]

In the chapter on *sin* (ethereal spirit), Heo described the etiology of *jeongwang* (madness) as disorders caused by *dameum,* or the lack of circulation of bodily fluids, *hwa* (fire), or *hyeol* (blood), which agitate the *sin* (e.g., consciousness), damaging the vital organs and later manifesting in mental disorder. Drawing on the *Huangdi neijing* and the *Nanjing* (Classics of difficulties), Heo further described *jeon* (madness) as disorders of yin excess and noted that the most common symptoms included withdrawal, depression, and syncope. He added that the term *gwang* (madness) represented disorders of yang excess and that the symptoms involved were excitement, agitation, and hyperactivity. According to Kim Tae-hyeon, the *Dong-ui bogam* prescribed a total of nineteen herbal remedies for treating *jeongwang* (madness). Heo's herbal remedies for treating *jeongwang* often included a concoction of cinnabar or mercuric sulfide with a variety of herbs and minerals such as panax ginger, alumen, gold, mastrix, poria cocos-root, and other native ingredients.[83]

In many respects, Korean traditional medicine had close links to Daoist philosophy, and Heo was drawn to the alchemy school of Daoism and its philosophy of *yangsaeng* (nurturing life). According to the historian Don Baker, Heo strongly recommended that "those who wished to remain healthy and enjoy a long life should focus their attention first on Daoist techniques for strengthening the production and harmonious circulation of vital energies within their bodies so that they would not need the healing techniques of medicine."[84] The *Dong-ui bogam* would lay the foundation for traditional Korean medicine during the Joseon period and would have a lasting impact until the introduction of Western medicine and physiology in the late nineteenth century.

By the late Joseon period, the field of medicine had become more professionalized, as the creation of the examination system suggests. Moreover, Korean physicians began to expropriate the information they culled from Chinese medical tracts to create their own synthesis. Most prominent was Heo Jun's role in synthesizing competing theories of medicine in East Asia that had been around for more than two millennia into a single compendium. If shamanism focused primarily on misfortune or bad luck to explain why someone suffered from some mental disorder, Heo's traditional medicine naturalized illness and death as part of the human experience. Heo drew on clinical experience with demonstrated efficacy in treating a wide range of health issues and showed not why but how each part of the body functioned in relation to the whole. Instead of being stigmatized, those who suffered from some kind of psychological sexual disorders such as nocturnal emissions could now seek a traditional medical doctor, who in turn could consult the *Dong-ui bogam* for specific case studies and prescriptions.

DOCUMENTING MADNESS

In his study of the *Samguk sagi* (History of the Three Kingdoms), Yi Bu-yeong suggests that historians need to read between the lines for subtle hints of madness. Because of the strict social censure against speaking ill about people in power, chroniclers always described rulers' mental health issues in psychogenic terms (e.g., attributing them to emotional or mental stresses). But the study of such instances can reveal much information about how mental disorders were treated. Perhaps the earliest example of a form of "psychotherapy" is recorded in an episode in the *Samguk sagi* during King Hyeondeok's reign (809–826 CE) in which Nok-jin, a lower-ranking official, used "noble words and utmost discussion" rather than *yongchitang* (dragon-teeth broth), a herbal concoction commonly prescribed by court physicians, to treat Jung Gong, a court official who was suffering from mental exhaustion "with scattered concentration, decreased volition and apparently a depressed mood."[85] In another study of mental disorders during the Three Kingdoms period and the Goryeo dynasty (918–1392), Hong Sun-hyang identified a total of twenty-seven cases of afflicted kings and high officials. Because these records were compiled for the sake of posterity, the descriptions he found in the official records were quite limiting in scope yet revealing. For example, there was one case of a "conversion disorder" involving the wife of Bak Je-sang, whom the chronicler described as "becoming as stone" (paralyzed in her lower extremities) after hearing of her husband's fatal death during his attempt to rescue a Silla prince in Japan. There is also the well-known story of Sadaham, a seventeen-year-old *hwarang* (flower boy) warrior who suffered from an acute stress disorder and depression after learning that his best friend Mugwan-nang had died in battle and who ended up committing suicide. Hong also offers some examples of kings who suffered from various mental disorders such as peritraumatic distress (Jeongjong), agoraphobia and paranoia (Mokjong), anxiety disorder and paranoia (Myeongjong), and psychotic disorder (Gongmin).[86]

In all four cases, their conditions contributed to their abnormal and sometimes destructive behavior, making it very difficult for them to rule. While these cases are very selective and represent a limited sampling of elite figures, it is clear that the narrators sought to paint these figures not merely as victims of unintelligible or uncontrollable forces and to suggest that their mental disorders were triggered by some kind of social or political event.

The way people understood and coped with mental disturbances shifted dramatically during the Joseon period (1392–1910) with the Confucianization of society, which set even more limits on the actions of individuals. The infusion of Neo-Confucian ideals into Korean society was most visible in the strict and rigid division of social classes and the reorganization of the family into a patriarchal system, which was now even more responsible for the welfare and behavior of its members. The tenets of Neo-Confucianism, defined by vertical, hierarchical, and generational differences, placed a great emphasis on *illyun* (moral imperatives) governing the relationships between sovereign and subject, father and son, husband and wife, elder and younger brother, and senior and junior to instill propriety and virtue.

For the elite *yangban* class, the responsibility of maintaining the lineage fell primarily on the eldest son. The burden of sustaining the prestige and honor of his household proved arduous, as the rigid rule of primogeniture, which singled out the eldest son as the preferred heir, "implanted inequality in the relationship among brothers."[87] In 1556, during King Myeongjong's reign, a Confucian student by the name of Yu Yeon was sentenced to death for killing his elder brother Yu Yu. The latter, who was suffering from a mental disorder, suddenly disappeared from home for about ten years and then reappeared one day. Although Yu Yu was able to reunite with his wife with the assistance of his sister's husband, his younger brother, Yu Yeon, had become so obsessed over the family inheritance that he plotted to kill his elder brother. While the *Myeongjong sillok* (The annals of King Myeongjong) does not provide an elaborate description of Yu Yu's mental condition, what is certain is that it did not preclude him from retaining the rights to the family inheritance.[88] In other words, the Confucian value of primogeniture stipulated in the Gyeongguk daejeon (National Code), the dynasty's first comprehensive legal law code, which was first promulgated in 1471, protected Yu's exclusive right of inheritance as the eldest son and "direct lineal descendant" despite his psychological state.[89]

The *Hyeonjong gaesu sillok* (The revised annals of King Hyeonjong) describes a case in 1672 involving the death of Min Yeop, a former military instructor. Min Se-ik, the only son of the deceased, suffered from some kind of mental disorder despite "being able to eat when he was hungry, clothe himself when he was cold, and even have his own children." However, family members contended that Min Se-ik should not be allowed to wear the chief mourner's outfit because of his unstable mental condition. After some deliberation, they decided to allow Min's grandson to assume the ritual duties. Unlike the previous case, which involved inheritance rights, this case appears to be more about the honor of the family's name, which could be extended to the ancestors.[90] That Min was able to get married and have children suggests that he may have been able to mask his disorder or that its onset occurred later in his life. Although it is not clear whether the hereditary basis of mental disorder was well recognized by Koreans during this period, it is telling that the family was eager to conceal him by denying him a public ritual role; this attitude would also exclude him from the marital pool if he was going to jeopardize the reputation of the household.

The Joseon court adopted the Great Ming Code to adjudicate legal crimes involving the mentally ill. As a rule, an insanity defense could not be used by an individual who had murdered any family members. The *Injo sillok* (The annals of King Injo) relates an incident that took place in 1627 involving a certain Mu Myeong, who was accused of killing his brother and striking his mother. Though Mu suffered from a serious mental disorder, three offices (State Council, Office of the Inspector General, and State Tribunal) sentenced him to death. Despite proof of his madness and inability to control his actions, such mitigating factors did not outweigh his crime.[91] In another case, the *Sukjong sillok* (The annals of King Sukjong) describes a grisly massacre of an entire household in Gyeongseong County, North Hamgyeong Province, that occurred in 1683. The mayhem started when Kim Myeong-ik lost his mind, killing his mother, his two daughters, and his female cousin (Baek Sam-gil's wife) with a knife. In a bizarre twist, Kim Myeong-ik's son, Kim Yun-baek, then stabbed his own wife. This triggered Baek Sam-gil to stab two of his sons and triggered Kim Myeong-ik's slave to kill his own child. According to the report, Kim Myeong-ik then also killed his slave and in the melee was stabbed by Baek Sam-gil. A total of ten family members died, forcing the court to dispatch an inspector to investigate the scene of the crime. According to the inspector, one of Kim Myeong-ik's sons had contracted smallpox and had started to ramble like a crazy person. Believing that his son was possessed by a wicked ghost, Kim Myeong-ik used a heated needle to drive out the spirit, a treatment that drove his son insane very suddenly; after this, everyone in the household started to draw knives on each other. It is not clear from this report if everyone had contracted smallpox. Kim Yun-baek survived the mayhem, and despite his claims that he thought his mother was a rabid mountain animal and that he had been instructed by his father to kill her, he was sentenced to death and beheaded. Baek Sam-gil was also indicted and charged with violating one of the "Ten Abominations" cited in the Great Ming Code.[92] Despite pleas of insanity caused by illness, "to strike or to plot to kill" one's immediate family members was a clear violation of the code, cited as the fourth "abomination" (contumacy), and was subject to harsh punishment.[93]

Several cases of family members in elite households suffering from some mental disorder are described in the official records and in miscellaneous writings by scholars. For example, the *Injo sillok* states that the son of the civil servant Yu Baek-jeung, who descended into *jeonjil* (madness) because "he had suffered at the hands of his stepmother," disappeared one day, and nobody knew where he lived or if he was alive.[94] In the *Yongjae chonghwa* (Assorted writings of Yongjae), Seong Hyeon (1439–1504), a literati scholar-cum-artist, described in detail the tragic story of a magistrate's aide, Kim Cheo, whose father, Kim Yang-hyang, died unexpectedly while traveling abroad. Overcome by grief after learning of his father's death, the son went crazy. His mind became blurred and he was unable to do anything. According to Seong, his condition deteriorated so rapidly that children in the county made a fool out of this once reputable man who now believed everything they told him. He was particularly afraid of one of his slaves and did everything he commanded. Whenever the slave reprimanded him, he would cower in fear, unable to move. Kim slept late into the morning, and whenever he got up would sing a *kasa* composed by Jeong Cheol entitled "Gwangdong byeolgok" (Song of Gwangdong), wave his sleeves at the skies, dance in a frenzy, and then weep very loudly. At night he would slowly recite the poems in a melancholic state and then take a stroll deep into the mountains, always acting restless and never taking a rest. One fateful day after encountering a sick man in the mountains and offering him water out of pity, Kim contracted the man's illness and died.[95] In both cases mentioned above, the afflicted person did not seek medical treatment and was left alone to fend for himself. Likewise, there is no evidence in any of the written records suggesting that there were state facilities to house the afflicted. Wealthy families either confined members at home or sent them off to Buddhist temples to convalesce or retire permanently, a practice dating back to the Goryeo period.[96]

Although various collections of *japgi* (literary miscellany) and *paeseol* (scribblings) written by scholars on the customs and everyday lives of commoners exist, there are very few accounts of how commoners coped with mental disorders. The official records do offer some descriptions of folk remedies, but these are described in such a way as to promote socially accepted practices like *hyo* (filial piety). For example, the *Sejo sillok* (The annals of King Sejo) offers an example of "the filial wife" of Kim In-deuk, who, after much grief over her husband's odd behavior, heeded the advice of a fellow villager by the name of Wi Yeong-pil to cut off her finger and mix her blood with medicine to nurture her mad husband. Regardless of the outcome, the state deemed her filial act worthy of recognition and cited her for a reward.[97] In another case, the *Jungjong sillok* (The annals of King Jungjong) cited a case of a soldier named Yi Gye-nam who agonized over his brother Gye-dong's madness and decided to grind his severed finger with medicine to nurture his ailing brother. He severed a second finger after his brother suffered another relapse; his act was reported to the king, and he was subsequently rewarded with gifts and praised for his filiality.[98] While there is no mention about the efficacy of such folk remedies, these two narratives reveal how officials combined folk culture and Confucian filiality to promote the values of devotion.

Regarding public cases involving state officials suffering from mental disorders, the *Jungjong sillok* cites the example of Yi Jeong-ho, an official who had a stellar public record that included stints as the *sijong* and *daegan* (posts in the Censorate); he was also employed in Hamgyeong Province as a military attaché. Yi had never shown any behavioral problems "until one day he started to act oddly" by separating from his wife and then writing a petition slandering another official by the name of Kim Jong-jik. The officials appointed to adjudicate this case recommended that Yi not be punished because his "bizarre behavior" was caused by *simjil* (acute anxiety) that had developed into *gwangjeung* (madness).[99] The *Hyeonjong gaesu sillok* (The revised annals of King Hyeonjong) provides another example from 1670 involving Yi Min-seon, an official who worked at the Hongmungwan (Office of the Special Counselors) and experienced *baljak* (suddenly went crazy): he started "to say bizarre things to other officials." Although some felt that his madness was the result of overwork, the court believed that his unstable condition would endanger others, so they relieved him of his government post and assigned him to another position in Goyang County, suggesting that a less demanding environment would help him recuperate.[100] While one could speculate that Yi could have been pretending to be mad to escape responsibility from work, what we can infer from the two examples above is that the court usually relieved those who suffered from mental disorders.

While it would take another book to psychoanalyze each of the twenty-seven kings of the Joseon dynasty, it is not an exaggeration to say that all of the them had to contend in one way or another with contentious factions and court intrigues, overbearing parents, zealous partners, ambitious siblings, manipulative officials, intrusive eunuchs and ladies-in-waiting, and pressures to behave like a "sage king." According to the sources, these kinds of internal and external pressures often triggered kings to suffer from anxiety, social withdrawal, wild mood swings, fear, feelings of victimization, and delusions. For example, King Seonjo (1567–1608) is said to have suffered from an acute case of *simjil* (anxiety), which worsened during the *Imjin waeran*, when Toyotomi Hideyoshi invaded Joseon. His symptoms are described in the *Seonjo sillok* (The annals of King Seonjo) as "being in a confused state of mind, unable to distinguish east and west, yelling incessantly, and running around like crazy." Despite his visible illness, different factions in the court prevented him from abdicating because they did not want the crown prince to take over the throne.[101]

Because the official records of the Joseon kings focus primarily on monarchs and heirs apparent, there is little information on the many princes and princesses of consorts in the palace. For example, Gyeongpyeong-gun, King Seonjo's eleventh son with the consort Onbin Han-ssi, is described in the *Gwanghae-gun ilgi* (The diary of Prince Gwanghae) as suffering from anxiety and madness after the death of his father at an early age of eight years. In one incident, Gyeongpyeong allegedly created a huge commotion after losing his home because of the expansion of the palace. Angered by the eviction, he raided the homes of several *sadaebu* (literati) homes and freed their slaves. Other odd behaviors he displayed included terrorizing court ladies, going on random excursions to the mountains and streams, and increasingly becoming a nuisance to people around him.[102]

Perhaps the two most famous kings suffering from madness who are mentioned in the *Joseon wangjo sillok* (The annals of the Joseon Kings) are Yeonsan-gun (r. 1494–1506) and Prince Sado (1735–62), the heir apparent to King Yeongjo (r. 1724–76). Yeonsan-gun has been regarded by many as one of the worst monarchs of the Joseon dynasty. He was notorious for instigating two bloody literati purges and executions to exact vengeance on those officials whom he thought had wrongly deposed and executed his mother, Queen Yun. The trauma of his mother's execution and his discovery of her blood-stained clothes is thought to have prompted him to become violent; he went on to kill not only his own grandmother, the Queen Dowager Insu, but also his loyal eunuch Kim Choe-sun, Jo Sae-seo, the royal tutor, and countless others. Between the two purges and before his ouster, Yeonsan-gun acted erratically, often neglecting "his duties in favor of hedonistic pursuits," kept hunting dogs and falcons in the palace, and forced the censoring bodies to evict hundreds of families near the vicinity of the palace walls "to prevent observation of the king's wanton frolics in the palace gardens."[103]

Like Yeonsan-gun, Prince Sado's spiral into the abyss of madness can be linked to politics in the court. Sado's abusive relationship with his father, King Yeongjo, can be attributed to the latter's obsession with accusations that he had acceded to the throne illegally as a prince-regent. Yeongjo's "high expectations and exacting demands" affected Sado immensely. He became delusional and suffered from nightmares, developed "clothing phobia," sexually abused and killed many court attendants in fits of rage, including the eunuch Kim Han-chae, and routinely left the palace in disguise. Sado's erratic and dangerous behavior compelled Yeongjo to seal him in a rice chest for eight days before he finally died. According to Jahyun Haboush, Lady Hye-gyeong, the widow of Sado, in her four autobiographical narratives (*Hanjungnok*) blamed her husband's insanity on his father. She claimed that "he lost his battle to meet his father's demands not because he did not want to comply, but because he desired so intensely to live up to his father's expectations that the constant disapproval was too great to bear."[104]

To fully understand the psychopathology of Yeonsan-gun and Prince Sado, it is important to understand how Koreans expressed distress in a local context. In modern psychiatric diagnosis, the symptoms Prince Sado exhibited might be interpreted as bipolar disorder or schizophrenia, while King Yeonsan-gun's condition might be characterized as post-traumatic syndrome or chronic mania. But because traditional Korean medicine did not identify specific disease entities but rather symptoms, both cases were diagnosed as an aggravation of the five emotions, which caused an imbalance in the viscera and developed into mental disorder. And lay people understood both conditions quite differently under the folk idiom of *hwabyeong* (fire illness), or an accumulation of pent-up or unresolved anger over some kind of unjust social situation, which had built up for a long period of time. The symptoms of *hwa* (fire) or distress included a wide range of emotions such as *eogul* (feelings of unfairness or victimization), *geunsim* (anxiety), *bigwan* (depressive mood), *bunno* (anger), *mium* (hate), *singyeongjil* (nervousness), *mugiryeok* (helplessness), *gongpo* (fright), *uisim* (suspicion), *gosaeng* (hardship), *moyok* (feeling insulted), and *joechaekgam* (guilt feelings).[105] The precipitating factors usually were conflicts in social relationships between husband and wife, father and son, housewife and mother-in-law, or master and slave; the death of parents; betrayal by a friend or relative; or an instance of social injustice such as a false accusation, forced submission to authorities, class and gender discrimination, widespread nepotism, the loss of one's freedom, poverty and hardships, or deprivation.[106] In these cultural interpretations of distress, a pervasive emphasis was placed on *jeong* (an emotive and psychological bond), *nunchi* (requiring tact), and *chemyeon* (face-saving) to maintain social harmony and keep from disrupt the collective *uri* (we), which will be discussed in more detail in chapter 3.

For Prince Sado, the suppression or displacement of anger over time induced a somatization process whereby the symptoms manifested physically in his body, making him feel irritable and nervous.[107] According to Korean doctors, while such symptoms of respiratory stuffiness (described as something pushing up in the chest) could be relieved temporarily by striking one's chest with one's fists, sighing, or crying, its continuing increase could have dire consequences, such as *hwapuri* (an aggressive outburst of anger). Sometimes the individual lapsed into *chenyeom* (unwillingness to resolve the problem anymore) or resorted to *salpuri* (disentangling evil through a *gut* or exorcism). But if one simply let this unresolved anger turn into *han* (everlasting woe), it could transform into other comorbid physical and mental syndromes. Both Prince Sado and Yeonsan-gun were eventually unable to suppress their anger and began murdering people.

According to the psychiatrist Min Seon-gil, folk idioms like *hwabyeong* (fire-illness), *hwajeung* (fire-rage), *uljeung* (melancholia), *ulbyeong* (depression), and *ulhwa* (pent-up anger) did appear in official records such as the *Joseon wangjo sillok* (The annals of the Joseon Kings). More specifically, Min points out that *hwabyeong* is mentioned in the annals six times while *hwajeung* appears twenty-one times. This suggests that these folk idioms of distress were used not only by lay people but by elites as well. The term *hwabyeong* first appeared in the annals during King Seonjo's thirty-seventh year of reign (1603) and is mentioned several times under the reign of Kings Gwanghaegun (r. 1603–23), Sukjong (r. 1674–1720), and Yeongjo (r. 1724–76). *Simdeukjil* (illness of the heart), which was believed to be caused by internal fire, had symptoms similar to those of *hwabyeong* and was mentioned in 1536 during the reign of King Jungjong. Likewise, *gyeokwa* (fire between the chest and abdomen), which has symptoms similar to the respiratory stuffiness described above, was mentioned in 1836 during King Hyeonjong's reign.[108]

Perhaps the most vivid description of *hwabyeong* is found in Lady Hyegyeong's memoirs as she recollected her husband's condition:

> Prince Sado's illness grew worse. Before he had completely recuperated from his recent bout of smallpox, the Two Highnesses passed away. He was saddened by these losses. He was also heavily burdened by the ritual duties of mourning. This affected him adversely. As his illness tightened its grip, his behavior often fell short of propriety.... During the five-month wake, after a wail at Kyŏnghun [Gyeonghun] Pavilion His Majesty would invariably drop by at Okhwa Hall to scold his son for whatever he happened to find irritating. Then, when the Prince went to T'ongmyŏng [Tongmyeong] Pavilion, the same scene would be repeated. How angry this made the Prince! His rage was kindled like a well-constructed fire. It was His Majesty's habit to rebuke his son in front of a large crowd. It was at T'ongmyŏng Pavilion, before all the ladies-in-waiting, where the Prince went to honor his grandmother's memory despite the relentless summer heat of the sixth and seventh months, that His Majesty's sharpest and most humiliating derision awaited him.
>
> No longer able to contain his rage, his mind helplessly seized by disease, Prince Sado started to beat his eunuchs severely.[109]

Lady Hye-gyeong's description of her husband's distress, which was characterized by a wide range of somatic and emotional symptoms, provides a glimpse into such culture-bound maladies. Similarly, doctors saw Prince Sado's outburst as the result of his reaching the human limits of suppressing the internal fire rising within his body and his inability to cope with his pent-up emotions.

By the end of the Joseon period, there was a slow shift from the personal, spirit-centered approach of shamanism to mental afflictions to naturalistic medical methods that focused on the processes of somatization. Whereas shamans sought to identify external forces (such as the invasion of angry spirits) as causes of mental suffering, naturalistic doctors probed the body for signs of a mental condition. With the development of the Neo-Confucian state and social institutions, there was also a perceptible stigma attached to recourse to shamans, and even more to individuals who experienced manifestations of *sinbyeong*, which signaled the calling of a shaman. In his "Notes on the Exorcism of Spirits in Korea" (1895), the missionary Eli Landis observed that an upper-class woman who contracted an initiation illness was more likely to die from it, not only because her family would isolate her from the outside world but also because, "if she belongs to a noble family as sometimes happens, they may probably, and very often do, kill her as the disgrace would be felt so keenly that the family would feel that nothing could ever wipe it out."[110] If before the Neo-Confucian period a woman who survived her *sinbyeong* would attain a certain level of prestige, now her illness would be a cause of deep shame and ostracism.

The development of traditional Korean medicine, which synthesized the differing canonical medical classics from China in its holistic approach, became a dominant form of preventive medicine until the introduction of Western medicine by missionaries in the late nineteenth century.[111] A group of Korean scholars who belonged to the *silhak* (Practical Studies) school—Yi Ik, Sin Hu-dam, Bak Je-ga, Jeong Yak-yong, An Jeong-bok, and Yi Gyu-gyeong, among others—were able to obtain Chinese translations of medical texts on human anatomy that transformed their thinking about the causes of mental illness. They were successful in securing physiology texts by physicians in Europe such as Andreas Vesalius, William Harvey, Thomas Willis, Jesuit priests like Matteo Ricci, Julio Aleni, Francesco Sambiaso, Johann Adam Schall von Bell, Diego Pantoja and Nicole Longobardi, as well as early Greek and Roman physicians like Alcmaeon, Galen, and Hippocrates. Combining all this newfound knowledge with their native experience, these scholars published the first public statement about mental illness on June 3, 1884, in the *Hanseong sunbo*, the first Korean-language newspaper and the official organ of the Joseon court.[112]

In this issue, the newspaper introduced a piece by the late Choe Han-gi (1803–77), a progressive scholar of "fallen *yangban*" background, a *silhak* scholar, and the author of *Injeong* (Personnel administration), who advocated opening Joseon and embracing the culture of other enlightened nations of the world. In an article entitled "The Mental Institution in England," Choe addressed the misery of being afflicted with mental illness and losing one's ability to act and speak freely, as well as the imposition of this enormous burden on family members who had to remain constantly vigilant and wary of the violent tendencies of the afflicted. In contrast to the situation in Joseon, Choe argued that preventive measures and policies had been implemented much earlier in the West and that various countries had established "mental institutions." Individuals afflicted with mental disorders were admitted to these institutions and put under surveillance. Choe based his article on seven different newspapers in England in which he had read about these institutions. He elucidated the current debates in Parliament over the number of patients and the management of these facilities. He noted that in the past these institutions had controlled their patients by handcuffing and shackling them and incarcerating them like prisoners but that now such practices were criticized for being too harsh and having no therapeutic effect on the afflicted. Recently, he reported, practices had shifted to support a more compassionate management of the insane. He estimated that there were roughly fifty-eight thousand mentally ill patients in the various institutions in England, a figure that he considered rather high. What intrigued him most was the fair treatment of all patients, whether they were alcoholics or lunatics. He also was impressed with the genuine sympathy and the amount of consideration put into the care of the afflicted, which included their clothing and food, but also the management of their properties while they were being treated. Choe also highlighted some criticisms in the editorials warning that Parliament would cut the budgets of these institutions if they continued to treat alcoholics.

Choe was most impressed with Small Side, a facility in the West End of London. Its facility included a garden with stuffed animals and birds that looked real so that the patients could enjoy their stay during their treatment. During the winters, the staff let patients use a fully windowed greenhouse with a variety of flowers and trees so that they did not feel lonely. Choe described the living room as very tidy and noted that the walls were all painted and adorned with images of mountains, water, flowers, and birds. There were books and newspapers from various countries in addition to famous paintings on the walls for patients to look at. Patients were encouraged to play chess, play an instrument, or kick a ball in their free time; the staff would have them play games and would offer prizes to those who won in order to make them more socially outgoing. Choe stated that the other hospitals were running similar therapeutic programs. Choe also noted that in Western culture men and women would sit next to each other during meals, though individuals deemed dangerous by the authorities took their meals in isolation. The mixing of sexes was deemed beneficial, and Choe noted that men and women even went on trips together without anyone violating the rules.

Not only were the patients required to maintain decorum during meals, but alcoholics were not allowed to drink. Because of the temperament problems of female patients, Choe noted that a staff member recommended building a wooden horse and making the chronic female patients ride it for amusement. As a means of treatment, staff members also took one to two hundred chronic patients deep into the forest to "play" and return at the end of the day. After a year of therapy, patients allegedly stopped fighting, and many of them became stable enough to be discharged. At one mental institution,

Choe noted that out of 494 patients 84 were women; 26 of them had fully recovered so far. Among these women, 10 had been charged with murder before their recovery, but because they had not been in their right minds they had received a much more lenient punishment, and the institution was able to rehabilitate them. Choe noted that the current institutions were much larger and fully equipped than those of the past. Each district was responsible for the expenses of maintaining these facilities, and every year a certain percentage of the taxes paid by its citizens was diverted to help defray the maintenance costs. In addition, wealthy merchants with good intentions offered donations, and these institutions hired only staff who were compassionate, completely replacing the old oppressive practices and instead treating the mentally ill with humane affection.[113]

The adoption of Western medicine by King Gojong (r. 1863–1907) at the end of the nineteenth century resulted in the creation of a medical school and the first psychiatric ward in 1913 at the Government-General Hospital under Japanese colonial rule. This new regime of Western psychiatry, introduced by missionaries and the Japanese, differed significantly from shamanism, which viewed patients' unresolved grudges (*han*) or misfortune, or their possession by spirits, as the cause of mental afflictions. It also parted ways with the holistic approach of traditional Chinese and Korean medicine, which advocated finding harmony between complementary energies. In all these instances, a shaman or traditional doctor expected that once acute symptoms disappeared from the afflicted (e.g., when the malevolent spirit had departed, or the body returned to its normal state), the individuals would return to their way of life and family. In contrast, modern medicine insisted on labeling such individuals as possessing a permanent or long-lasting defect or chronic condition; thus the mentally ill had to be incarcerated over the long term for the good of state and society.

TWO

Madness Is...

Under observation madness ... is judged only by its acts....
Madness no longer exists except as seen. The proximity instituted by the asylum, an intimacy neither chains nor bars would ever violate again, does not allow reciprocity, only the nearness of observation that watches, that spies, that comes closer in order to see better.

    MICHEL FOUCAULT, *Madness and Civilization*

In the manifold missionary activities of the Church in the Far East there are but two or three institutions devoted to the care and treatment of the insane. Nevertheless it is, I believe, the case that the insane have a special claim upon the Christian Church. It is repeatedly recorded in the Gospels that Christ himself cast out evil spirits, and that He committed to those whom He had appointed to preach and to heal a like authority and obligation. While there are, I know, some difficulties in identification of the phenomena described in the New Testament as "possession by evil spirits" with those we now describe as insanity, such is the conclusion to which I myself have come; and I hold my belief together with another; namely that the New Testament in so describing the condition speaks in a more fundamental language than does our modern terminology.

    CHARLES I. MCLAREN, "The Problem of Insanity and the Responsibility of the Church"

What convinced me of the superiority of the clinical method of diagnosis (followed here) over the traditional one, was the certainty with which we could predict (in conjunction with our new concept of disease) the future course of events. Thanks to it the student can now find his way more easily in the difficult subject of psychiatry.

    EMIL KRAEPELIN, *Psychiatry: A Textbook for Students and Physicians*

IN APRIL 1931, *Byeolgeongon* (Another World), a popular leisure magazine, published a short essay by Chae Man-sik (1902–50), a novelist known for his satirical pieces about his two visits to the psychiatric ward (previously known as East Ward Number Eight) of Keijō (Gyeongseong) Imperial University Hospital. In "Dongpalho sil jamipki" (My report: Sneaking into East Ward Number Eight), Chae offered his readers a glimpse of the psychiatric ward— one of the few descriptions available of the facility and the patients. Aware of the alarming statistics published in the daily newspapers about the number of Koreans suffering from *jeongsin isang* (mental disorders), Chae felt compelled to visit this infamous ward. He wanted to "see for himself" those who had lost their minds and experience what it was like to be trapped in a "pathetic and pitiful world," devoid of human emotions and "unable to enjoy the tranquility of spring." His first visit forced him to reevaluate his preconceived prejudices: to his amazement, the asylum was not an overcrowded madhouse bursting at the seams but rather two modest brick buildings located in back of the university hospital and surrounded by old untrimmed pine trees. During his second visit, he was accompanied by a Japanese doctor who was conducting his weekly rounds. The latter served as his guide, taking him to the male ward, which was located in back of the building, where he rang a doorbell. Two eyes suddenly appeared in a small rectangular hole, which was the size of a mailbox slot, and a guard unlocked a padlock and allowed them to enter the ward. Anticipating a ward full of crazy people "crying, singing, dancing, or fighting with each other," Chae recalled seeing five patients sitting calmly in a large *tatami* room. During his first visit, he had been shocked to see two male patients playing a game of *go* (*baduk*), but this time he was even more perplexed to see two patients playing a game of *rokpaekku* (*yukbaek*), a complicated version of *hanafuda* (*hwatu*). "I was at a loss for words!" Chae remarked.

Chae was fascinated by the diversity of male patients housed in the ward and by their odd behaviors. The Koreans included a young boy suffering from epilepsy, a delusional man anxiously waiting for the police chief's car to arrive, a middle-aged patient talking gibberish to himself, and another suffering from *jobalseong chimae* (early dementia praecox) who had recently set a house on fire. The Japanese patients also exhibited strange symptoms: one counted his fingers repetitiously while another complained incessantly about people cursing at him. There was even a former Japanese policeman who had been incarcerated for eight years (the longest duration of all the inmates), According to Chae, the hospital administrators did not segregate the

Japanese patients from the Koreans but locked up the more violent patients in a room with a bolted door and steel-barred windows. Male patients who were "completely cured" were kept in a separate room for final observation with female patients before they were discharged. The other categories for discharged patients included "improved" or "went out with prospect of certain death."

In one interesting episode, Chae described how a Korean male patient "whose outward appearance would fool anyone" asked the doctor accompanying Chae to help him get married. The doctor promised to introduce him to a beautiful lady and arrange a marriage. Bemused by the interaction between the two, Chae inquired whether it was a realistic possibility for a mental patient to get married; to this the doctor sarcastically quipped, "What point is there to her being pretty? All he wants to do is [...] her ... ha, ha!"

Chae also provided vivid descriptions of female patients in the ward, including a woman in her twenties suffering from a type of obsessive-compulsive disorder, a Japanese woman who babbled all day to herself, and an elderly woman from Pyeongan Province who was completely obsessed over her money. Having been called crazy once by a patient, Chae ended his essay by asking his readers if money could indeed drive one crazy.[1]

The patient profiles offered by Chae provide a window into the new state of affairs in the field of psychiatry in the 1930s: the medical community no longer viewed the mental ward at Keijō (Gyeongseong) Imperial University as a custodial institution offering long-term care to chronic patients. Instead, it treated the space as a holding cell for a select group of patients for clinical research. Debates about the efficacy of psychiatric treatment at Keijō Imperial University Hospital (later renamed Imperial University Hospital) and fears about the increasing number of chronic and incurable patients on the streets assumed greater urgency especially in light of the growing tendency to segregate undesirable elements in society. Indicative of this trend was the construction of twenty-one prisons throughout the peninsula, including the Seodaemun prison, the largest penitentiary in the colony, and the creation of a leper colony on a remote island in South Jeolla Province in 1916. Neglect of the mentally ill, in contrast to the attention paid to criminals and individual with contagious diseases, frustrated Koreans: not only did the Government-General fail to create legislation to enforce home confinement (a legally accepted practice in Japan until 1950), but it broke its promises to construct large asylums in the cities for the sake of public health and safety. Even as late as 1938, a writer for the *Donga ilbo* remarked on the increasing number of *gwang-in* (lunatics), including "a naked woman yelling gibberish and dancing in joy," making a huge scene and roaming the streets of Masan.[2]

This chapter will examine the transformation of clinical psychiatry in Korea during the colonial period, which involved competing medical and national agendas regarding the purpose of institutions such as hospitals and psychiatric wards and the appropriate models of diagnosis, treatment, and care of mentally ill patients. It will argue that the opening of the first psychiatric ward at the Chōsen sōtokufu iin (Chongdokbu uiwon, Government-General Hospital) in 1913 was initially motivated by the goal to treat and care for mentally ill patients. Rehabilitation was also the central goal of Protestant missionary doctors who opened their own psychiatric ward at Severance Union Medical Hospital in 1923. Smaller in scale than its colonial counterpart, the missionary hospital emphasized the healing of both body and soul; unfortunately, it did not have the resources to pursue medical treatment commensurate to its lofty goals. The paths of the colonial state and missionary hospitals diverged radically when the Japanese authorities converted the former into a full-fledged university clinic and made it part of Keijō (Gyeongseong) Imperial University Hospital in 1926, formalizing the training of professional doctors in the field of psychiatry. In place of its custodial ambitions, the colonial hospital now aimed to construct the perfect laboratory in which to study patients and train medical doctors in psychiatry. This shift to pedagogy led the hospital to adopt a German-style approach to psychiatry, including its emphasis on diagnostic nosology and its emphasis on congenital and degenerative causes of mental disorders. Funding was shifted from treatment of the mentally ill to quantification projects (e.g., statistical surveys on the etiology of illness), new therapeutic technologies, the creation of professional journals and associations, and laboratory research (the epitome of German psychiatry). Ironically, as mentioned above, this shift to a pedagogical and research emphasis coincided with the trend of institutionalizing "dangerous elements" such as political criminals and people with contagious illnesses like leprosy. However, the Government-General chose not to allocate resources in the institutionalization of the mentally ill, arguing that they should be relegated to the care of their families, in accordance with the practice in Japan.

The treatment of the mentally ill as research objects of the colonial powers and their stigmatization by the new medical knowledge would have a profound impact. Korean society not only lacked a solution to the problem of the mentally ill but also came to associate psychiatric institutions not with treatment but with exploitation and discipline. The departure of Japanese and Western missionary doctors during and after World War II also left a dearth of qualified Korean doctors trained in psychiatry (only thirteen at the end of the war). To understand the trajectory of psychiatry in Korea, this chapter will examine the traditions on which two models of psychiatric practice in Korea (rehabilitation versus pedagogy research) were built, and the impact of the Japanese model of the latter at Keijō Imperial University Hospital that revealed the gulf between the goals of the empire and the expectations of its colonial subjects.

EARLY DEVELOPMENTS IN CONTEXT

The separate paths of psychiatry's development in Japan and America would come together in Korea as doctors there offered competing models for the treatment of the mentally ill. The traditional practice of home confinement of the mentally ill had a long history in Japan. While cities during the late Tokugawa period established custodial-charity wards to house vagrants, the mentally ill, and the destitute, the vast majority of Japanese families continued the indigenous practice of confining the afflicted in private cells or cages (*sashiko*) in their homes.[3] Changes in the laws did little to stop these practices or to address the specific needs of the afflicted. For instance, the enactment of the Penal Code and Code of Criminal Instruction in 1880 provided a statutory framework to protect those who lacked mental capacity to commit a crime (e.g., were unable to discriminate between right and wrong); moreover, Article 39 of the Penal Code (enacted in 1907) stipulated that an act of insanity by an incompetent person was not punishable by law.[4] However, in neither case did the juridical system provide any provisions for those who were acquitted. On the basis of the Mental Patients' Custody Act (1900), a law that allowed families to confine the mentally ill at home and that remained in effect until 1950 released prisoners returned to their residences, leaving them vulnerable to retaliation for their crimes and leaving the general public at risk from their further crimes.

Because Japan had a very long history of confining the afflicted, on the eve of the Meiji Restoration (in 1868) its large cities already contained twenty-nine medical and religious custodial institutions that offered services to the mentally and physically ill, vagrants, and the destitute.[5] In 1905 Akihito Suzuki noted that 5,500 patients were in various institutions compared to 12,000 patients who were in home confinement. Furthermore, two laws enacted by the state—the Mental Patients' Custody Act of 1900 and the Mental Hospital Act of 1919—offered families the option of either keeping the afflicted at home or institutionalizing them. The law stipulated that a "competent custodian," usually a family member, had to take full responsibility for the afflicted.[6]

Concerned about the conditions of confinement, Dr. Kure Shūzō (1865–1932), a professor of psychiatry at Tokyo University who had also studied abroad in Germany, lobbied senior officials in the parliament to create a national policy on mental illness that would compel families to transfer the afflicted detained in inhumane domestic cells to public mental hospitals. Kure's famous report on home confinement and public security issued in 1918 emphasized the importance of early detection and intervention, which could curtail violent crimes and keep certain individuals isolated in hospital wards. Compelled by Kure's report, the state enacted the Mental Hospital Act (Seishin byōin ho) in 1919, giving the state power to provide partial subsidies to local governments and to the private sector to build more hospitals. While this act did not abolish the Private Custody Act, and many families continued detaining the afflicted in domestic cells, it did empower a group of "doctors of the mad" to articulate a new rhetoric of care, especially in diagnostic procedures, thrusting psychiatry onto the national stage as a legitimate discipline in the sciences and as a separate department in the hospital. Moreover, the authors of this act argued that hospitalization would help the afflicted to resume a productive life, an important position taken by psychiatrists who sought to expand their influence in hospitals and to gain more legitimacy and state recognition.[7]

Kure had studied under both Emil Kraepelin (1856–1926) and Franz Nissl (1860–1919) in Heidelberg, Germany; Kinnosuke Miura (1865–1950) had been a student of Jean-Martin Charcot (1825–93) at La Salpêtrière in France. Together the two men founded the Japanese Society of Neurology in 1902.[8] Kure's introduction of Emil Kraepelin's diagnostic classification of mental illness, which would be widely accepted by Japanese psychiatrists, was also adopted as the standard method for diagnosis in colonial Korea. Several of Kure's students, including Suitsu Shinji, the first director of the Government-General Hospital, would cross the straits to Korea to become the caretakers of the new psychiatric ward at Keijō (Gyeongseong) Imperial University. By the 1920s in Japan, increasing numbers of people were entering psychiatric institutions themselves or bringing family members there.[9]

As noted earlier, a complex traditional Oriental medical system with its own methods of diagnosis and treatment and folk remedies for treating mental disorders had existed for many centuries on the Korean peninsula. The creation of Western-style medicine in Korea began with the opening of the ports in 1876 to Japan and the arrival of Western missionaries in the 1880s.[10] Traditional Korean medicine, though gradually marginalized, remained influential in the field of mental illness in large part because neither the Japanese establishment nor the missionary doctors had the resources to allocate or cultivate proper treatment programs and educational opportunities for future Korean psychiatrists. Discrimination against Korean medical students and the monopoly of psychiatry by Japanese doctors meant that there would be very few trained Korean psychiatrists at the end of the Japanese colonial occupation, and this scarcity had a significant impact on future developments.[11]

Another important element in the development of psychiatry in Korea was the role of Western missionary doctors. According to one narrative of Protestant missions in Korea, which reached near-mythic proportions, Western missionary medicine made its first successful debut on the peninsula when Horace Newton Allen (1858–1932), an American missionary, saved the life of a Royal Court family member after an aborted coup in 1884. Horace Grant Underwood (1859–1916), another missionary who had difficult relations with Allen, remarked, "The story of Dr. Allen's arrival, providentially just previous to the émeute of 1884, and his success in saving the life of the favorite cousin [sic] of the queen, holding the position equivalent to Prime Minister, is too well known to need repetition."[12] The inability of traditional herbal doctors to heal the prince and Allen's appointment as the physician to the Royal Court allegedly led to a willingness on the part of the Royal Court to consider the introduction of Western medicine in Korea.[13] Hence, at Dr. Allen's request, in February 1885 King Gojong officially endorsed the opening of Gwanghyewon (Royal Hospital), which was later renamed Jejungwon (the House of Universal Relief), the first Western-style government hospital that was equipped with several operating rooms and wards.[14] In his first annual report of the Jejungwon, Allen listed a total of eighteen diseases most common among Koreans who frequented his outpatient clinic, which included smallpox, parasites, leprosy, syphilis, and malaria, as well as "diseases of the nervous system" such as delirium tremens, hysteria, hysteria globus, insanity, mania, dementia, melancholy, insomnia, and nervous prostration.[15] Despite this list of ailments, there is very little information on how Allen treated patients, especially those suffering from nervous disorders.

What is known about Allen is that he graduated from Ohio Wesleyan University in 1881 and subsequently received his MD following a one-year program at the Miami Medical College. Notably, he never received formal training in surgery, let alone in the specialized field of psychiatry.[16] Allen himself admitted in his sketches entitled "Things Korean" that he made medical mistakes when he performed procedures in which he was not really trained: for instance, he described pulling out a healthy tooth alongside a rotten one, an error that caused him to be "most depressed." With respect to his patients, the missionary doctor observed that Koreans "seem to operate on principle of no cure no pay"—a ruinous policy for the hospital in terms of both cost and time. To "prevent curiosity seekers from taking up valuable time at the hospital," and to instill in them a modicum of appreciation for his efforts, Allen instituted a small fee for all treatments. He was distressed to learn that, contrary to his goals, the patients considered the fee as "conferring a favor rather than that we had placed them under a debt of gratitude."[17] If Allen could not cure the chronic nervous disorders presented to him, there was also the danger that patients who paid their fees would feel cheated and deceived.

Dr. Oliver Avison (1860–1956), a medical professor from the University of Toronto who became the fourth director of the hospital in 1893, also listed a number of nervous disorders treated at the outpatient clinic in the *Annual Report of the Imperial Hospital* (1901). These included epilepsy, insanity, facial paralysis, spastic paralysis, hypochondria, neuralgia, sciatica, hemiplegia, and debility.[18] He noted that out of the 123 total cases treated at the hospital between May 1, 1900, and April 30, 1901, 46 patients were completely cured, 33 improved, 8 died in the hospital, and 5 left with the prospect of certain death.[19] Aside from these facts, there are no other documents that discuss in detail how Avison and other doctors at the hospital treated mental disorders.

In 1899, the Greater Korean Empire (Daehan) opened the Gwangjewon (House of Extended Deliverance), a new Western-style hospital and established a three-year medical program at the Uihakgyo (medical school), which accepted a total of nineteen students. During his furlough in North America in 1900, Avison worked tirelessly for greater investment in medical training of doctors and hospital expansion in Korea. Louis H. Severance, the Cleveland millionaire and founding member of Standard Oil Trust and a sulfur magnate, attended one of Avison's lectures and decided to offer a generous donation to realize the latter's dreams. Notably, that same year the Department of Home Affairs sought to modernize the Korean medical system by allowing both "practitioners of traditional Korean medicine and modern Western medicine [to] coexist" by requiring a medical doctor's qualification and registration.[20] On September 3, 1903, when the money from America arrived, the Jejungwon was renamed the Severance Memorial Hospital and Avison was named the new director; the latter opened a new medical school to train modern physicians in line with his goals. Four years later, on March 15, 1907, the Greater Korean Empire, by order of Emperor Gojong, merged the Uihakgyo (medical school), Gwangjewon, and the Red Cross Hospital and created the Daehan uiwon (Daehan Hospital), whose real authority lay in the hands of the Tōkanfu (Residency-General) after Japan inherited Korea as its protectorate in 1905. By 1909, the Daehan uiwon had seven departments, a faculty of seventeen physicians, seven professors, and nine pharmacists and a rigorous four-year medical curriculum. The first formal course in psychiatry was offered in 1910 to medical students during their final year.[21] It was at that time part of the medical training and not a special or separate specialization, although things would change by the early 1920s.

As observed in the previous chapter, the language of psychiatry began to seep into the report of Protestant missionaries in Korea who dealt with the mentally afflicted in their work. At the same time, some came to the conclusion that "insanity" stemmed from demonic possession just as it had in the time of Christ. For example, Charles F. Bernheisel, who worked as a missionary in Pyeongyang, related this incident, employing a blend of medical and religious terms: "The method of cure is unique. The Christians call for volunteers and then they divide themselves into bands which may consist of one or two persons, and then these bands take turns staying with the patient so that at no time day or night till recovery is complete is the patient left alone.... This continuous cannonade of prayer, Scripture reading, song, testimony, and exhortation finally prevails and the demon promises to leave, sometimes giving the very hour on which he will take his departure."[22] In place of the biblical term *healing*, Bernheisel chose the word *cure*. He also used the medical term *patient*, which suggested a person who required medical treatment, even as he described an exorcism. Sung-Deuk Oak says of Protestant missionaries in Korea that "their biblical literalism and field experiences ... led them to accept a Christian version of exorcisms" that "overrode their backgrounds in medical science and theology."[23] In other words, missionary doctors' triumphant narrative about their victory over primitive superstition did not tell the full story of Christianity and medicine in Korea.

JAPANESE PSYCHIATRY IN KOREA

Western-trained Japanese doctors began to arrive in Korea after 1876, primarily to treat the Japanese military.[24] Although these doctors did not generally treat native residents, official documentation of Koreans receiving treatment for psychiatric disorders appeared in an 1877 document at the Saiseiin (Jesaengwon), a clinic for Japanese expatriates and naval officers in Busan. However, there are no detailed accounts of how these Japanese doctors treated their patients and if the mentioned individuals required convalescent care.[25] Following Japan's annexation of Korea in 1910, the colonial authorities began to reform the medical system by modernizing existing institutions and enacting new legislation: they reorganized the Daehan uiwon and renamed it as the Chōsen sōtokufu iin (Chongdokbu uiwon, Government-General Hospital). The Uihakgyo was also given a new designation—the Joseon Chongdokbu uiwon busok uihak gangseupseo (Government-General Hospital of Joseon and Attached Training School), which later became the Gyeongseong uihak jeonmun hakgyo (Gyeongseong Medical College) in 1916. The hospital's director served as the school's rector, and the doctors simultaneously worked in the hospital and served as faculty members at the medical college.

On June 21, 1911, the Government-General enacted the Jesaengwon Act (Ordinance No. 77), the first attempt by the new colonial state to engage in charity work that involved "caring for orphans, educating the blind and mute, and [providing] relief for the mentally ill."[26] This approach was influenced by the spirit of social reform and humane philosophy that characterized early Japanese psychiatry.[27] The Government-General purchased the Gyeongseong Orphanage from Yi Pil-hwa (a Korean) and changed its name to the Jesaengwon. According to Yi Bu-yeong, there is no official record of how the Jesaengwon treated the mentally ill, but its changing policy became clear: by February of 1912, the Government-General decided to separate the mentally ill from the orphans, the blind, and the mute by placing the former under the jurisdiction of the Government-General Hospital. By May of 1914, the Government-General transferred the funds of the Jesaengwon to a separate account, and the following year it dispersed monies to specific projects such as a fund for poor relief (3,093,919 *won*), a fund for Hansen's disease (300,000 *won*), a fund for the mentally ill (150,000 *won*), and the Jesaengwon fund (333,446 *won*).[28] In other words, unlike the other recipients of charity, the mentally ill became classified as wards of the medical establishment, in recognition that they required some level of medical treatment.

In 1913, the Government-General Hospital allowed the psychiatric unit to branch out of internal medicine and create its own department. Suitsu Shinji, a graduate of Kyōto Imperial University and a former student of Kure Shūzō, became the director of the Department of Psychiatry and provided one Korean assistant (Sim Ho-seop) and four nurses. East Ward Number Eight was composed of two wards and an attached wooden building that was 170 *pyeong* in size (approximately 6,049 square feet) with twenty rooms for both men and women. The rooms looked quite ordinary and could accommodate a total of thirty-five patients at any time. There was a restraining room, a diagnosis room, a nurses' room, a bathing room, and a toilet. An *ondol* (charcoal brazier heating system) gave the building a more traditional feeling and was much more cost effective than an iron space heater.[29]

The profile of the patients changed over time as the medical and police regimes began to cooperate more closely. The first group of patients admitted to the ward were primarily Japanese male expatriates who suffered from alcoholism. However, the second annual report of the hospital shows a significant increase in the number of Korean patients as police precincts started to refer to the ward individuals with particular behavioral problems—from habitual stealing to sexual deviancy and arson. In addition, other departments in the hospital such as obstetrics and gynecology and internal medicine transferred to the psychiatry ward patients whom they deemed to be mentally unfit. While some of the behavioral problems cited in the report were observations documented after patients' admission, such as engaging in violent fights, wandering around the ward, displaying homicidal tendencies, or trying to escape, there were also patients who suffered from chronic disorders. According to the hospital annual report, a total of ninety-nine patients with antisocial behavior were admitted to the ward between 1912 and 1913.[30]

The annual report also listed patients diagnosed with dementia praecox, paralytic dementia, manic depression, epileptic mental illness, acute mental derangement, internally (somatically) caused mental illness, morphine addiction, and other debilitating mental problems.[31] This list of mental disorders suggests the adoption of Emil Kraepelin's system of taxonomies of mental illness as early as 1912, especially the inclusion of chronic disorders such as dementia praecox (later termed schizophrenia by Eugen Bleuer) and manic depression, a less pernicious form of psychosis.

In 1901, Kure Shūzō created two sewing rooms for female patients at the Tokyo Metropolitan Sugamo (later named Matsuzawa) Hospital, and within two years most of the mental hospitals in Japan started to offer occupational therapy to their patients.[32] Administrators at East Ward Number Eight also adopted Kure's "soft" therapeutic programs, which included outdoor activities such as weeding, farmwork, gardening, and horticulture for male patients; female patients were assigned domestic tasks such as laundering and knitting. Some of the activities were coed: male and female patients sat in the same room to seal envelopes. The most skilled were able to seal an average of 281 envelopes a day, while the less skilled managed to seal 50 envelopes. Patients were paid meager wages as an incentive, and although their supervisor kept most of their earnings in a savings account, they were allowed to spend up to forty *jeon* to purchase basic necessities.[33] While these tasks were not labor intensive and were designed to keep patients motivated, some of the other recreational activities that included walking were designed to induce natural fatigue.[34] Doctors sought to correct a wide range of "abnormal" behaviors through these kinds of "soft" occupational therapies.[35] The reports also mention the use of hypnotherapy and hot bath therapy for more debilitated patients. Those who were likely to become recidivist offenders were transferred back to the prison or police stations.

According to the *Government-General Hospital Annual Report,* by 1916 the number of patients referred to the ward for antisocial behavior had gradually begun to diminish. As table 1 shows, by 1926, in the Government-General Hospital's Department of Psychiatry, there were over three times as many outpatients as inpatients among those referred for antisocial behavior, suggesting that many patients who had previously been confined for this reason were now being categorized differently and treated as outpatients and that the inpatient clinics were being used primarily for patients with acute

TABLE 1 Numbers of Inpatients and Outpatients Referred to the Department of Psychiatry, Government-General Hospital, 1913–27, for Antisocial Behavior

	1913	1914	1915	1916	1918	1921	1922	1923	1926	1927
Inpatient	71	83	77	88	69	100	131	139	141	128
Outpatient	0	20	15	29	67	104	114	188	447	448
Total	71	103	92	117	136	204	245	327	588	576

SOURCE: Jeong Won-yong, "Geundae seoyang jeongsinuihagui jeongaewa byeoncheongwajeong—1920-nyeondae chobuteo 8. 15 gwangbok ijeonkkaji" (PhD diss., Seoul National University, 1996), 42.

illnesses. For example, in 1922 the majority of patients admitted to the inpatient ward suffered from chronic disorders, primarily cases involving dementia paralytic and dementia praecox, as well as different types of syphilitic mental disorders.[36] As one writer for the *Joseon ilbo* noted, East Ward Number Eight was the only facility in Korea where those suffering from chronic disorders could get treatment. While nobody seemed to be able to pinpoint the origins of mental illness, the author noted that madness, which had once been the domain of the philosopher, had become the domain of scientists, who were now engaged in numerous treatment experiments.[37] Despite this optimism, the annual reports between 1914 and 1928 showed successful treatment programs only for certain disorders; in most chronic cases, especially those of inpatients with dementia praecox, the cure rates were extremely low. For example, in 1923, out of fifty-eight patients admitted to the clinic, only four patients left it fully cured. In 1927, the cure rate was even lower, with only three out of sixty-eight patients being discharged as "fully cured."[38]

Despite the sparse official descriptions of the ward and the patients who were admitted to East Ward Number Eight, popular newspaper articles that aimed to familiarize the public with this space, like the article whose description opens this chapter, provide a general sense of the facility. The ward was not attached to the main hospital building. It could be entered only through a main gate, and all of the windows were secured by metal bars like those of a "zoo or prison." Security guards were responsible for opening the padded locked doors. In addition to the doctor who was on duty making his rounds for the day, there were usually four to five nurses working their shifts at the ward. Unlike in Japan, the patients were not forced to dress in asylum uniforms, and many opted to wear traditional Korean clothes. Some of the female patients wore colorful *jeogori* (Korean traditional jacket) tops.[39] Several of the patients were known outside the institution for their crimes, which were often reported in the daily newspapers. Certain types of criminals, such as arsonists, murders, and violent criminals with chronic mental disorders, were usually referred to the ward by police precincts.

Newspaper reports' descriptions of patients' behavior and, occasionally, guesses at their inner state and feelings, covered a wide spectrum—from "pathetic looking" to emaciated, sedated, disheveled, depressed, agitated, and overly excited.[40] Writers observed that in fits of rage the patients would curse at visitors or break the windows with objects. Sedated patients often drooped their heads or would engage in repetitive acts like twiddling their fingers or talking endlessly to themselves. The ages of adults ranged between nineteen to sixty years, with the majority of the patients in their early twenties, although one newspaper article noted a child as young as nine years.[41] Some were from well-to-do Japanese families, like the son of Mr. Takeshi, a lawyer, who was admitted to be treated for neurasthenia but was diagnosed by the hospital doctors as suffering from mental illness instead. His reasoning for trying to escape was his unhappiness being around "abnormal" patients at the ward.[42]

During the 1920s, East Ward Number Eight usually housed between twenty to thirty patients, with about half of them usually being Korean. Often men outnumbered women, and the sexes were housed in separate floors. Not all patients survived in the ward, and sensational stories of patients' suicides, such as one involving Jeong Seong-nam, a beautiful nineteen-year-old girl from Jinju who succeeded in hanging herself before a nurse could rescue her, were reported in the press.[43]

According to the Korean newspapers, the colonial authorities distinguished between the mentally ill who posed a threat to the colonial authorities and those who were merely pathetic and harmless. When mentally ill people were harmless and lived in the countryside where shamanic practices persisted, authorities allowed villagers to take them to a shaman for exorcistic rites. The authorities viewed these kinds of practices as an extension of Korea's backwardness and superstitious culture, but they saw no need to interfere: in these cases, the afflicted were not rounded up and sent to East Ward Number Eight.[44] However, when the idioms of madness involved some threat to the Japanese or colonial authorities even in a distorted form, the reaction was swift and uncompromising. Incarceration awaited the man who was caught loitering around the Joseon Hotel with a bat in his hand claiming to have an appointment with the Governor-General. Similarly, a woman who posed as a general wanting to use a sword against those "Japanese sons-of-bitches" who had stripped her son (allegedly the heir apparent to the throne) of power prompted the police to react to her as a "dangerous" element in society.[45] In an editorial in the *Joseon ilbo*, one writer observed that Korean patients in the mental ward seemed to harbor some political grievances toward the Government-General. He argued that their mental illness was induced, not by personal problems such as marital discord or lovers' quarrels, but by the desire to drive out the Japanese out of town or publicly rebuke them for their abuses of power.[46] It is difficult to gauge from newspaper reports when those who were incarcerated actually suffered from mental illness and when they employed madness as a disguise under which to express dissent against the Japanese authorities.

SEVERANCE UNION MEDICAL COLLEGE AND HOSPITAL: A NEW PHASE (1909–45)

Between 1909 and 1945, Severance Medical College and Hospital admitted a total of 909 Korean students; 65 of them would eventually become doctors. According to J. D. VanBuskirk, by 1925 Severance was one of the largest hospitals "of the whole missionary field" and "probably the largest charity service of a single institution in Korea."[47] The appointment in 1923 of Charles Inglis McLaren (1882–1957), an Australian psychiatrist and missionary of the Presbyterian Church of Victoria at Severance Union Hospital, led to the creation of the first department of neurology and psychiatry at the institution. McLaren's humanistic approach to patients' rights and his ardent attempts to combat social stigma attached to mental illness shaped the character of his psychiatric ward, which differed significantly from East Ward Number Eight.[48]

McLaren had earned his doctorate at the University of Melbourne under the guidance of Richard Starwell and had experience working as a resident medical officer at the Royal Melbourne Hospital and Children's Hospital. Upon arriving in Seoul, he taught courses in neurology and psychiatry in addition to pediatrics and orthopedics at Severance Union Hospital and Medical College. According to the course catalog, all fourth-year medical students were required to take a course in psychiatry during their third semester for two hours a week.

McLaren wanted to introduce a type of treatment program that differed from the rigid German-style biological approach offered at the Japanese schools by emphasizing a focus on the soul as well as the body. His model of treatment had to address the cry, "Physician, canst thou not minister to a mind diseased?" In 1928, McLaren wrote: "It is almost axiomatic in the thought of many medical men that where mental disease is, there necessarily abnormality of the brain cells must be, and be in a causal relation to the disease." However, he rejected the hypothesis that there was necessarily "a causal organic basis" (such as the "deterioration of the brain cells") to mental illness. Instead, he argued, "Mental abnormality may arise from abnormality of psychism and a strong confirmation of this fact is the other fact that grave disease of mental function is constantly being cured by direct appeal to the psyche." In his view, physical injuries of the brain often simply exaggerated or muffled existing attributes of someone's personality.[49]

Besides "qualities in the personality," McLaren distinguished "things in the environment" that could produce "devastating effects on the susceptible mentality." For instance, quoting from the Anglican Book of Common Prayer, "From all blindness of heart, from vain glory and hypocrisy; from envy, hatred, and malice, and all uncharitableness; from fornication and all other deadly sin, and from all the deceits of the world, the flesh and the devil, Good Lord, deliver us," McLaren contended that some individuals' hyperconscientiousness about such sins and struggles to fulfill the "infinite requirements of holiness" resulted in mental derangement.[50] Adopting a humanistic position, McLaren emphasized the importance of rehabilitation in all mental illnesses rather than viewing certain afflictions as chronic and incurable.[51]

In 1923, drawing on a generous donation from Caroline B. Adams, a philanthropist from Berkeley, California, as well as several anonymous donors, McLaren established his long-sought psychiatric ward with ten beds at Severance.[52] Although the ward was not as big as East Ward Number Eight at the Government-General Hospital, McLaren felt that it was satisfactory and suitable to treat patients. Careful thought was put into making the facility hospitable, from the private garden to the fresh paint on the walls to the paintings in each room. Safety was also paramount: the ward had a security guard, was fireproof and soundproof, and had barred windows and locked doors to prevent patients from escaping. Staff were not only experienced professionally but also oriented to help make the life of each patient as dignified as possible. The goal was to relieve the afflicted of their mental tortures and to return them to the ranks of productive citizens.[53]

McLaren developed several models of treatment. The first he termed "spiritual treatment." It involved "an elucidation and interpretation of the psychic history of the patient, a sympathetic understanding of his difficulties, and encouragement and direction in facing and overcoming these difficulties." This meant helping patients confront their fears, whether these fears were based on real threats in their current lives or on imaginings from their past. Unless patients were "delivered from the past," they could not be reoriented in the present. McLaren described one patient who seemed to be suffering from neurosis; physical symptoms were present, but "the whole aspect of the case proclaimed its psychic origin." After he gained the patient's confidence, he drew out the man's past from him. It turned out that the patient, who was a widower, had committed adultery in his loneliness and depression. McLaren's "spiritual" therapy consisted of attempting to reorient the patient toward "forgiveness and new hope." As he wrote, "The treatment for false self-accusation is not assurance of forgiveness but deliverance from morbid self-depreciation and condemnation and reinstatement in merited self-respect."[54]

For McLaren, such encounters proved that Korean patients were no different from patients in the West: "those same maladjustments concerning sex, livelihood, disappointed hopes, responsibilities which have been demonstrated as the potent causes of neurasthenia in the Occident are seen exercising a like baneful influence with like results in Korea." He attempted to offer his patients both spiritual and psychological solutions, modeling his approach on Jesus's own treatment of the ill and downtrodden. As McLaren put it, "His [Jesus'] teachings about sex, money, the family, fear, economics, and the other problems, which constantly appear and reappear in a psycho-neurological clinic, are strangely apposite, constructive, and vital."[55]

Most important, McLaren believed that there was always a cure for what he deemed psychic diseases. His biographer and fellow missionary Esmond W. New related one incident that demonstrated McLaren's faith in the power of a treatment approach inspired by Christianity: McLaren accepted a young medical student who had suffered from a nervous breakdown two years prior. When the medical faculty rejected his decision to take the recovered patient as an assistant, McLaren challenged their refusal to reinstate the man: "In our attitude, a patient who has suffered from psychosis, to accept it as inevitable and beyond remedy, and to sit down under the shadow of a dreaded recurrence is not the kind of help we should extend towards sickness. To deny the hope of a cure seems that we have not emerged from a fatalism scarcely to be distinguished from superstition. It denies the faith alike of scientific medicine and of Christianity, for both of them teach that nature is understandable and can be brought under control."[56] McLaren optimistically believed that spiritualized psychotherapy was the most effective treatment for all psychic problems, and he considered it critical to train medical students to practice it.[57]

In 1929, during his sabbatical, McLaren himself undertook postgraduate study in Vienna, where he learned new treatments like fever therapy and psychoanalysis. He was particularly interested in learning how to treat progressive paralysis through the work of Julius Wagner-Jauregg (1857–1940), and he followed the therapeutic methods of Joseph Dejerine (1849–1917), Alfred Adler (1870–1937), and Sigmund Freud (1856–1939).[58] Dejerine viewed emotional trauma as the cause of neurosis and advocated "cathartic expression" as a means to free patients from their harmful feelings. Like Dejerine, McLaren also advocated an "exhortative, trusting relationship between himself and his patients" and urged them to believe in their "eventual cure."[59] McLaren also learned about Adler's approach of using friendly conversation to discover distortions in neurotic patients' thoughts and feelings, a line of therapy that he preferred to Freud's approach of working toward an "integrated awareness of unconscious thoughts."[60] And although McLaren and his students spent a lot of time consulting with patients on spiritual matters, they also, according to the annual reports of the hospital, experimented with other, more physically focused treatments, such as electroshock, insulin shock therapy, and pharmaceutical medications such as phenobarbital.[61]

McLaren was also alert to potential underlying medical problems that caused patients to present as if they were suffering from mental illness. In "Lessons from the Neurology Clinic," McLaren described a visitor to the Neurology Department whose "whole bearing stamped the diagnosis of 'sinkyung-soi-yak,' . . . an exact translation of our own high-sounding but not very sensible term 'neurasthenia.'" During the consultation, McLaren realized that the patient suffered from a serious lung disease that was in fact the real problem. He described him as one "who a moment before had been torn with a desperate anxiety about ills which others might deem and dismiss as imaginary."[62] McLaren's faith in both medical science and Christianity blended to create a special atmosphere of optimism and hope in his psychiatric ward.

In an article directed at foreign missionaries, McLaren provided a glimpse of an average day on a busy Saturday morning at Severance Hospital that highlighted his role as instructor, mentor, and healer. After exchanging pleasantries with a Canadian man who was the secretary-treasurer of the hospital, McLaren headed to his office to find a letter from the head of the Department of Neurology at Peiping (Peking) Union Medical School, informing him that Yi Jung-cheol, his first student and "the man to succeed me in the department," had excelled in postgraduate study at the university and was returning to Seoul. Yi eventually became one of the first Korean doctors formally trained in psychiatry but would die at the tender age of forty-one in 1945. McLaren expressed joy about the news of his protégé and began his morning round with a group of new interns.[63] The medical college, which modeled its curriculum on an American medical school, had started to offer internships in 1914.

The first part of McLaren's round with his interns focused on patients with physiological conditions. His first patient of the day was a man suffering from hemiplegic paralysis. After offering a clinical explanation to the interns, the teacher confirmed his diagnosis by showing them reports of the chemical blood findings from the bacteriological laboratory. Next he treated one of the nurses in the hospital who had been suffering from a type of paralysis. McLaren demonstrated the importance of the x-ray department to the process of making a clinical diagnosis; on the basis of an x-ray he was able to discern that the patient suffered from an acute case of beriberi, a treatable condition. He then examined a former student who had been diagnosed with tuberculosis, an urban scourge afflicting many young men in Korea. As he came to the end of this ward, he supervised interns who drew spinal fluid from a patient with meningitis. Next McLaren visited the clinical laboratory, where he examined the eggs of a rare parasite extracted from a patient, and then the outpatient clinic, where he prescribed a cough mixture to some "foreign" (Western) child.

Finally, McLaren attended to an unusual case of a young girl "with a strange sort of hysteria" that he confessed he had never encountered before in Korea. He hypothesized her symptoms to be those of St. Vitus Dance or chorea minor, a disorder characterized by rapid, uncoordinated jerking movements of the face and hands. McLaren decided to admit her into the inpatient ward for further observation and treatment. According to

VanBuskirk's report, roughly half of the patients received free care, and those who were charity patients stayed in the hospital an average of 21 days each, compared to 9.5 in cases of those who could pay for their care. It is unclear whether this girl was a charity patient.[64]

After completing his round at the outpatient clinic, McLaren met with the dean of the Medical College to schedule his lectures for the following semester, which were to begin in two weeks.[65] By 1928, all medical students at the college during their third year had to take a yearlong course (three semesters) in neurology and psychiatry for one hour a week. Students in their fourth year were also required to take a course in psychiatry for two hours a week that included lectures and bedside training (as described above).

McLaren's day had not yet ended: he returned to his office and examined a plan for placing violent mentally ill patients in a small ward of their own to segregate them from patients being treated in the General Hospital. McLaren continued his routine of examining patient case histories with his student assistant before meeting with patients for consultation. The first patient was a typical neurasthenic young man who had abandoned his studies and was incapable of working. Aside from some anemia and hookworms in his blood tests, the patient had no physical ailment; still he claimed that "something [had] gone wrong with his brain and so he [was] incapacitated." In this particular case, McLaren declared that potent therapy would not be helpful; instead he resorted to the "spiritual treatment." The doctor encouraged him to look to examples of "people who have been weak [who] claim to have become strong." Equally important, he urged the patient to "be consistently associated with faith in and obedience to the Christ."[66] As in his other spiritual treatments, he was recommending a course of action that would reconcile the patient with Christ and Christianity's lofty ideals. The patient's response to this advice is not recorded.

McLaren's final patient of the day was a carpenter whom he had seen the previous week. The latter claimed to be suffering from sleeplessness and nervousness. After drawing out the patient's personal history (presumably using psychoanalysis), McLaren ascertained that the cause of mental derangement was not distress over how to provide for his aged mother (as the patient must have complained) but rather his doubts over "the validity of the supreme claims of the Church." As a Roman Catholic Christian, he was pained to see priests "whose actions and motives belie the claim that they represent another order of life than our common mundane one." Unable to offer the patient "indubitable proof," McLaren asked the patient to read the Gospel of St. John and to consult with him later after he had thought about it.[67]

McLaren's Saturday ended with disappointment when one of his student assistants bid him farewell. This was the assistant who, as described above, had had a mental breakdown and a two-year hospitalization at an asylum. Despite McLaren's protests, the faculty in the college had decided not to readmit him.

McLaren was forced to resign from Severance Medical College in 1939 for arguing against Japan's enforcement of emperor worship. After he had served a seventy-day sentence, the Japanese authorities expelled him to Australia in 1942.[68] Up to his last day in Korea, the missionary doctor worked "feverishly against the time," attempting to train as many Korean doctors as possible in both medicine and Christianity. Esmond New recalled, it had become increasingly evident to his friend that "there might be no second generation of Western experts to carry on the work of Western education."[69] To the end, McLaren pondered the burning question: "How can we make the power of God work in the mental diseases to which man is prone."[70] McLaren's missionary psychiatry may have left a deeper mark on Korean society than previously imagined. In Korean Christian communities, mental illness came to be seen as a form of spiritual malaise (not unlike the traditional explanation). According to one study conducted in 1986, Koreans responded that the most effective methods of treatment included "isolation, rest, prayer, and penitence"—a cure reminiscent of McLaren's approach.[71] At the very least, one can argue that McLaren lay the foundations for a Christianized understanding of mental illness, accompanied by the basics of Western psychotherapy.

KEIJŌ (GYEONGSEONG) IMPERIAL UNIVERSITY

The other major institution that laid the foundation for modern psychiatry in Korea was created at the initiative of the Japanese colonial authorities, who incorporated the German model wholesale, retaining a biological approach to the bases of mental illness. In 1924 the Government-General of Korea officially established Keijō (Gyeongseong) Imperial University, the sixth imperial university and the first outside Japan, followed by Taihoku (Taipei) University in 1928. It was the only university in Korea with two faculties (the faculty of law and humanities and the faculty of medicine).[72] That same year, the Government-General Hospital became the Associated Teaching Hospital of the Medical College of Keijō (Gyeongseong) Imperial University, the highest institution of medical education in the colony. On May 1, 1926, the medical college started to offer its first courses in neurology and psychiatry. Dr. Kubo Kiyoji, who had been offered a position at Hokkaidō Imperial University, decided to take the position in Korea as the head instructor at the new medical school and hospital and was joined by Watanabe Michio and Hattori Rokuburo, a graduate of Kyūshū Imperial University whose extensive research focused on the treatment of malaria fever and paralytic dementia. East Ward Number Eight, which had originally been built to treat patients, was renamed Keijō (Gyeongseong) Mental Ward in 1928, marking a shift in its priorities from treatment to research. Thus stronger ties were forged between the mental ward and the university and laboratory—the former serving as the observation center for the latter. The Department of Neurology and Psychiatry moved into a new building on the west side of the Associated Teaching Hospital of the Medical College. It was equipped with thirty beds, a restraining and inspection room, library, conference room, and research laboratories modeled after the German *klinik*.[73]

The curriculum of the medical school in psychiatry was more extensive than that of the Severance Union Hospital Medical School. All medical students were required to take a course in psychiatry and neurology for one hour a week during the second and third semesters of their third year. They also had to take another course in neuropsychiatry, which included bedside training, for three semesters during their fourth year for two hours a week. Starting from the second semester of their third year, students received training at the outpatient clinic as well.[74]

Although Japanese was the official language of instruction at the university, instructors used German extensively in the classrooms and practicum. According to Yi Bu-yeong, all the clinical reports of patients were written in German, so students needed to have at least proficient reading knowledge of the language.[75] All Japanese students in the medical college were required to take eight hours of German a week during their first year, while their Korean counterparts were required to take only four hours, thus making the latter less prepared for the psychiatric field. During their second and third years, Japanese students had to take an additional four hours a week of German while Koreans only took three hours. In their fourth year, only Japanese students enrolled in two hours a week of German. Before graduation, Japanese students were required to have taken a total of thirty-six hours a week of instruction in German while their Korean counterparts were expected to have completed twenty hours a week.[76]

According to the historian Liu Si-yung, the Meiji state had from its beginnings endorsed a German university-based system, which gave greater prominence to scientific training and laboratory work, over the system of clinical medicine in Great Britain, which was much more hospital based. By the 1880s, German was the lingua franca of the Japanese medical profession and medical students were expected to be fairly fluent in it. The Meiji state also encouraged students to go study abroad and enroll in medical schools in Germany and offered generous scholarships.[77] Quite apart from the inadequate preparation for Korean students to compete with Japanese, open discrimination ensured that graduates could not secure teaching or research positions. Such patterns of discrimination continued in the following decades: as Ho Young Lee has observed, Japanese doctors "monopolized" faculty positions at the Medical College until the end of World War II. When these doctors departed the peninsula, they left a gaping hole in the field of psychiatry, for there were only thirteen trained Korean psychiatrists to take their place.[78]

Research and Treatment at the Klinik

Professors in the Department of Neurology and Psychiatry at Keijō (Gyeongseong) Imperial University and Gyeongseong uihak jeonmun hakgyo (Keijō Medical College) viewed themselves not only as members of the university faculty and physicians but also as natural scientists. They published their research findings in the *Chōsen igakukai zasshi* (*Joseon uihakhoe japji*), the official journal of the Chōsen (Korean) Medical Association, the largest professional medical organization, which published its first volume in 1911 and its last in 1943. In 1926, the journal switched its serial format from annual to monthly installments. Suitsu Shinji, Sim Ho-seop, Kubo Kiyoji, Kitamura Yojin, Manjirō Sugihara, Hara Shinsho, Hikari Shingo, An Jeong-il, Yi Jung-cheol, and Hattori Rokuburo, who all worked at some point as faculty members at the university and medical college, contributed articles to the journal. The topics ranged from narcotics addiction to St. Vitus Dance (chorea), alcoholism, the procedure of cisterna magna puncture (to collect cerebrospinal fluid), Ringer's solution, *verschamte Manie*, torticollis, various dissociative disorders, schizophrenia, malaria treatment, alkaloid treatment, the Wasserman reaction, scopolamine and luminal (barbiturates), sulfuric acid treatment, neurasthenia, and hysteria. These articles were influential in enlightening other physicians about the etiology, symptoms, and therapeutic treatment of mental illness. Japanese professors like Kubo Kiyoji and Manjirō Sugihara had the opportunity to present their research at the annual meeting of the Japanese Society of Psychiatry and Neurology in Tokyo.[79] Faculty were also encouraged to experience *ryūgaku* (foreign study) because it provided Japanese psychiatrists with professional role models and values and, according to James Bartholomew, "inspired commitment to particular kinds of research."[80]

Some of the faculty produced their works in other medical journals such as *Man-Sen no ikai, Mitteilungen aus der Medizinischen Akademie zu Keijo* (1917), *Acta Medicinalia in Keizo,* the *Keizo Journal of Medicine* (1930), and the *Journal of Medical College in Keijō*. Korean doctors also published their research results in the *Joseon uibo* (Korean medical journal), while missionary doctors like Charles McLaren published more widely in Christian and international journals such as the *China Medical Journal,* the *Australian Journal of Psychology and Philosophy,* and the *Korea Mission Field*.[81] Japanese professors like Kubo Kiyoshi and other faculty at the university and medical college also translated important textbooks by Eugen Bleuler (*Lehrbuch der psychiatrie*), Emil Kraepelin (*Psychiatrie: Ein Lehrbuch fur Studierende und Arzte Band IV* and *Klinische Psychiatry*), S. A. Hunter (*A Manual of Therapeutics and Pharmacy*), Henry Maudsley (*The Pathology of Mind*), Oswald Bumke (*Handbuch der Neurologie*), Wilhelm Griesinger (*Die Pathologie und Therapie der psychischen Krankheite*), Karl Jaspers (*Allgemeine Psychopathologie*), and others into Japanese. These texts were available in the university library.

The German framework for understanding mental illness differed significantly from McLaren's spiritual framework. For example, Wilhelm Griesinger's works claimed that every mental disease was rooted in brain disease, an assertion that inspired students at the college to conduct research in brain pathology.[82] The well-known Japanese psychiatrist Kure Shūzō's work on Kraepelinian nosology also had a huge influence on psychiatry in Korea.

Other popular approaches, including Morita (Masatake) Shoma's studies on neurosis (later developed into the "Morita therapy method"), were readily available at the university library as well. Having suffered from chronic neurasthenic symptoms himself, Morita, a student of Kure, developed a therapy whereby the patient would be able to "overcome his symptoms, gain insight into his disease and realize his true self." This "life normalization method" involved a stage of rest therapy, which was also being advocated by psychiatrists like Otto Binswanger (1852–1929) and Silas Weir Mitchell (1829–1914). That stage was followed by stages of occupational therapy that oriented patients to the present, helping patients to decentralize the self and to understand that although it was "normal" to have certain feelings, and although feelings should be acknowledged, they did not have to influence action.[83]

The newspapers often reported summaries of important doctoral theses of students such as a Dr. Ikeda, a recent graduate of Keijō (Gyeongseong) Imperial University, who had submitted a thesis on treating syphilitic mental illness through intravenous therapy.[84] Taken together, translations of important Western theories and treatments for mental disorder as well as publications of important texts by Japanese psychiatrists played a decisive role in developing psychiatry as a medical field at the university.

In addition to their teaching and publication, Japanese professors and their students spent a considerable time in the psychiatric *klinik*, which functioned as an examination room as well as a research laboratory. The laboratory allowed faculty and students to engage in physiological examinations; it was a place where they could conduct experiments in histology and pathology. Students also learned how to perform autopsies, conduct blood samples, and examine microscopic samples.[85] Equally important, cadavers of Japanese and Korean patients were readily available for autopsies, and those working on experiments in neuropathology preserved many of the brains for further research. The institutional need for the quick availability of cadavers required a surplus number of chronic patients in the ward at any given time.[86] Postmortem autopsies was treated as a part of clinical practice that enabled students to evaluate the accuracy of a particular clinical diagnosis or, as Eric Engstrom aptly notes in the German context, "to discover something that the patients had not been unable or willing to supply" and to use the results as "surrogates for patients' description of their own illnesses."[87]

The routines in the clinic became streamlined for the most efficient study of the mentally ill subjects. Whenever a patient was admitted to the ward, a hospital staff member, usually the head nurse or a student completing his weekly practicum hours, measured and recorded the patient's blood pressure and pulse with a kymographion and a sphygmograph respectively. Doctors and their students also had to become well versed in laboratory techniques, including new methods of sampling, measuring, and chemically analyzing cerebrospinal fluid and blood. Because so many of the male patients seeking treatment in the inpatient clinic suffered from syphilis, it became mandatory practice to perform a lumbar puncture on them and to analyze the obtained fluid.[88] These tests were considered crucial because, although doctors were still unable to determine whether syphilis or mental illness was curable, they could at least establish with far great accuracy whether the patient would require long-term care. Chronic patients were considered a liability after 1926 because the university mental ward was relatively small and because they were not considered to be useful for clinical teaching. At the same time, the lumbar puncture test offered the hospital and psychiatry a means to profit financially by expanding their outpatient ward to treat alcoholics, syphilitic, and drug users.

The acceptance of Emil Kraepelin's nosology and biological framework in the 1920s as well as his longitudinal study of patients gave doctors at the university hospital a coherent system of diagnostic techniques, disease categories, and therapeutic strategies. They could now show their students patients with acute disorders and instruct them in identifying a disease, elicit certain symptoms, document the disease's progression and regression, and offer treatment based on the data collected before the chronic phase set in. Because of this pedagogic shift to diagnostic examination, doctors expected their students to take clinical bedside instruction very seriously. Unlike doctors in the United States and Great Britain, the faculty at the hospital rarely invested their time in the personal lives of the patients (in contrast to McLaren's interactions with his patients described above) and focused primarily on conducting the earliest possible intervention to cure acute diseases, without regard for patients' rights. The lack of personal attention to patients was highlighted when East Ward Number Eight's director, Suitsu Shinju, was asked about how a nine-year-old girl, who had been admitted a year earlier for setting fire to twenty or so establishments, had escaped from the ward; he simply expressed regret to a reporter from the *Donga ilbo*, admitting human error and claiming that he could not keep track of all his patients.[89] To train students effectively, the ward required a certain percentage of acutely ill patients to be readily available for students' instruction, but when "they were no longer considered research worthy" the hospital discharged them.[90]

While there is very little information about the laboratory instruction that students received, Yi Jung-ho's detailed study of Keijō (Gyeongseong) Medical College shows that all medical students were required to take a variety of courses in anatomy, physiology, medical chemistry, microbiology, pharmacology, pathology, and hygiene and preventive medicine, which were held in large lecture halls and often involved clinical demonstrations.[91] By taking these science courses, students were able to see that the same laws of causality governing the natural sciences could be applied to psychiatric cases. Government-General annual reports record that doctors also experimented with new techniques that they had learned during their postgraduate work at German universities, such as insulin shock therapy, metrazol/cardiazol shock, electroconvulsive therapy, malaria therapy, chloral hydrates, chemical bromides, and sedation by barbiturates. According to the historian Akihito Suzuki, shock therapy was offered to well-off patients and their families in Japan because such prospects of treatment appealed to them.[92] It is not clear if this was the case in Korea. Doctors also worked closely with pharmaceutical companies to develop placebo pills (usually a mix of bromides) for hypochondriacs and prescribed over-the-counter drugs from Japan such as *mohirarin* (mozarin), a painkiller for morphine addicts; *Kennogwan*, a pill that "could cure headaches, sleeping disorders, loss of memory, and weariness"; and a variety of other pills to cure various "brain" and "nervous" disorders.[93] According to Bou-Yong Rhi (Yi Bu-yeong), clinical psychiatric management and treatment developed alongside therapies in Europe starting with occupational and sleep therapy in the 1910s for psychotic patients, Manfred Sakel's insulin coma therapy in the late 1920s and early 1930s, and fever, sulfur, and malaria therapy for general paresis, which became popular in the 1930s.[94]

In short, the development of psychiatric medicine in Japanese-controlled institutions was shaped largely by a tradition of German theories, techniques, and cures. Over time, the humane approach disappeared completely, replaced by the relentless research agendas of faculty and staff.

Therapeutic or Custodial Institution?

Despite some advances made in clinical research and instruction, the lingering question of how to deal with incurable, long-term chronic patients plagued colonial authorities and doctors alike. In the parallel case of lepers, in 1916 the Government-General transformed an old Protestant sanatorium on the island of Sorok in South Jeolla Province into one of the world's largest leper colonies, housing at its peak in 1929 a population of eight hundred inmates. The government was, however, less successful in procuring funds to build mental institutions on the peninsula.[95] The statistics on patients who were admitted to the

TABLE 2 Patients at the Government-General Hospital and *jahye uiwon* (provincial charity hospitals), 1925

Diagnosis/Gender		Inpatient			Outpatient		
		Korean	*Japanese*	*Foreigner*	*Korean*	*Japanese*	*Foreigner*
Mental Illness	Male	47	44	0	110	107	0
	Female	25	36	0	59	61	0
Nervous Disorder	Male	101	74	0	3,272	2,346	23
	Female	36	62	0	1,182	1,918	6
Opium Addiction	Male	49	19	0	159	43	2
	Female	21	13	0	63	22	0
Total	Male	197	137	0	3,451	2,496	25
	Female	82	111	0	1,304	2,201	6
	Total	279	248	0	4,845	4,497	31
Total Patient Figures	Male	3,432	4,017	43	80,512	51,503	591
	Female	1,434	3,959	8	40,939	55,955	135
	Total	4,886	7,976	51	121,451	107,458	726

SOURCE: Jeong Won-yong, "Geundae seoyang jeongsinuihagui jeongaewa byeoncheongwajeong—1920-nyeondae chobuteo 8. 15 gwangbok ijeonkkaji" (PhD diss., Seoul National University, 1996), 158.

Government-General Hospital and provincial charity hospitals, which were compiled in the aftermath of the March First Movement (1919), show that many more people suffering from mental disorders sought outpatient services than inpatient services. For example, in 1925, 4,845 Koreans sought outpatient treatment services for mental illness, nervous disorders, or opium addiction, while only 279 patients sought inpatient care (table 2). One reason for this significant disparity was the exorbitant cost for an average citizen seeking inpatient care, even hospitalization for one day. Whereas at the Government-General Hospital outpatient services cost 674 *won*, the cost for inpatient care was 1,858 *won*. At the provincial charity hospitals the situation was almost the same: 406 *won* for outpatient services, 1,848 *won* for inpatient services. To put things into perspective, the average daily wage for a farmer's entire household was 4 *won* and 83 *jeon* a day; most farmers earned roughly 49 *jeon* to 1 *won* a day. In other words, a farmer would have to spend his entire annual earnings to seek treatment at a hospital.[96] From hospitals' point of view, the accumulation of chronic patients also posed a huge financial risk; doctors did not want to see wards turned into carceral institutions.

Given the financial burdens placed on patients and their families and the pragmatic concerns of hospitals, the public debate focused on three overlapping solutions. Newspaper editorials called for strict custody laws to treat and protect the mentally ill, financial support for the improvement of treatment programs, and the construction of large asylums. From a study completed by the Department of Hygiene in 1926, the *Sidae ilbo* reported that an estimated 2,411 Koreans (1,855 males and 556 females) and 87 Japanese (41 males and 46 females) suffered from some kind of mental disorder. Although the writer praised East Ward Number Eight for doing something to treat the afflicted, he noted that the ward did not have the resources and staff to handle the surge of people who experienced a fit of mental illness (*balgwang*) during the summer monsoon season, prompting them to commit murder, theft, arson, and other violent crimes. One writer urged the Government-General to expeditiously approve a custody and protection law—Japan already had a quite effective one, but Korea had none—arguing that hospitalization would provide an effective form of crime prevention.[97] In its own study, the *Donga ilbo* estimated that 2,500 Koreans were suffering from mental illness. Comparatively speaking, of neighboring regions Japan was ranked highest with 57,800 mentally ill patients, followed by Korea, Taiwan (2,300), Hokkaidō (1,460), Karufuto (Sakhalin, 100), and Nanyang (72). If there was a correlation between civilization and mental illness, Korea was catching up, and the writer pressed the colonial government to create facilities to house dangerous lunatics, who were "wandering aimlessly around Seoul scaring ordinary people."[98]

With the easing of publication laws in the aftermath of the March First Movement, surveys and censuses conducted by different bureaus in the Government-General Office were made available to the wider community through the press. Compiled statistics fueled the perception of madness as a growing social problem. Though the Government-General Hospital claimed that its East Ward Number Eight was solving the problem of insanity, policies of admission and discharge did not adequately account for chronicity. This became clear with the announcement that the Government-General Hospital and East Ward Number Eight would be transferred to the Keijō (Gyeongseong) Imperial University. If the annual budget for maintaining twenty-two patients was 12,000 *won* a year, the new hospital could no longer serve as a custodial institution, and from 1926 onward the state attempted to transfer mentally ill patients to charity hospitals and other private facilities.[99] According to one report, the restructuring of East Ward Number Eight signaled a radical shift in treatment policy: acutely afflicted patients, who were deemed more pedagogically useful for research, were kept in the new ward, while others suffering from incurable and chronic diseases were discharged and left on the streets to fend for themselves.

This approach in turn angered the public, for it saw the Government-General's new policy as endangering Korean lives.[100] Even by 1929, writers continued to express frustration with the colonial state for neglecting the afflicted and not implementing any hospital or custodial laws to incarcerate people they considered to be dangerous lunatics. Drawing on a recent study by the Department of Hygiene, one writer for the *Donga ilbo* noted an increase not only in the numbers of mentally ill but in the intensity of the disease as manifested in public life. He argued that patients suffering from *jogwangseong* (mania) posed the greatest threat to public security, placing huge burdens on the police precincts to monitor them and ensure that they did not commit any crimes. Despite these daily threats, the writer argued in frustration that unlike Japan the colonial state had yet to create any *gajeong gamchi* (home confinement) laws. Despite the Department of Hygiene's recommendation to construct a large mental hospital to house the afflicted, the writer complained, the Government-General had decided to pass such responsibilities on to the general population by asking Koreans to solicit funds to build such a facility.[101]

In the absence of custody laws, asylums, and a rigid criteria of curability that governed institutional psychiatric care, a new rhetoric of care emerged in the 1920s. Psychiatrists attempted to use their diagnostic skills to address the larger sociopolitical questions of the times. Citing statistics on the dangers posed by madness and other, related urban scourges such as alcoholism and venereal disease, psychiatrists drew on degenerative theory and empirical hereditary prognosis to expand their jurisdictional reach beyond the hospital and laboratory. Fears that mental illness and criminality were or were linked to hereditary and congenital diseases allowed psychiatrists to enhance their professional status by becoming experts in mental hygiene. In addition, they could impose their diagnostic skills on new groups of "degenerates" in the urban centers such as the feeble-minded, neurasthenics, hypochondriacs, hysterics, and overburdened students and children. Psychiatrists claimed that many urban dwellers had their delicate nerves stretched to a breaking point by the pressures and temptations of urban, modern civilization, a topic that will be discussed in detail in chapter 4. Instead of having to deliver on their earlier promises of therapy and treatment, doctors now shifted their focus to social prophylaxis and public enlightenment to explain congenital disposition and the pathogenesis of psychiatric disorder.[102]

On August 26, 1921, *Joseon ilbo* reported that Kim Yeong-chul, a sixteen-year-old from North Chuncheon Province who was suffering from a mental disorder, had been sent to Kim Du-hyeon, a man known in the village for treating those afflicted with mental illness. To the cacophonous banging of gongs and drums, the shaman struck the child with three nine-inch-long branches from a peach tree. The beatings resulted in severe internal bleeding, a concussion, and ultimately the death of the boy the following day. *Chukgi* (to drive away the evil spirits from the body) and other folk remedies, which had existed for many centuries on the Korean peninsula, continued to be practiced by many despite their marginalization as superstitious and ignorant. But although traditional medicine and shamanism persisted, the emergence of modern psychiatry with the establishment of the first mental ward under Japanese colonial rule began to affect how people thought about insanity. In Korea, unlike the metropole, which had its own home custody laws for the mentally ill, early administrators of the mental hospital were plagued with referrals from police precincts and other departments in the hospital of patients suffering from antisocial behavior. As admission policies began to route such patients to outpatient services, questions over the growing number of chronic patients concerned doctors who were seeking to establish their own professional standards and to secure psychiatry as a separate field of study and practice.

Protestant missionaries, who had been in Korea for more than two decades, also grappled with to the treatment of patients with chronic mental disorders. Doctors like Charles McLaren attempted to take a more humanitarian approach that employed a form of spiritual psychoanalysis. Although McLaren was unable to secure funds to open a large ward with a holding cell for violent patients, his modest psychiatric ward at Severance Union Hospital offered treatment to a dozen or so chronic patients. His approach to mental illness through a spiritual framework may have influenced Korea's new Christian communities. McLaren championed the "necessary connection between healing the body and healing the soul," relating it to Christ's earthly ministry devoted to preaching and healing. For McLaren, psychiatry was an extension of spiritual redemption, and he sought to "replicate the New

Testament miracle of healing" through "humble ministrations" to the mentally ill.[103]

By the mid-1920s, the admission policies for patients changed again when the Government-General Hospital became part of the new imperial university. The field of psychiatry was fully integrated into the newly designed curriculum for medical students at Keijō (Gyeongseong) Imperial University in 1926. The doctors, who also served as faculty at the medical college, focused on research, making chronic patients their laboratory specimens while selecting suitable patients with acute disorders for clinical instruction. With the full adoption of Kraepelinian nosology and its well-defined procedures of examination and documentation, rapid diagnosis would come to characterize the university clinic, whose approach differed remarkably from McLaren's humanitarian and spiritualized care of individual patients. With growing frustration in the community over the lack of facilities and treatment programs for chronic patients, the discourse among psychiatrists started to shift from one of custody and therapy to one of socio-hygienic concerns about heredity and degeneration.

FIGURE 1. Bridge of Life (Mapo Bridge), Seoul, 2014.

FIGURE 2. Bridge of Life (Mapo Bridge), Seoul, 2014.

FIGURE 3. A madman in the countryside (ca. 1920s).

FIGURE 4. The Government-General Hospital, Seoul, 1927.

THREE

A Touch of Madness

THE CULTURAL POLITICS OF EMOTION

> Emotion, it is argued, can be and often is subject to acts of management. The individual often works on inducing or inhibiting feelings so as to render them "appropriate" to a situation. The emotion-management perspective draws on an interactive account of emotion.... It allows us to inspect at closer range ... the relation among emotive experience, emotion management, feeling rules, and ideology. Feeling rules are seen as the side of ideology that deals with emotion and feeling. Emotion management is the type of work it takes to cope with feeling rules.
>
> ARLIE R. HOCHSCHILD, "Emotion Work,
> Feeling Rules, and Social Structures"

> *Chemyeon charida gulmeo jungneunda* (By trying to save face, one can die of hunger).
>
> A popular Korean *sokdam* (adage)

> The term *face* may be defined as the positive social value a person effectively claims for himself by the line others assume he has taken during a particular contact. Face is an image of self delineated in terms of approved social attributes—albeit an image that others may share, as when a person makes a good showing of his profession or religion by making a good showing for himself.
>
> ERVING GOFFMAN, *Interaction Ritual*

IN JANUARY 1926, the popular literary journal *Gaebyeok* (Genesis) published a short story by Hyeon Jin-geon (1900–1943), one of the most prolific writers of modern Korean realist literature, entitled "Sarip jeongsin byeongwonjang" (The director of the private mental hospital). It was republished later that year in an anthology of his works, *Joseon ui eolgul* (The faces of Korea). Set against the backdrop of an oppressive colonial society, the story explores one man's slow descent into madness, as exposed through the mundane conversations of old school friends. The voice of a semidetached narrator "*na*" or "I" probes the subtle, yet powerful "feeling rules" that govern the social interactions among friends from the same town,[1] the delicate performance of "face work" to maintain emotional harmony, the breakdown of emotional control, and the consequences for violating accepted norms and etiquettes. Here, as in Hyeon's other stories, "madness" is but a stone's throw away as the characters struggle hopelessly against unrelenting socioeconomic forces, beyond their control under Japanese occupation, that wreak havoc on their emotional stability.[2] As we shall show below, the suffering of Hyeon's characters might be read as the result of their failure at self-management or conformity to the rules of the emotional regimes (to borrow William Reddy's concept) that govern their lives[3]—with the plural usage indicating the conflicting emotional ideals, norms, and rituals of Korean society and Japanese colonial power.

This chapter will examine mental illness through literary and legal representations of the emotions, especially engagements with indigenous Korean emotional constructs such as *jeong* (affective bonds), shame and *chemyeon* (social face), *nunchi* (the subtle art of gauging another's mood), and *han* (intense suppressed anger). Although these constructs were deeply rooted in Korean culture, they assumed new meaning and significance during the early twentieth century under the influence of Japanese colonialism, new psychiatric knowledge, the rise of modern bourgeois culture, and the discovery of "individualism," which introduced new ways of perceiving the world and one's place in it. Employing Korean modernist literature, film, and judicial cases, this chapter will examine three "social types" that culture cast as especially vulnerable to mental breakdown during the decades of occupation—Korean male scholars, women (especially young wives and mothers), and the struggling poor. Narratives about their difficulties in navigating multiple, often conflicting, emotional regimes reveal yet another largely unexplored dimension of colonial modernity: the reconfiguration of the individual's relationship to others and "the relocation of the responsibility for illness" in a rapidly changing milieu.[4]

A GENEALOGY OF THE HISTORY OF EMOTIONS

The study of emotions remains a nascent field in Korean history (and East Asian history in general),[5] whereas in American and European history it has produced such a wealth of literature that scholars are already "invoking the term 'emotional turn.'"[6] At the most fundamental level, various disciplines—

from cognitive psychology to anthropology, from sociology to history—have asked the question: What are emotions? Until recently, studies have been framed by variations of nature-versus-nurture binary propositions—biology versus culture, universalism versus constructionism, or expression versus experience. Influential in this debate was Paul Ekman's pioneering study of emotions (conducted in the 1970s), which claimed to have identified six "basic emotions" universal to all cultures. From his study of facial expressions, Ekman concluded that these were happiness, sadness, anger, fear, disgust, and surprise.[7] Culture, he acknowledged, shaped *how* these universal emotions could be expressed. First, "cultural display rules"—that is, cultural norms and conventions—"interfered" with *innate* feelings, shaping what emotions individuals displayed. Second, cultural learning shaped individual "coping" with emotions such as anger. Finally, he posited universal "emotion elicitors" in very broad, abstract terms.[8] Ekman's sweeping universal claims, however, attracted criticism even from fellow cognitive psychologists—Alice Isen and Gregory Diamond, for instance, who argued that what appeared to be spontaneous, irresistible, innate emotions were in fact the result of "overlearned processes," akin to "a deeply ingrained, overlearned habit."[9]

Social constructionists, especially in the fields of anthropology and sociology, also began to turn from biological factors to culture and social structures to define emotions. For early practitioners in the 1970s, emotions represented "cultural artifacts" (to cite Clifford Geertz), which emerged "as socially shaped" but could also function as "socially shaping in important ways."[10] As Michelle Z. Rosaldo explained, "What individuals can think and feel is overwhelmingly a product of socially organized modes of action and of talk."[11] That is why she and other anthropologists stressed the importance of understanding local, indigenous frameworks: the unique concepts of *liget* among the Ilongot tribe in the Philippines, *aloha* among Hawaiians, *amae* among the Japanese, or *jeong* among Koreans.[12] The broad concept of culture, however, seemed too essentialist and limiting to some. Catherine Lutz and Lila Abu-Lughod reframed their inquiries, identifying and analyzing discursive fields to illustrate how certain modes of power can shape and create "meaning systems" that establish and regulate feeling and display rules through institutions like the family and other social processes.[13]

Historians, influenced by developments in social history, women's and gender studies, and the new cultural history, also sought to understand the emotional lives of people in past times by employing their own approaches and methodologies. In one *American Historical Review* "conversation" entitled

"The History of Emotions," six scholars discussed several important questions that are relevant to this present study.[14] First, is it "possible to go beyond emotional *expressions*—usually conveyed in language—and attain some assurance that these are indicative of actual emotional states?" What do the gaps between experience and expression reveal about the structures of power? According to Nicole Eustace, "Shifting patterns in who expresses which emotions, when, and to whom provide a key index of power in every society. Every expression of emotion constitutes social communication and political negotiation."[15]

Second, how do non-Western epistemological contexts change how we think about the category of emotion? Eugenia Lean observes that emotions can provide an entryway into examining broader issues of gender and politics. Her work on the rise of popular sympathy in twentieth-century China examines a period when "Confucianism was being debunked as official state ideology," accompanied by the emergence of a new commercial culture and imported ideas about "private and public," self and family, and collective identity and social organization. These issues also came under scrutiny in Korea under Japanese colonialism and modernity.[16]

Finally, what analytical tools and models have been influential in understanding emotions in historical context? In the 1980s, Peter N. Stearns and Carol Z. Stearns sought to differentiate between emotions (which they defined as partly mediated by biological factors) and what they called "emotionology"—that is, "attitudes or standards that a society, or a definable group within society, maintain toward basic emotions and their appropriate expression; ways that institutions reflect and encourage these attitudes in human conduct."[17] Since it was difficult to access actual emotional experiences through historical sources (for statements could not be taken at face value), their approach was to analyze the emotional standards of societies. Why and how did a society "either promote or prohibit some kinds of emotions, while remaining neutral or indifferent to others"?[18]

William Reddy built on this idea by articulating the notion of the emotional regime, which he defined as "the set of normative emotions and official rituals, practices, and 'motives' that express and inculcate them: a necessary underpinning of any stable political regime."[19] He argued that an emotional regime demands conformity and imposes penalties on those who deviate from the norm, causing them emotional suffering.[20] This model works well for the modern period, observed Jan Plamper, when the "prototypical political regime is the nation state."[21] However, according to Barbara Rosenwein the model not only is too rigid with its state/society binary and one norm for all but also overlooks "varieties and localism."[22] She prefers the concept of "emotional communities" or "social groups that adhere to the same valuations of emotions and how they should be expressed."[23] By identifying emotion words in texts, Rosenwein analyzes various patterns—the context in which they are used, how they are expressed, and so forth.[24] All these models—with their distinctive insights and sharp critiques—provide a solid analytical tool kit with which to approach emotions in colonial Korea.

EMOTIONAL REGIMES IN TRADITIONAL KOREA

In his now famous article "Munhak iran hao" (What is literature?), which was published in several installments in the *Maeil sinbo* (Daily News) in 1916, Yi Gwang-su, a young fiction writer and essayist, launched a scathing critique of Confucianism for obstructing Joseon's (Korea's) modernization. Yi argued that this powerful ideology was impeding the emergence of great literature, which constituted "a country's spiritual civilization" and served as the underpinnings of the nation. So what was literature (*munhak*) in the modern age? According to Yi, the answer was simple yet profound: "Human emotions are the very foundation of literature." The goal of literature was not to "*study* things; rather we *feel* them."[25] Confucianism, which relegated *jeong* (a broad range of individual human emotions) to the margins while prioritizing the other two higher faculties of the human mind in *ji* (knowledge) and *ui* (will), had "weakened Korean culture" and enslaved it to "Chinese thought." Yi conceded that he could blame not only the Chinese but also the inhospitable Korean climate and unfavorable living conditions. In another article, "The Value of Literature," he explained why the development of literature in Korea had been so slow: "Climates vary across the East Asian region, whose lands are barren. Living in such unfavorable conditions, people in our country and others like it have largely focused their efforts upon obtaining materials that can provide them clothes, food, and shelter. This narrowly focused interest on such materials, in turn, has resulted in the prioritization of knowledge (*chi/ji*) and will (*i*) over emotions (*chŏng/jeong*). Emotions, in other words, have been disregarded or ostracized. Thus literature—as an embodiment of emotions—has been seen as a mere recreation or pastime."[26] In Yi's view, what made the literary canons of the West superior was their "affirmation of feelings," leading writers to draw their materials from everyday life (as in Tolstoyan realism).

Yi also observed that Confucianism, which enforced a rigid moral system, lacked the appropriate framework for the development of *gaeseong* (individualism). Calling for the "fulfillment of emotions," Yi emphasized the important relationship between the writer and the reader whereby, in Tolstoy's words, "one man consciously, by means of certain external signs, hands on to others feelings he has lived through, and … other people are infected by these feelings and also experience them."[27] Experiencing emotions through literature, he stressed, served several purposes. First, it helped people "understand the subtleties of human affairs," especially the lives of people from different socioeconomic backgrounds and cultures. It also provided educational knowledge about how to adapt to society and facilitated feelings of sympathy, "a driving force behind virtuous acts." Literature could also enrich virtue, "free our minds from injustice," help individuals overcome addiction, and impart important lessons about morality (even as it did not *aim* to teach). Above all, reading literature was to be for the pleasure of wandering "imaginatively through an ideal world, experiencing the lives and thoughts of others."[28]

For these reasons, Yi was critical of the primary function of literary works in Joseon, which revolved around a particular set of ideals principally based on "encouraging good and punishing evil" (*gwonseon jingak*).[29] These metaphysical and ethical concerns, first articulated by the Chinese Neo-Confucian scholar Zhu Xi (1130–1200), became a point of controversy during heated debates between renowned Joseon scholars such as Toegye Yi Hwang (1501–70) and his disciple Gobong Gi Dae-seung (1527–72), Yulgok Yi I (1536–84), and Ugye Seong Hon (1535–98). At the core of their disputes was what constituted human nature and the role of the mind and feelings in governing everyday life. The initial controversy between Toegye and Kobong, better known as the "Four-Seven Debate" (*sadan/chiljeong*), stemmed from disagreements over the relationship between the two categories of human emotions: the "Four Beginnings" (commiseration, shame, courtesy/modesty, and discernment of right and wrong) and the "Seven Emotions" (basic human feelings or *jeong*, such as pleasure, anger, sorrow, fear, love, hatred, and desire that could be aroused), mentioned in the *Book of Mencius* and the *Doctrine of the Mean* respectively.

According to Toegye (drawing on Mencius), the "Four Beginnings" represented the original state (*bonyeon jiseong*) of human nature, emanating from *li* ("principle," or the rational or moral order of things), so they were pure and good. They could be found in the mind-and-heart of all human beings (rendered as *sim*) and were best illustrated by Mencius's famous example of people's reaction to seeing a child fall into a well. Anyone, without exception, would experience feelings of alarm and distress and would spontaneously rescue the child with no time for calculation or deliberation. Such "goodness," Mencius contended, allowed an individual with erudition to cultivate [his] mind to achieve sagehood. Without these four dispositions, "one is no longer human." As a passage in the *Book of Mencius* stated:

> A person without the "mind-and-heart" of commiseration is not human; a person without the mind-and-heart of shame and dislike is not human; a person without the mind-and-heart of courtesy and modesty is not human; and a person without the mind-and-heart of right and wrong is not human. The mind-and-heart of commiseration is the beginning of benevolence; the mind-and-heart of shame and dislike is the beginning of righteousness; the mind-and-heart of courtesy and modesty is the beginning of propriety; and the mind-and-heart of [moral discernment of] right and wrong is the beginning of wisdom. All human beings have these Four Beginnings just as they have their four limbs. If one who has the Four Beginnings is unable [to develop them], one destroys oneself.[30]

While human beings, more specifically "men," were said to possess these virtues naturally, the problem of "moral evil and human fallibility" had to be addressed. Toegye proposed that in contrast to the "Four Beginnings," with which one was born, the "Seven Emotions," which stemmed from *gi* (the generative material force that gives things their substance), emerged during one's lifetime.[31] In the case of the Seven Emotions, he observed, "good and evil were not yet fixed." That is, they were not in themselves good or evil but over the course of one's life, as one became wise or mature, could be brought into harmony with the good.

Gobong challenged this dualistic approach, for he believed it created an artificial division between the "Four Beginnings" as "belonging to principle" and the "Seven Feelings" as stemming from material force. Defining the "Four Beginnings" as emotions, he suggested that they were part of the Seven—the only difference being that they were the "good ones among the revelations of *ki* (*gi*)."[32] While these debates revolved around how to integrate human nature with the Neo-Confucian cosmos through the concepts of *li* and *gi*, the problem of how to rein in excess and bad influences required these philosophers to prescribe a standard code of ethics and "feeling rules" that would govern social interaction and family relations.[33]

The Emotional Management of Jeong *and* Uri

Among all social relations, the family during the Joseon period (1392–1910) became the most important unit for social life because duty and obligation dominated Confucian family ethics. As the philosopher Tu Wei-ming observes, "The role of the wife [had] to be preceded by that of the daughter-in-law. If children [were] involved, the role of mother [had to] take precedence over that of the wife."[34] This emotional regime required the appropriation of dignity depending on one's personal rank throughout all of society. Bruce Cumings notes that "knowing 'one's place,' an idea that we abhor, nonetheless was something honorable, dignified, a locus where human beings could realize themselves. Hierarchy without shame, hierarchy that is self-conscious but without conscious abuse, without necessarily infringing on what it means to be human."[35]

The Confucianization of Joseon, with its links to patrilineage and patriarchy, instilled a deep sense of *uri* (we-ness), prioritizing group achievement over the individual, while accentuating the significance of hierarchical relationships between social classes, age groups, and gender, which in many respects facilitated as well as constrained emotional life. Martina Deuchler puts it this way: "These were the relationship between sovereign and subject guided by righteousness (*ui*), the relationship between father and son guided by parental authority (*chin*), the relationship between husband and wife guided by the separation of the functions (*byeol*), the relationship between elder and young brothers guided by the sequence of birth (*seo*), and the relationship between senior and junior guided by faithfulness (*sin*)."[36] This kind of solidarity to the group held sway and dominated all forms of communication and social relationships. It led to feelings of intimacy and oneness—so much so that the Korean word *uri* was (and still is used today) in place of "I" or "mine."

Much as the Nguni Bantu tribes in southern Africa described a shared feeling of *ubuntu* or humanity toward others, Koreans developed their own nuanced term of *jeong* to explain the dynamics and importance of interpersonal relationships, which superseded the individual while prioritizing *hyeoryeon* (blood-kinship ties), *jiyeon* (regional or hometown ties), and *hagyeon* (ties of school or learning).[37] *Jeong* is most closely analogous to the emotional state of *amae* or *ninjo* among the Japanese, in which the self is conceived as part of a larger social context. Individuals must learn to communicate their *ma-eum* (state of mind) using their *jeong* to instill a feeling of *uri* (we-relationship), subordinating personal desires to "fitting in" with others. As the psychiatrists Christopher Chung and Samson Cho observe, the "location of *jeong* seems to be between individuals," which makes it different from anxiety and depression and more in line with "extra-psychic and inter-psychic emotions."[38] Because of the "inter-individual location" of *jeong,* it is keenly felt in all aspects of communication and interaction, as individuals must learn how fellow members of the collective *uri* are feeling and adjust their behavior. In other words, in any relationship interactants can only "be attached to *jeong*" (*jeong deulda*) or literally "fall out" or "be put off by it" (*jeong tteoreojinda*).[39]

This feeling of *jeong* is first felt through the mother-infant *jeong* relationship (*mojeong*) before being extended to other members of the family. As the famous Korean adage goes, there is nothing greater than a mother's *jeong* for her children; she can read her infant's mind and attend to the infant's needs because her *jeong* is *muhan* (boundless).[40] Mothers who do not demonstrate such strong feelings of attachment and unconditional love toward their children are often labeled as *mujeong* or "heartless." Cultivating feelings of dependency and attachment to the mother creates a feeling of *ilchegam* or "togetherness" as the *jeong* is then extended to other members of the family, who are expected to "open their hearts without any reserve" (*sogmaeum eul teononoko*).[41] Through this process of acculturation, the relational term *uri* (we-ness), a plural pronoun, is used in place of "I" and is combined with other subjects and objects such as *uri nampyeon* (our husband), *uri manura* (our wife), *uri jip* (our house), *uri gohyang* (our hometown), and the like to express *jeong* as it extends beyond the individual to include others.

These seemingly altruistic motives of concern for others' feelings and situations are governed by complex interpersonal and group relationships that differentiate *uri* (in-group) from *nam* (other out-groups) because the "valence and direction of emotional arousal depends on the attributions made by actors for confirmation or disconfirmation of their relative status."[42] Even in informal settings such as casual greetings, it is very common for Koreans to ask if you had your meal or where you are going, questions that might be seen as intrusive in other cultures but are simply a ways for individuals to express feelings of attachment, empathy, and affection. For example, the presence of *jeong* is constantly reinforced in social gatherings like the *suljari* (drinking party), where individuals engage in rituals like the passing of the shot glass.[43]

The *uri* membership is profoundly felt when *simjeong*, a Sino-Korean compound consisting of the two characters *sim* (heart) and *jeong* (affection), is activated. This emotional arousal is usually triggered by a specific behavior or event and is expressed in various ways such as "a disappointed *simjeong*, under false accusation *simjeong*, rejected *simjeong*, heartless *simjeong*, or unfairly treated *simjeong*."[44] Expressing one's *simjeong* assumes a "sharing of the mind" and must invoke empathy from others, especially those who have experienced similar situations. For example, a mother-in-law should be able to empathize with her daughter-in-law's *simjeong* because she probably experienced similar emotional ups and downs and can offer some solace. She can tell her daughter-in-law that *"geureolsudo itji anneunya"* (such things can occur) and then engage and narrate past events and pour out her *ma-eum* (state of mind).[45] Through the mechanism of *hasoyeon* (appealing for sympathy), individuals can narrate their *simjeong* to a third party as a way of justifying their actions or soliciting sympathy and the reassurance that they are not wrong.

Emotional Navigation and the Feeling Rules of Chemyeon *and* Nunchi

The sociologist Erving Goffman describes how people make use of the "front," or "that part of the individual's performance which regularly functions in a general and fixed fashion to define a situation for those who observe the performance."[46] When individuals assume an established social role, they must engage in emotion management to maintain a presentation of self that conforms to a set of culturally sanctioned rules to minimize the chance of disagreement or an embarrassing scene.[47] This means that people assuming the role find "a particular front that has already been established for it" and through "dramatic realization" behave accordingly to the environment in which they are embedded.[48] Through "defensive practices," individuals learn a code of subtle verbal and nonverbal expressions and gestures on the basis of their relative position and authority vis-à-vis others to maintain proper behavior and avoid embarrassing situations.

From this vantage point, individuals must adhere to a set of complex rules called *chemyeon* (saving face), a Sino-Korean compound consisting of the characters of "body" and "face." In Goffman's terms, each person tends to act out a "line" or "a pattern of verbal and nonverbal acts by which he expresses his view of the situation and through this his evaluation of his participants, especially himself."[49] Although the concept of one's face (or a "social face," according to Goffman) exists in every culture and is perceived as an external expression of one's inner nature, it is much more accentuated in its function and social contexts among Koreans, for whom one's behavior must comply with the expectations of *uri*.

Because of the inclusive nature of *uri*, shame and guilt, or what William Reddy calls "induced goal conflict," are used as the primary social sanctions to bring individuals into conformity with the group.[50] These mechanisms operate not only in the family or in institutions but in daily interactions through the passive and inhibited form of communication called *nunchi* or "the situated sense of tact" as interactants become highly conscious of what others think of them.[51] As the psychologist David Matsumoto notes in his study of the Japanese, often doing anything is constrained by the "fear of its impact, actual or perceived, on someone else"; the threat of shame "becomes the primary social sanction."[52] Executing a "*nunchi* act" allows an individual to imply through nonverbal, facial, and bodily expressions, a series of messages delineated by the rules of the *uri*-group and a personal assessment of the situation at hand. Because this is an indirect form of communication, it requires others to be able to read "the act," hold back, deliberately display more than they actually feel, or manipulate *chemyeon* to meet the expectations of others to maintain the *uri* dynamic.

The Emotional Suffering of Han

The feeling of *han*, what William Reddy calls "emotional suffering," can be described as the other face of *jeong* and is central to the psychological makeup of Koreans.[53] It is bound up with the emotional regime of *uri*, which ensures that "correct" emotions serve the goals of the collective. Rendered in the Chinese character as a heart that is splintered by a vertical line, *han* can be described as an intense suppression of anger that arises from the violation of *jeong*. It includes feelings of victimization and helplessness, coupled with intense negative feelings of hate, unresolved resentment, chagrin, and anger against injustices suffered because of an unfair social situation.[54] Such feelings of impotence can be felt individually or realized in the form of a collective consciousness that can have fatal consequences if "one harbors the *han*" (*haneul pumda*) or if it becomes "tangled and cannot be untied" (*hani maechinda*).

People are described as suffering from *han* when they stoically undergo hardship and suffering that they just have to live with and passively accept as fate (*palja*). For example, a mother is said to suffer from *han* after she finds out that her son did not get admitted to a top university. The same can be said about a son who laments after the death of his father for his lack of filial piety while his father was alive. A wife can feel *han* if her husband is involved in an extramarital relationship because he has damaged his reputation as well as that of his family (*paega mangsin*). From parents who have a disabled child to a bar girl who has to pour drinks for her male customers to a jilted lover who sees her partner marry someone else, there are a variety of reasons why people suffer and encounter *han*. These feelings of resentment, shame, anger, hate, humiliation, scapegoating, or frustration accumulate over time, creating residues in the mind.[55] One mechanism to unknot the *han* (*hanpuri*) is through the cathartic process of *hasoyeon* (appeal for sympathy to a third party), as will be discussed below in Hyeon Jin-geon's short story "The Director of the Private Mental Hospital," or through narration of one's *eogul* (oppression) over a past *han* that one has had to endure with those who share a similar *simjeong*.

Han has also been characterized as an intersubjective feeling or ethos of "collective sorrow" most felt during particular periods in Korean history. The anthropologist Clifford Geertz observes that collective sorrow is "the tone, character, and quality of [the collective's] life, its moral and aesthetic style and mood; it is the underlying attitude toward themselves and their world that life reflects."[56] Historically speaking, those living on the Korean peninsula, who for centuries have had to endure foreign invasions by neighboring states as early as the Han period, followed by the incursions of the Khitans, the Mongols, the Jurchens, the Japanese, and most recently the Americans and the Soviet Union, who contributed to a bloody civil war and national division, all cite *han* as evolving from these encounters. The losses of family members to war, poverty, forced labor, and ideological conflicts among Koreans all have contributed in one way or another to this ethos of lamentation.

Others have pointed to the penetration of Confucian ideals during the Joseon period (1392–1910) as playing a central role in creating the feelings of helplessness, injustice, and victimization. These feelings stemmed most visibly from the organization of rigid social classes that increasingly concentrated wealth and power in the hands of a few, an oppressive patriarchal family system that sought to maintain the prerogatives of social class, the discouragement of illegitimacy, and the domination of men in inheritance matters. These predetermined and unchanging rules, which forced people into relationships of subordination, were said to have also contributed to feelings of *han*.

On a socioeconomic level, the pressures of eking out a living under extreme situations, rigid gender expectations, or limits placed on mobility also could trigger feelings of impotence and frustration. For example, a tenant farmer's inability to pay off his debts to his landlord, a merchant's desire for upward mobility, or a mother-in-law's selfish and discriminatory behavior toward her daughter-in-law could create these vicarious feelings of helplessness in one's *ma-eum*. The suppression of this unresolved anger is described as *eogul*, which literally means "bearing resentment toward" someone or something. This kind of "forced demobilization of anger" often results in psychosomatic illnesses such as *hwabyeong* (fire illness), which is discussed in greater detail in chapter 1.

Folk Culture as Emotional Refuge

During the Joseon period, one way commoners coped with these feelings of suppressed anger triggered by an oppressive class and gender system, was to turn to cathartic play (or what William Reddy calls an emotional refuge) in order to sublimate their *han*.[57] This was achieved through performances and artistic expression such as *pansori* (epic song), *nongak* (traditional farmers' music), *inhyeong-geuk* (puppet shows), *minyo* (folk songs), folk painting, vernacular fiction, *yadam* (unofficial histories), *madang* theater, and *talchum* (masked dance). As in Mikhail Bakhtin's "carnival" or inverted world, where all rules, inhibitions, hierarchies, and sanctioned behaviors are suspended, oppressed groups were able to interact and freely express themselves through play. Through slapstick and satire, commoners parodied the venal *yangban* class and freely engaged in mockery of social conventions that the ruling class would otherwise find unacceptable.[58]

The *pansori* (epic song), traditionally sung by a *gwangdae* (singer) and accompanied by a *gosu* (drummer), was performed on a stage for several days if the repertoire consisted of twelve works or stories (*madang*). Reminiscent of a shaman's song, this oral narrative offered a realistic depiction of problems commoners encountered in their everyday lives, often caricaturing Confucian ideals and social taboos. Satirical, witty, and humorous, this musical art form, which drew its material from folk culture and popular songs, hit a responsive chord with both commoners and elites alike because of its depth and versatility. As Hŭng-gyu (Heung-gyu) Kim notes, *pansori* also drew on "tragic language that touche[d] the soul and expresse[d] the dark side of life."[59]

Drawing on a long oral tradition of *pansori,* impoverished literati storytellers played an important role in developing traditional vernacular fiction and the *yadam* (unofficial history), which also depicted "human types and social conditions in a more realistic manner" and poked fun at the old order and the rigid status system. *The Tale of Hong Gildong,* by Heo Gyun (1569–1618), considered the most popular vernacular novel of the times, "depicts a will to resolve the contradictions of contemporary society through a historical figure in a fabulous mode."[60] According to Peter Lee and Kim Hŭng-gyu, Heo's disregard of Confucian morality and its downplaying of human instinct and emotion compelled him to focus on "negative human types such as malcontents, dissenters, outlaws, and rebels." Critics castigated his work as morally harmful because "it depict[ed] passions, fantasies, and dreams that are best suppressed; it present[ed] a distorted version of the real world." It also engaged in fantasies and improbabilities such as "the traffic between human beings and the dead, ghosts, and other supernatural beings." Moreover, vernacular fiction like *The Tale of Hong Gildong* received censure for laying bare "people's instinctual behavior, especially sex and stimulat[ing] base desires, a hindrance to moral education." In other words, it "created a world other than that sanctioned by authority and therefore offer[ed] an unofficial view of reality."[61]

Much like Heo's vernacular fiction, the characters in masked dance, whose comical face masks represented a wide range of male and female characters from the different social classes—the *yangban* (literati class), the *chwibari* (old bachelor/prodigal), the *bune* (usually a concubine or *gisaeng*), the *gaksi* (bride), the *seonbi* (scholar), the *jung* (monk), the *imae* (village idiot), the *choraeng-i* (servant), the *miyalhalmi* (old widow), the *baekjeong* (butcher), and the like—mixed the sacred with the profane, drawing on village rituals and shamanistic traditions. The dance evoked anger and resentment toward the oppressive class and social system as well as sympathy toward those suffering from injustices of class discrimination, poverty, evil mothers-in-law, and other social ills. Without any written scripts, these roving performing troupes, mostly composed of members of the lower social classes, including monks (who joined these groups during the early Joseon period when the new Neo-Confucian state sought to suppress Buddhism), moved from village to village seeking large audiences. These masked dancers, who were accompanied by a musical band, would engage with their audiences with mock fights and sexually explicit plays. Their acts, which were dramatic and cathartic, had similar storylines, such as the confrontation between the old monk and the old bachelor, the concubine and the old widow, or the scholar and the servant, ending in a dramatic denouement as the oppressed triumphed over the oppressor.[62]

These plays used "satire, uninhibited vulgarism, and word play" and mirrored the everyday lives of commoners. Characters displayed "heightened emotions," and their "confrontation[s] between social norms and everyday desires" could elicit both sympathy and disgust from the audience members, many of whom engaged with the stories as temporary respite from their own lives, an expression of some of their own feelings, and the most vivid form of vicarious experience.[63] As Hŭng-gyu Kim (Kim Heung-gyu) notes, "[The plays'] main themes [were] satire of the ruling class, a realism that asserts a worldly life while negating empty ideals, and an accusation of the oppression by a patriarchal society," and they expressed "popular sentiment against the social ills of late Chosŏn [Joseon] when the Confucian ruling order was slowly dissolving."[64]

Given the subversive content behind these public performances, the Japanese colonial state issued an ordinance in 1911, cracking down on performances held during the late evenings and allowing groups to host masked dances and other artistic performances only during certain holidays, and even then only with official approval by the local authorities.[65] In addition, the lack of social foundations necessary for the transmission as well as survival of these roving troupes led to their demise, as these spaces for play and catharsis could not compete with modern forms of entertainment (e.g., cinema and radio). As a result, many performers and artists could no longer attract an audience and sought professions in the new entertainment industry or dispersed into the general population.

JAPANESE COLONIALISM AND MODERNITY: CHANGES IN THE EMOTIONAL REGIME

The modernization and accelerated pace of industrialization and urbanization that accompanied Japan's colonization of the peninsula had a profound and unprecedented impact on the psyche of Koreans. The population of Gyeongseong (Keijō) had almost quadrupled from 246,251 in 1914 to 988,537 in 1944. Built around visual spectacles (modern buildings, factories, hospitals, public conveyances, banks, department stores, and cafes), new people (the "crowd," consumers, and urban workers), movement (shopping, strolling, gazing, and the circulation of commodities), and new feelings (stress and anxiety), these *ilsang ui gonggan* (everyday spaces) promoted new "urban sensibilities." These in turn changed the way people thought about themselves and others. However, modern developments also possessed a visible dark side, constraining emotional life for many, while contributing to the rise of new social and behavioral pathologies. The very process of modernization fostered a completely different emotional regime with its own rationale and normative frames, as people started to redefine traditional social forms of emotions and feeling rules in specifically modern ways and as individualism/individual identity started to undermine the deep ties of *jeong* to the family and the collective unit (*uri*).

Feeling as "Symptoms": Subjective Well-Being and the Marketing of Emotions

As rural-urban migration took place on an unprecedented scale, the possibility that contagious diseases would become epidemic in the urban centers became a huge concern for the colonial state, which sought to curb disease transmission through prevention campaigns and mobilization of a huge police force.[66] The emergence of germ theory and the discovery of microbial pathogens through the pioneering work of Robert Koch, John Snow, and Louis Pasteur, among others, in the late nineteenth century "provided convincing experimental proof" about the role "living microorganisms play in the cause of many human and animal diseases." Nancy Tomes suggests that the new field of bacteriology "produced an explosion of knowledge about disease transmission and prevention," prompting a new public awareness not only of germs as the cause of disease but also of how disease spread.[67]

Fear of urban scourges like tuberculosis and nervous disorders like neurasthenia, with purported links to degeneracy, hereditary insanity, and social pathology, started to gain currency by the 1920s, especially with the easing of censorship laws by the colonial state and the rise of the vernacular press. Worries about emotional ailments or insanity fueled a lucrative business for pharmaceutical companies. Advertisements promoting the efficacy of Kennōgan (healthy brain pill), a psychotropic drug, appeared almost daily in popular newspapers and magazines, promising to "reconstruct the mind" of the afflicted whose nerves had been stretched to their limits.[68] Also by the 1920s, neurasthenia had become the most ubiquitous expression for mental discomfort among urban denizens. In Bak Tae-won's popular novel *Soseolga gubossi ui iril* (1934; A day in the life of Gubo the novelist), *taedium vitae* underpins the narrative of the protagonist Gubo after he returns to Gyeongseong (Seoul) from Tokyo. Here, Gubo's neurosis intervenes and undermines what little happiness he has been able to acquire from *kultur* (a term that encompasses not just civilization but also science and technology), for his neurotic behavior springs from his deep frustration with his pathetic status in colonial society as an emasculated Korean man.

By the 1920s, social stigma was no longer limited to physical abnormalities. It included "blemishes in the individual character perceived as weak will, domineering, or unnatural passions, treacherous and rigid beliefs, and dishonesty, these being inferred from a known record of, for example, mental disorder, imprisonment, addiction, alcoholism, homosexuality, unemployment, suicidal attempts, and radical political behavior," any of which could later ruin the reputation of a family.[69] Daily newspapers and popular magazines compiled police reports to expose the rise in numbers of "abnormal" people with emotional and mental problems. They particularly highlighted persons posing serious risks to themselves and others, such as arsonists, pathological gamblers, kleptomaniacs, vagabonds, and exhibitionists, whose impulsive behaviors were said to be driven by narcissistic self-gratification or emotional anomie. The disorders of these individuals often resulted in crime, physical violence, or suicidal acts, which could be carried out in public spaces such as Sajik and Jangchungdan parks and the Han River Foot Bridge, two of the most popular hotspots for suicides (see chapter 4).

In the nascent field of psychiatry, "mind doctors" introduced the public to a new language of mental hygiene that linked emotions such as anger and sadness to nervous disorders. Like their counterparts in sociology and criminology, psychiatrists engaged in data collection to obtain statistics critical to achieving their goals in public health—that is, "rates of mortality and morbidity, yields of internment and rehabilitation, a taming of risk, and a maximization of reward."[70] Behind this feverish activity was the desire to widen the scope of criminality and to confine the "abnormal," aims justified in terms of social and biological determinism, especially genetic susceptibility to mental health problems and specific causal factors such as stressful life events, anomie, or poverty.[71]

In spite of the desire of the colonial state and medical science (i.e., psychiatry) to demarcate what constituted normality, it was extremely difficult to navigate the shifting "mental" state of Koreans who were attempting to negotiate the challenges of modernity. They felt the seductive allure of a more modern society with a new emotional regime that offered greater individuality, but this modernity was inextricably intertwined with Japanese colonialism. At the same time, they longed for emotional authenticity and stability in the face of the decline of the traditional emotional regime and its feeling rules, as we will see below.

EMOTIONS IN KOREAN SHORT FICTION

Modern fiction provided one venue in which to define and explore the conflicting emotional regimes in colonial Korea. Despite Yi Gwang-su's impassioned call for Korean literature to "treat human emotions realistically," it is striking that writers often cast "unacceptable" emotions in traditional Korean culture, such as external rage (as opposed to internalized *han*) or violations of "feeling rules," as abnormal or mad. They also began to employ the language of psychiatry (such as "depressed state of mind") or descriptions of the mentally ill to convey certain emotions. It could be argued that they were simply employing the trope of madness to describe the malaise of modernity like their counterparts in Europe.[72] Moreover, in light of Yi Gwang-su's assertion that Confucian morality prevented Koreans from freely expressing their "thoughts and emotions," Korean writers' use of themes of "mental illness" may have sometimes been the workings of a strong habitus that evaded direct confrontation with problematic emotions. Yet the colonial subtext suggests a more complex reading. Perhaps some writers sought to defuse the threatening actions or emotions of their characters by marginalizing them as mentally unstable. This provided a perfect camouflage for the hidden scripts, giving free rein for the "mad" character to speak truth to power, critiquing both Korean society and the Japanese colonial administration.[73] To reiterate Nicole Eustace's observation, "Every expression of emotion constitutes social communication and political negotiation."[74] In Korean fiction and film, three social types were portrayed as especially prone to mental instability and illness in the modern age: colonial intellectuals, those suffering from economic hardships, and women.

Korean Colonial Intellectuals, Displacement, and Madness

In Korean fiction, colonial intellectuals represented one group that was particularly vulnerable to madness because of their collective experience of displacement both during their years of study abroad in Japan and upon their return home. According to Ellie Choi, "The cultural and economic unevenness between the metropole (*naichi*) and the colonial periphery (*gaichi*) was so pronounced that the homecoming experience was akin to traveling backward in time."[75] In many respects, colonial intellectuals occupied an interstitial space of identity that resisted normative definition as a result of their travels back and forth, both literally and metaphorically. Korean writers, many of whom, like Yi Gwang-su, had studied in Japan, focused on the inner worlds of these intellectuals—their isolation, loneliness, marginalization, and disappointments in terms of mental instability and contemplation of suicide. As some scholars have observed, the inner world of the fictional colonial intellectuals often resembled that of their real-life writers.

Displacement as a formative experience of the colonial intellectual during his student years is most poignantly captured in Yi Gwang-su's short story "Ai ka" (Maybe love; 1909). Published in *Meiji Gakuin*'s *Shirogane gakuhō*, Yi's school newsletter, when Yi was just seventeen years old, the story explores a Korean student's homosocial desire for his Japanese classmate, which is brutally crushed through "heartless" rejection at the end of the school term.[76] The orphaned protagonist, Mun-gil, a precocious *yuhaksaeng* (student studying abroad) in a middle school in Tokyo, begins to have feelings for Misao, a good-looking *sempai* (senior), after encountering him at a school sports event. Mun-gil's profound isolation and loneliness, which often has induced violent weeping, is replaced by feelings of "joy and pleasure" as "boundless hope filled his breast."[77] The story explores one mundane but startling moment that changes Mun-gil's hope to despair: a nervous Mun-gil paying a visit to Misao at his boardinghouse the day before his return to Korea at the end of the term. Instead of the warm reception that he is expecting, he is met with rejection. Misao, who is obviously in the house, does not even deign to come out and greet him. Mun-gil's "latent weariness and depression" becomes full blown as "physical manifestations of shock and depression"; he becomes "listless and melancholic, a young man once talkative but now taciturn, unwilling to have anything to do with others." Like Anna Karenina, he feels that he has no other choice but to commit suicide on the railroad tracks.[78] Although "Maybe Love" is considered secondary to Yi's other great works like *Mujeong* (The heartless), it is through the appropriation of a queer subjectivity that Yi is able to critique the hegemonic order and exposes the limits of imperial desire. Mun-gil's longing for love and acceptance conflicts with the traditional emotional regime, since such modern expectations of love not only between two men but also between colonized and colonizer are impossible, compelling the protagonist to commit suicide. The story also contrasts the genuine and authentic emotions that Mun-gil experiences with Misao's heartlessness—his inability to feel love and compassion. For Yi, who valued human feelings and emotions above all else as the true sign of civilization, the depiction of Misao was a harsh critique of his colonial masters.

Another prominent theme in modern Korean literature was the isolation of colonial intellectuals driven to madness by their inability to fit into society. This was the subject of Yeom Sang-seop's short story "Pyobonsil ui cheonggaeguri" (The green frog in the specimen room, 1921), which appeared in the literary journal *Gaebyeok* (Dawn of History). Yeom Sang-seop (1897–1963), like Yi Gwang-su, studied in Japan, where he completed high school and matriculated at Keio University in Tokyo; however, after only a semester he left the university to create his own literary journal (*Pyeheo,* Ruins) in July 1920 with his friend Hwang Seok-u. Soonsik Kim observes that "The Green Frog in the Specimen Room" appears to "depict the author's psychological state of mind after returning to Korea from Japan," employing literary naturalism and psychology.[79] In this story, Yeom examines the lives of two young Korean male intellectuals, the narrator "I" (*na*) and Kim Chang-ok, who have become misfits in colonial society. The narrator lives a most erratic life, suffering from ennui, finding temporary solace in alcohol and tobacco. He is so paralyzed by fear and anxiety that he hates to leave his home. Even the most minor objects cause him uneasiness and even panic. Whenever he sees a needle or small objects that "look like chicken poop," they conjure nightmarish flashbacks of his middle school teacher in a laboratory pulling out the wriggling organs of the frog one by one as it lay there helplessly with its four limbs pegged down by pins. The narrator struggles to become unpinned and unmolested by exposure to prodding and pulling by becoming a recluse. Seclusion isolates him, but it also bars others from access to him; he can passively ignore them or actively exclude them from his society.

Yeom's narrator suffers from nervous disorder, which is linked to his chronic insomnia, depression, and suicidal thoughts. Aware of his condition and his need for a change of scene, his friend "H" drags him out of solitary confinement to accompany him to Pyeongyang despite his initial protests. The narrator finally decides to accompany "H" to the town of Nampo, where they meet "Y" and "A." This is where he first hears about a *gwang-in* (crazy person) named Kim Chang-ok, who was once known in town as a child prodigy—the real focus of the story. Although Kim hails from a well-to-do merchant family, his father squandered all of his fortune on women and alcohol, forcing Kim to drop out of school. Despite the promise of his intellect, he falls victim to circumstances beyond his control: he is forced to become a menial drill instructor at a local school after his mother's death. He remarries following the tragic death of his first wife but cannot enjoy his newfound life because the police detain him for some crime. Though he is acquitted of all charges, when he returns home four months later he discovers that his second wife has run away to become a prostitute. Dejected, Kim refuses to leave his home and goes crazy (*balgwang*). His reclusiveness eerily resembles that of the narrator. The latter hears that Kim has become very active in his idealism by preaching about world peace. Envisioning a merger of Tolstoyism and Wilsonism to save the world, Kim has created the East-West Friendship Society, of which he is president and sole member. He has built himself a three-story home based on a Western model near a red-light district with merely three *won*.

Two months after the narrator returns home from his trip from Nampo, he receives a letter from "Y" informing him that Kim Chang-ok has set his house on fire and is reported missing. The story ends with the narrator roaming his hometown in a depressed state of mind (*u-ulhan simjeong*), ruminating about his recent trip to Pyeongyang, where he saw a disturbed-looking man with long hair loitering around the Daedong River. Although no one seems to know Kim's whereabouts, the narrator suggests that the mysterious man he encountered was probably Kim. He suspects that Kim has gone to Pyeongyang, where his second wife's parents live, and is barely eking out a living, sleeping under a stack of straw and begging outside Botong Gate.[80] A man of great promise has been reduced to nothing, his intellectual entrails and sanity torn to shreds (like the green frog) by a world that has no place for his grand ideals.

Because Yeom's writing is rich in symbolism and metaphors, "The Green Frog in the Specimen Room" has elicited multiple interpretations, both literal and allegorical. Some point to the disillusionment that colonial intellectuals felt when they understood the disconnect between their ideals and the "absence of conditions for putting them into effect."[81] The author does not reveal why the narrator in "The Green Frog in the Specimen Room" is suffering from dysfunctional ennui and emotional fatigue, but one might perhaps guess from Yeom's own life story that the narrator's depression could have been triggered by the failures of the March First Movement in 1919, a period when many Korean male intellectuals felt totally disillusioned and incapacitated. In contrast to the ambiguous origins of the narrator's despondency and depression, Kim Chang-ok's condition is much clearer, as the narrator and his friends dissect his mental state like the proverbial frog in the laboratory: much of the evidence points to his madness as being socially induced and exacerbated by family problems, a "condition" experienced by many male intellectuals who felt emasculated and stripped of their powers under Japanese colonial rule.

At its very core, Kim Chang-ok represents a new type of *gwang-in* (mad person) whose symptoms are remarkably different from those of people in other eras. Characters suffering from mental disorders (*jeongsin isang*) started to appear with striking regularity in the works of many writers such as Baek Sin-ae, Hyeon Jin-geon, Bak Tae-won, Yi Gwang-su, Yi Tae-jun, and Yi Sang. They identified particular symptoms to mark distress and impairment, producing a particular discourse on mental health, illness, and disease as no longer springing from supernatural forces or malevolent spirits but derived from concrete conditions. In the case of Kim Chang-ok, the disconnect between the intellectual's ideals and colonial reality drive him to madness exhibited through his pyromania, bizarre preaching, and wandering. Here we see again the clash of modern/colonial expectations with the traditional emotional regime, where mental illness becomes the only way out for male intellectuals to fulfill their desires, regardless of promises and social conventions.

Colonial intellectuals' displacement led not only to madness but to their infantilization. In "Nalgae" (Wings), Yi Sang (1910–37), a trained architect and gifted artist, poet, and fiction writer, provides a glimpse into the life of a young male intellectual who bears an uncanny resemblance to the author himself. The protagonist's withdrawal from society has made him impotent. He suffers from emotional aloofness and seeks to escape the everyday world of "frustration and negation." Like the narrator of Yeom's story above, he lives a life of "uneasiness, suspicion, boredom, a life without money or ambition," which can also be read as an allegory of social and economic contradictions of the intelligentsia under Japanese colonial rule. Here, the "wings" represent "a liberation of self" and release.[82]

The language of the text, like the consciousness of this emasculated protagonist, is convoluted, "a dismembered discourse incapable of communicating openly [that] ventur[es] out from its hiding places to express, only half coherently, ideas and urges it must keep repressed."[83] The protagonist lives a "silent and passive" existence and is unaware that his wife is prostituting herself next door. He spends most of his time in seclusion and detached. This "genius," who has become infantilized and no different from "a stuffed specimen," according to Henry Em, represents the self-knowing subject who is "unseen or unrecognized by the Other (his wife), who perceives only the emasculated shell of her husband."[84]

Much like Yeom's protagonist who is afraid of leaving his room, the narrator in Yi Sang's "Wings" becomes completely disoriented during one of his several forays to the city. Wandering in a daze for two hours or so, he is almost hit by several automobiles on his way to Gyeongseong Train Station before ending up at the roof of the Mitsukoshi Department Store around noon. In a revealing passage, the narrator explains his timorous and languid state: "My wife and I are a pair of cripples destined to be out of step with each other. There is no need to assign a logic to my wife's behavior or mine. No need to justify it either. Isn't it enough to keep moving through this world, endlessly limping along with whatever truths and misunderstandings in our tow?"[85] For Yi Sang, this reference to cripples can be read as a predicament shared by the narrator and his wife but also more generally by colonized Koreans, who were "all reduced to the status of children" by the Japanese and "pressured to sell themselves to survive,"[86] and whose identities were profoundly changed by modernity and colonialism. Much like Kim Chang-ok in Yeom's story, Yi's protagonist is caught between two very different emotional regimes, emotionally isolated, emasculated, and no longer capable of navigating this new terrain of colonial modernity.

Shame, Madness, and the Emotional Navigation of Economic Hardships

Modern Korean writers also depicted individuals who had experienced socioeconomic reversals because of their inability to adapt to the colonial economy as particularly prone to mental instability and illness. Hyeon Jin-geon's short story "The Director of the Private Mental Hospital" (1926), which chronicles the economic hardships of one man, explores the emotions of shame and alienation that lead to madness. The story opens inside the mind of the narrator (the first-person *na*), who is visiting his hometown. His detachment from home, a consequence of colonial modernity, is immediately apparent. The sight of straw-thatched huts lined next to each other in what he once regarded an idyllic village no longer moves him. These structures seem even less conspicuous than "the poplar leaves fluttering during the fall season," conveying a sense of estrangement from his surroundings, which now seems more like a forlorn and desolate place to this urban dweller.[87] The narrator's relationships with his elderly father and young stepmother lack the familiar attachment (*jeong*) between parent and child; he feels like a guest who is a burden to an old couple struggling to make ends meet. The narrator finds an excuse to meet his childhood friend "L" and other former classmates who have gathered near his parents' home. His feelings of discomfort are replaced with *ujeong* (friend's attachment) as "L" and other members of his *gurakbu* (circle) welcome the narrator "unconditionally" as they embrace him as they catch up on things happening in Seoul, his writings, his thoughts, and what has been going on with friends.

The story, however, is less about the narrator than about his friend "W," who struggles to survive in the harsh, uncaring environment of colonial Korea. During the intimate conversation between friends, "L" divulges a few troubling details about their mutual friend "W," who has experienced a series of financial and personal setbacks during past year. "L" recounts that the series of unfortunate events began when "W" got fired from his job at "T Bank," which had paid him a modest salary of 25 *won*, enough to feed his three young children and wife. The strain and pressures of work as well as the shame of living with his financially strapped in-laws (*cheoga sari*) compelled him to relocate his family to a shabby attached unit to a house, further increasing his *budam* (responsibility) as the sole provider for his family. Such precarious economic conditions made it necessary for "W" to accept an unusual job through his friend "P," a man who was born to privilege but incapacitated by mental illness.

During the next *suljari* (drinking party), one of "W's" acquaintances, "S," reveals to the narrator that "P" hired "W" for a monthly salary of ten *won* and a bag of rice to be his personal caretaker. Through a series of episodes that occur during the evening, which include the appearance of "W" at several of these drinking rounds, Hyeon offers his readers a glimpse into the Korean psyche, the dominant feeling rules that govern interpersonal relationships, and what people can achieve by "doing emotions." In the next round of *suljari*, "W" is urged by "S" to pour out his *simjeong* (heart-and-mind) about his new job as "the director of a private mental hospital." Assuming that his tales of woe will elicit sympathy from his friends (*hasoyeon*), "W" drops his guard and describes his struggles of taking care of "P," whose condition is more serious than previously thought. He explains that "P" is suffering from an acute case of social paranoia. Over time, his *heoyak* (feebleness) has gradually deteriorated into *jeongsin byeong* (mental illness). "P's" family members did not feel comfortable being around him because of his frequent tirades. Feeling guilty about leaving him alone or confining him (*gamgeum*), the family decided to hire "W" as a full-time attendant. Desperate to narrate his *simjeong* to his friends, "W" startles them by describing an incident that occurred on a day after "P," "the *michin nom*" (crazy person), experienced *balgwang* (went completely berserk). He locked all the doors of his house without "W's" knowledge and tried to assault him with a fruit knife, only to faint in front of him, losing consciousness because of how much energy he expended during his *jiral* (insane fit). While W's pouring out of his *simjeong* does elicit some sympathy from the narrator, his lack of *nunchi* (tact) leads him to drink too much that evening. His emotions erupt in anger and violence, violating the bonds of *jeong* and *chemyeon* (saving face) of the group, as we will see below.

Because maintaining one's *chemyeon* involves positive self-evaluation and social approval by others, W has always felt pressure to guard his integrity. This has been all the more so because of his precarious existence and low social status. When the narrator first meets his friend "L" in the absence of "W's" company, they talk freely about the latter's personal and financial problems. It is during the course of these conversations that the narrator realizes that "W" has been putting up a front all along with his jovial demeanor despite all his personal troubles. To avoid further embarrassment of his *chemyeon*, "W," even after being fired from the bank, finds a way to borrow money to move his family to an annex away from his wife's parents' home.

In another episode, when "W" finally appears at one of the drinking parties, his friend "S" starts to poke fun at him, calling him the director of the private mental hospital and asking him sarcastically if he has "just gotten off work."[88] Even in the exchange of pleasantries, people with higher status can claim more *chemyeon* over their subordinates, as in the case of "S," who maintains his authority by continuing to ridicule "W." At the same time, individuals must take into consideration the actual or anticipated response of their superiors and must behave in such a way as to maintain the *chemyeon* of both parties. This can entail a series of "fronts" ranging from formalized behavior to ostentatious showboating and self-aggrandizement to protect one's personal integrity and ability or to disguise one's actual inferior status. To protect himself against his friends' devaluation or their misconception of his ability and personal problems, "W" simply laughs it off, not once but several times, with no signs of resentment. The narrator observes that "W," despite his gaunt appearance, always beams and smiles, a "front" used to disguise his financial and personal woes. Through the careful management of personal relationships and constant self-scrutiny and calculation, "W" always maintains his *chemyeon*.

The conflicts between *chemyeon* and *nunchi* come into play during the group's final binge at the Haedonggwan, "K's" favorite restaurant. As a frequent patron, "K" ostentatiously hires three *gisaeng* (geisha) to entertain the group and pour the drinks. Despite the festive ambience, the narrator describes how his *ma-eum* (state of mind) becomes troubled after he hears out "W's" *simjeong* (outpouring of heart-and-mind). Well aware of "W's" low tolerance for alcohol, the narrator is even more concerned to note that "W" is drinking excessively that evening. As people start to leave one by one after a night of drinking, "W" in a drunken stupor summons a waiter to bring him some newspapers and starts to gather all the leftover appetizers to take home. Insensitive to "W's" desire to give the remaining rice cakes and *yaksik* (sweet rice with nuts and jujube) to his children, "K" tells "W" that his tactless behavior is making him feel *changpi* (shame), and as a frequent patron of this restaurant he asks "W" to stop what he is doing.

"W" does not seem to feel any compunction about his actions and tells "K" he is simply taking what he has paid for. However, when one of the *gisaeng* at the restaurant sneers at him, announcing that "the director of the private mental hospital is going to throw a banquet at his house," the defense mechanisms of *chemyeon* and *nunchi* can no longer contain "W's" humiliation as he launches forward in rage to slap her face.[89] "K" tries to detain "W," but, having lost his own *chemyeon* earlier, he assaults "W" instead. "W" immediately strikes back, and the two have to be separated by the narrator and his other two friends "L" and "S." After sending off "K," the three try to calm down "W" by trying to restore his *chemyeon* as the narrator hands over the wrapped leftovers to "W" to take home without making any reference to his children. Humiliated and frustrated, "W" throws the wrapped food to the ground and buries his face in it, shouting, "Bokdal-ah! [the name of his daughter], it's okay if you don't eat this. It's okay if you don't eat these rice cakes. You can live without it!"[90] In a fit of rage, "W" turns pale, starts foaming at the mouth, and asks his friends if he should kill his children. The following day "S" tells the narrator that "W" not only battered his wife that evening but also tied his three children to a beam and threatened to set them on fire. Not knowing what to do, the narrator returns to Seoul. Five months later, he gets a letter from "S" that "W" went mad and stabbed his friend "P" with a knife, killing him.

In this particular story, the emotional regime of *jeong* and *uri* and the feeling rules of *chemyeon* and *nunchi* can no longer harness "W" to the goal of conforming to the group as he descends into madness. Even more, the relentless exigencies of modernity, coupled with the economic hardships precipitated by Japanese colonialism and the expectations on "W" as the family's patriarch, contribute to the protagonist's mental breakdown and a compromise of his integrity among his friends.

Women and Madness as Liberation

Women, specifically young wives and jilted lovers, were yet another category of people who were depicted as vulnerable to mental illness in Korean literature. In his short story "Bul" (Fire, 1925), Hyeon Jin-geon explores the notion of descent into madness as liberation.[91] The protagonist is Suni, a fifteen-year-old bride who suffers "nightly assault" by her husband. She is too exhausted from the onerous household labor imposed on her by her wicked mother-in-law to wake up during the assault: "[Her] hips throbbed and twinged. When an iron club pushed her innards aside and thrust into her chest, her mouth fell agape, her body convulsed. Normally, this much pain would have roused her, but her daily rounds of labor—carrying a water crock on her head, pounding grain, treading the watermill's wheel, carrying meals to farmhands in the rice paddies—had worn her out, and she could not wake up much as she tried."[92]

Suni initially keeps her feelings of *han* inside her, obeying without question. She jumps to attention at her mother-in-law's beck and call like a "soldier intently awaiting a commander's order" (3). As one film scholar has observed, "*Han* is passive. It yearns for vengeance, but does not seek it. *Han* is held close to the heart, hoping and patient but never aggressive. It becomes part of the blood and breath of a person. There is a sense of lamentation and even of reproach toward the destiny that led to such misery."[93]

Suni's *han* transforms gradually into external rage that must be vented. The first clue of this transformation takes place at the brook, where she sees minnows "floating fearlessly on the surface" (4) and experiences pangs of jealousy. Jealousy turns into anger when she fails to scoop them up in her hands. Finally, when she succeeds in catching one because it lands on her palms, she lets the fish jump her palm until it grows exhausted: "Suni was amused. Soon, the poor, tired thing became still in her hand; Suni then hurled it cruelly to the ground" (4). Seized by horror at what she has done,

Suni draws her water and hastens home. However, she feels the "ghost of the dead minnow," which "hovers before her" (5). She feels the "sensation of someone... pulling her hair from behind" (5). This ghostly presence may be pangs of guilt for having violated the feeling rules of *han*. The killing of the fish portends a more serious act of rage.

On her way to take a tray of rice and soup to the farmhands, she encounters the minnow that she has killed, "looming before her in the shape of a gigantic rockfish that blocked her path" (6). Her *han* has turned to vengeance that haunts her, causing her to faint and break her mother-in-law's china bowls. She wakes up in the room of her nightly terrors, "the room of her enemy" (6). Her husband is no longer described as a disembodied face above her but rather as her foe. Even his "soft, compassionate" look of concern over her accident has no effect on the transformation of her *han* into fear and rage: "The breathless Suni, like a chicken grabbed by a hawk, had no room to appreciate his kind expression" (8).

Reminiscent of the narrator in Charlotte Perkins Gilman's *The Yellow Wallpaper*, Suni sees the room as her source of all her troubles. "Were it not for that room, he would have no place to torment her. Was there any way to get rid of that heinous room?" (8). She displaces her rage from her husband who has perpetrated the violence onto the room itself.

The moment that Suni goes mad is described in terms of "strangeness." As she is about to check the rice in the kettle, "a strange idea flashed through her mind.... Was it not strange that such an idea had never occurred to her before?" (8). Her physical gesture confirms her insanity: "She smiled" (9). Like the mad women in the attic in English literature, she sets fire to the house. Her *han* is no longer passive and her vengeance is complete. "Just outside the hedge of the next house, Suni stood, her face never more radiant than now. Her heart bursting with delight, she stamped with joy" (9). Pushed to the limits, Suni descends into madness, and it becomes her "weapon of the weak" that enables her to retaliate. Instead of internalizing her rage (*han*), she is liberated by madness.

The story was not far removed from real events reported in newspapers and police reports, in which Korean women committed a significant number of violent crimes. The reports suggest that women with little recourse to address their grievances resorted to arson or murder to escape from their unbearable circumstances. While it is difficult to ascertain from these public records how long women waited before they decided to end their abusive relationships, several court records offer some details of their emotional state and motives for committing the crime.

In the case of one "heartless mother," lawyers presented the feeling rules and emotional displays in the opening arguments of the legal hearings. On April 25, 1928, the *Donga ilbo* reported on a preliminary hearing at the Chuncheon district's public prosecutor's office involving Kim Seon-gyeong, a thirty-two-year-old woman who had abandoned her children so that she could live with another man. She was later charged with brutally murdering her son. According to the court proceeding, Kim lacked the *jeong* that a mother should have for her children, and she was labeled an "unfaithful wife" because she was more interested in saving her *chemyeon* than the honor of her husband. The newspaper narrative sought to explain the reason for her outrageous behavior. The previous year, the authorities had imprisoned her husband, Bak Bong-dal, for larceny, leaving Kim to take care of her two sons and daughter. Unable to endure *saenghwalgo* (the hardships of life) and frustrated over not receiving any support from her husband's family, she abandoned her children and eloped with Yi Yeong-seok, who lived in Hwangseong-gun.

Kim's elopement was not the end of the story: the report claimed that on March 3 the three children were able to find their mother. Gi-nam, the eldest of the three children, went to plead with his mother to take them back without thinking of her *chemyeon*. Instead of embracing her children, Kim allegedly displayed no signs of *jeong* and instead treated them in a heartless manner, driving Gi-nam and his siblings away from her new home. Shocked by his mother's verbal abuse and holding a deep resentment toward his mother for her lack of *jeong*, Gi-nam felt compelled to return to his mother's new home and plead with her for sympathy, as any nine-year-old boy would naturally do (*cheol eomneun*), clinging to her legs. Instead of feeling any guilt, Kim dragged Gi-nam ten *ri* away from the village to save her *chemyeon* from her new husband and urged him to leave with his siblings.[94] Unable to convince him to leave, Kim allegedly struck Gi-nam with a stone, killing him instantly. According to the district attorney Motohashi, Kim could have felt conflicted over giving her *jeong* to her children of her previous marriage because it might offend her new husband. However, such circumstantial evidence proved unimportant because she had committed murder against her own son. Hence, instead of looking at the evidence "that moves us to pity" (*bulssang han ma-eum*), Motohashi felt it imperative to investigate this case more carefully as a murder and a grisly crime, even suggesting, in an attempt to refocus the case around the act itself rather than the motivation, that Gi-nam might have not died from the initial blow and that Kim might have been drowned him in a pond later.

As this murder case illustrates, the emotional regime of *jeong* and the feeling rules in *chemyeon* and *nunchi* were important concepts regarding the Korean psyche and social relations that the Japanese district attorney had to understand to be able to prosecute Kim. As Arlie Hochschild observes, "If we conceive of feeling not as a periodic abdication to biology but as something we do by attending to inner sensation in a given way, by defining situations in a given way, by managing in given ways, then it becomes plainer just how plastic and susceptible to reshaping techniques a feeling can be."[95] In a profound sense, as this chapter has shown, the individual can exist only in relation to the *uri* (we-ness) and is cemented by feelings of *jeong*, which are key to any interpersonal relationship and are crucial for maintaining a vertical society. This comes with a cognitive awareness of one's social status and position, nourished by way of constant self-introspection and self-scrutiny (*chemyeon* and *nunchi*).

COLLECTIVE EMOTIONAL SUFFERING UNDER JAPANESE COLONIAL RULE

As noted above, the feeling of *han* can be described as the other face of *jeong*. Perhaps the most popular film produced in the early twentieth century to reconstruct this sentiment of "collective" *han* is Na Un-gyu's silent film *Arirang*, which was produced by Kinema Production of Joseon and released in 1926. Written and directed by Na Un-gyu (1902–37) when he was only twenty-five years old, it was perhaps the single most discussed film of its day and evoked the *simjeong* of its spectators as a *byeonsa* (silent-film narrator) narrated a story of *han* through its mentally ill heroine, Yeong-jin, who was also played by Na.[96]

Influenced by the Japanese *shimpa* (melodrama) genre and popular imported films of the day, the plot revolves around the protagonist, Choe Yeong-jin, a student who becomes mentally ill while studying philosophy in Seoul. Although Na claims in an interview with *Samcheolli* that the script he wrote intended to suggest that Choe went insane because of his studies, spectators and critics alike assumed that he had been imprisoned and tortured by the Japanese police for his involvement in the March First Movement of 1919, mirroring Na's own experience as a participant in the movement.[97] In the film, unable to complete his studies, Choe returns to his hometown to be cared for by his father, who was once a middle-class farmer but ended up in serious debt to a landlord by attempting to finance his son's education in Seoul. Demoted to the status of a tenant farmer, Choe's father and his beloved sister Yeong-hui are barely able to eke out a living and are constantly harassed by O Gi-ho, the *mareum* or "running dog" who collects taxes for the landlord. O Gi-ho not only collaborates with the Japanese police but offers to pay off the debts of Yeong-jin's father in exchange for Yeong-hui, whom he covets and desires to be his bride. In the meantime, a love relationship starts to develop between Yeong-hui and Yun Hyeon-gu, a college student on summer vacation who is a good friend of Yeong-jin. Hyeon-gu's relationship with Yeong-hui gets thwarted by O Gi-ho, who becomes extremely frustrated and angered by the rejection and attempts to assault Yeong-hui during the autumn harvest festival. The climax of the film occurs when Hyeon-gu attempts to wrestle with the rabid Gi-ho. During the melee, Yeong-jin appears in the final scene, regaining his sanity only to strike Gi-ho with a sickle and kill him. The film ends with the Japanese police arresting Yeong-jin and taking him away to prison.[98]

If Na's *Arirang* eluded government censorship, its release in 1926 coincided with the deaths of Yi Wan-yong, Joseon's most notorious "traitor," who had signed the Japan-Korea Annexation Treaty in 1910, and the Emperor Sunjong, the last living monarch of Joseon. It also coincided with the June 10 Manse student demonstrations throughout Seoul, which made the film timely because spectators could collectively lament their *simjeong* in the theaters. According to one review in the *Joseon ilbo,* Na was able to evoke numerous emotions from his viewers. Whether it was Yeong-jin's unexpected mental breakdown, his father's exasperation at having mortgaged all his land to finance his son's education only to see him return home without a degree, or the unscrupulous behavior of O Gi-ho, viewers were able to experience vicariously through the film their own feelings of helplessness, sorrow, hardship, and a yearning for revenge.[99] While the final scene could be seen at some level as cathartic for viewers because Yeong-jin exacts vengeance by killing Gi-ho, the story ends in tragedy. Under such unfortunate circumstances, the protagonist is able to reclaim his sanity, but his actions cannot be overturned, for he is bound by a rope (perhaps a metaphor for the knotted *han*) and led away by police. This scene, which encapsulates the shared Korean sentiment of lamentation, triggered audience members to display their collective *simjeong* by weeping and singing out loud the folk song "Arirang."[100]

Korean historians have only recently engaged with the new field of the historical study of emotions. A handful of studies—primarily in the fields of psychology and pastoral studies—have attempted to identify several key emotions such as *jeong* and *han* as indigenous Korean constructs. This chapter has attempted to illustrate that Koreans found it very difficult to navigate multiple, often conflicting emotional regimes; often they lacked the mechanisms to cope with the immense economic, political, social, and cultural changes that were taking place under colonial modernity, which profoundly affected the ways people thought about themselves and their relationships with others. Writers employed the theme of a gradual descent into madness as a response to emotional suffering: some depicted it as liberating, while others depicted it as debilitating to Korean advancement.

FOUR

Madness as a Social Epidemic

"스토-ㅂ" [Stop], This is the last port. From time to time, ownerless hats hang on the railings fluttering in the wind bidding adieu. At the base of the pillars, large weeping bowls have been placed for young girls...

KIM GI-RIM, "The Han River Footbridge"

"Suicide" is the term applied to any case of death resulting directly or indirectly from a positive or negative act, carried out by the victim himself, which he was aware would produce this result.

EMILE DURKHEIM, *On Suicide* (1897)

ON JULY 27, 1927, the *Donga ilbo* reported that a woman sporting a trendy *hisashi-gami* hairstyle had leapt off the Han River Bridge around 3:00 a.m. the previous day. A policeman from the Yongsan precinct who was making his daily rounds had spotted her drowning in the river and had rescued her. The woman, later identified as Kim Seong-hui, had been a student at Gyeongseong Girls' High School and was the wife of Cho Geun-seol. According to the police, Kim and Cho, both natives of North Hamgyeong Province, had moved to Seoul three years after they were married. Kim had demonstrated her resourcefulness and industriousness by enrolling at a vocational training center and later working at a fabric store. She had scrimped to save 400 *won* to pay for her husband's high school education and had financed his trip to Japan so he could complete his university studies in Tokyo. Just one month before her suicide attempt, Kim received the devastating diagnosis of myofascitis (a chronic inflammation of muscles and fascia, causing acute muscle spasms), which led to a series of misfortunes. The husband whom she had supported for years demanded a divorce, claiming that he could no longer live with a sick person. When her illness worsened and she lost her ability to earn a livelihood, a despondent Kim wrote a suicide note describing her cold-hearted husband and her miserable life. Unable to locate any family members, the Yongsan precinct detained Kim, placed her under a suicide watch, and offered to pay her hospital bills.[1]

Was Kim a *michin yeoja* (crazy woman), or was her suicide simply part of broader "social phenomena" affecting a modernizing Korean society? During the Japanese colonial period (1910–45), a modern medical discourse, influenced by the birth of the mental clinic in Korea, emerged and by the 1920s had become prominent in Korean print culture. As the Korean press adopted psychiatry's diagnostic labels and biomedical explanations, the public became acquainted with new frameworks for understanding criminality and suicide risk, as well as behaviors that had previously been considered merely as eccentric, strange, or unusual. By affixing psychiatric labels to certain behaviors, experts often lumped together symptoms that ordinary Koreans had previously not understood as a singular, coherent condition, let alone as a medical illness. Biological reductionism, which provided a proper descriptive basis for normative judgment, replaced the complex vernacular vocabularies of afflictions; the public was made to believe that the mind was subject to disease, debility, or even death.

Psychiatry also offered expert help for mental disorders, claiming to supersede traditional approaches to understanding and treatment. The press urged ordinary people to "seek out" a doctor who specialized in "mental illness," admit "unwanted family members" to the hospital and get them medicated, and refrain from engaging in "superstitious" treatment practices of the past, which would only trigger unnecessary "commotions in the household."[2] Lay people were not qualified to assess the mentally ill by themselves: as one newspaper article warned, "Unlike common physical ailments, the symptoms of mental illness are very difficult to discern," and their "etiology is very hard to pinpoint."[3] Nor could patients' own judgment of their condition be relied upon, for although some patients, such as those with neurasthenia, tended to be "quite conscious" of their illness, many with more severe disorders "have no idea of their disease and do not think that they are ill."[4] Family members would first have to look for signs of abnormality, and many articles offered checklists of symptoms that indicated the need for a doctor's consultation: for example, the mentally ill "do not eat their meals, don't like to bathe, like to lounge about in one place for days, and become less affectionate to their parents, siblings, wife, or children." They might "become lazy," "laugh spontaneously," or start to show signs of paranoia, "accusing friends of slandering them" or of "exposing a secret in the newspaper."[5] The specialist, once consulted, could discern the complex constellation of symptoms that would lead to a specific diagnosis; only then could one know how to "nurse" the afflicted with "patience and compassion."[6] Many mentally ill people could not be left alone, for "if one allows them to do whatever they please, there is no way of knowing what kinds of acts they might commit."[7]

This chapter will examine the medicalization and criminalization of mental illness in the social sphere. Fueled by sensationalist accounts of bizarre and frightening behaviors in newspapers and other mass cultural texts, a galvanized medical community sought to diagnose them, giving culture-bound ailments scientific labels and identifying new social pathologies. The model of biological psychiatry, shaped by Darwinian notions of evolution, held that all mental illness was physical in origin and that mental defects and weaknesses had a strong hereditary component. These new discursive constructions were useful in dealing with a troublesome class of vagrants, criminals, and other "social deviants" who had to be differentiated and categorized because of their aberrant behavior. Focusing on their disheveled look, rude manners, facial expressions, or odd speech patterns, this new grammar of classifying insanity not only analyzed individual behavior but also reflected social prejudices that led to identifying certain maladies like hysteria in gendered terms. For the first time, surveys and studies of Korean mental health, crime, and genetic illnesses proliferated and were subjected to intense scrutiny in the press. As these discourses became increasingly embedded in everyday life, they prompted a fear of stigma and also a desire to absolve oneself of the duty to care for those diagnosed as "mentally ill." In short, this chapter examines the intersection between scientific knowledge and the social imperatives of a colonized but also modernizing nation that sought to control unruly elements of the population, as well as the impact of a new psychiatric discourse on everyday social relations and the politics of caring for the mentally ill. It examines the Korean press's contribution to criminalizing the mentally ill through sensational stories that created fear and anxiety among the populace, its explanations for the alleged rise in the cases of mental illness in Korea, and its construction of suicide as a social ill that was plaguing a society under colonial rule.

CRIME AND MENTAL ILLNESS

According to a recent study by Yi Bang-hyeon, a total of 1,183 articles on mental illness appeared in three of the major colonial newspapers (the *Donga ilbo*, *Maeil sinbo*, and *Joseon ilbo*) between 1920 and 1945.[8] Many of these articles were about acts committed by those suspected to be mentally ill. Local police provided the first diagnosis of these individuals; those whom they judged to be a threat to society were sent on to a psychiatric hospital. In contrast to the privacy laws today, there were no restrictions on private information, so the press could obtain the information on these individuals from local police stations and publish a biographical sketch of each suspect or victim that included his or her name, gender, age, and address. In addition, each report revealed the *jeungsang* (symptoms), the *balbyeong wonin* (cause of the disease), and its *balsaeng* (trigger), which usually involved the suspect's experience of *gwangpokseong* (a smoldering sensation of fury).

Statistics as well as sensational stories on the mentally ill started to appear frequently in the press. In an editorial in 1926, the *Donga ilbo* estimated that some 2,500 people in Korea were mentally ill. While this figure was significantly lower than the estimate of 57,850 for Japan, the editorial warned that it was probably far too low because it did not include the large numbers of mentally ill vagrants roaming the streets and countryside.[9] In 1933, the *Joseon ilbo* reported that there were more than 3,000 *gwang-in* (crazy people) in Korea and that 50 of the most dangerous were currently incarcerated in the infamous East Ward Number Eight at the Government-General Hospital because of the threats they posed to the public if they were allowed to roam the streets. The writer expressed his concern that the state planned to reduce its current 213,000 *won* maintenance fee the following year even though there was a need to construct another hospital to house 300 more dangerous people in Seoul.[10] Using terms such as *gamho* (care and custody), writers called for the *gyeogni* (isolation, segregation) of these people because they had no insight into their psychiatric disturbances and behaved very differently from the *botong saram* (ordinary person).[11]

Newspapers also provided alarming figures for the prevalence of insanity in the global population. For example, in 1934 the *Donga ilbo* reported that a famous psychiatrist in New York City had predicted that because of the astonishing numbers of mentally ill people globally, an estimated 30 percent of the total population during the previous decade, by the year 2139 the entire earth would be populated by the insane.[12] According to another report in the *Joseon ilbo* in the same year, one writer calculated that 20 percent of the world population was mentally ill. He urged readers to contemplate these numbers and to realize that globally twenty people out of a hundred, or an even more frightening ratio of two hundred people out of a thousand, were mentally ill.[13]

Newspapers presented those suffering from *jeongsin isang* (mental disorder) as likely to engage in destructive and injurious behavior and to be "at risk" of harming themselves and others. The "mad" would suddenly experience confusion in the mind, which would trigger them to behave in unpredictable ways. Relatedly, public tolerance for bizarre and disruptive behaviors decreased as these were attributed to mental illness. Stories abounded of "strange" or "dubious" acts committed by crazy people: demanding money from strangers, for example, or claiming a false identity. In one case, someone with mental illness claimed to be a police officer and presented fake ID. In another, a Ms. Kang claimed to be a female general and queen dowager whose "son had to abdicate because of the Japanese bastards."[14] In still another case, a woman who was reportedly "going mad" left her home so she could "become the wife of the governor-general."[15] "Abnormal" (*isang*) people like these were always taken to the local police precinct first and interrogated before they were deemed mentally ill.

Pyromaniacs got their fair share of coverage. Stories of people deliberately starting fires for gratification alarmed the public.[16] In one case, a *balhwagwang* (igniting-fires maniac) who had already been responsible for setting twenty-four fires in the previous three months was reported enjoying the spectacle of his neighbors trying to put out the fire that he had set in his bathroom.[17] Another story reported the arrest of a wandering beggar by the name of Bak Su-dong who was wanted for several fires in the neighborhood. Not only was he an arsonist, but he was deemed mentally ill, which heightened neighborhood fears. According to the suspect, he enjoyed setting houses on fire because it induced euphoria and because he enjoyed watching the spectacle of fire engines coming to the scene of the crime to put out the fires.[18] In another case, the *Donga ilbo* reported that the police had arrested a *michin yeoja* (crazy woman) for setting her own house on fire. The suspect was identified as Yu Seong-nyeo, Kim Kyeollim's wife, who lived in Gochang County, North Jeolla Province. Everybody in town knew that from time to time Yu would suffer from recurrent attacks of madness and cause all kinds of problems, often destroying family possessions. The police immediately took Yu into custody (*gugeum*) and placed her under surveillance (*gamsi*) after concluding that she had hurled a brazier onto the roof of her house and set it on fire.[19] In cases of deliberately set house fires, the arsonist was usually a family member: one Seon Yeong-hui, for instance, was taken into custody by the police after he set his own house on fire.[20]

Accounts of homicides and attempted homicides triggered debates not only among the experts but among ordinary people, who were now learning the language of crime and mental illness. Were these crimes premeditated? Did they lack any rational motive? In all criminal cases, the police released information to the public after conducting their investigation, which usually took two to four days. In cases of suspicious death, if the victim did not leave a suicide note, the police interviewed family members and neighbors to determine whether the suspect had any mental disorders. When the police did not release an autopsy report, the press often speculated and informed its readers that "in all likelihood, the cause was mental illness."[21]

While accounts of violent outbreaks and suicides by patients locked up at the infamous East Ward Number Eight of the Government-General Hospital made headlines, nothing was more frightening than reading stories of "crazy people" confined in their homes who were just waiting to kill themselves or others.[22] From police reports, the majority of the victims killed by the mentally ill were family members, and these killings were often particularly gruesome and cold-blooded: a father who unexpectedly stabbed his daughter, a boy who beat his father to death thinking he was a tiger, a father who bludgeoned his eldest son and daughter with a cudgel, a mother slaying her daughter (a story that "would give anyone goose bumps"), a son stabbing his mother ten times in the abdomen and head, a sixteen-year-old boy who used a kitchen knife to slay his family members.[23]

Several reports of such crimes in the press emphasized families' need for unwearied vigilance to keep the mentally ill from harming themselves or other family members. Even if family members left the afflicted person unguarded only for a moment, he or she might become violent and attack someone. The *Donga ilbo* reported, for instance, that Yu Hwak-sil, the eighteen-year-old daughter of Yu Gyeong-jeong, had "unexpectedly" gotten ill sometime in July and had started to exhibit some bizarre symptoms of mental illness. This concerned family members, who feared she might seriously injure herself. One day, however, her parents left her alone with her twelve-year-old brother for several hours. Yu took her brother to the field and stabbed him with a kitchen knife. When her parents returned home, they found Yu splattered in blood, dancing in glee while waving the knife around the corpse of her brother. The police, finding it "pointless to scold a crazy person," returned Yu to confinement in her family's home while the family prepared for her brother's funeral. It is unclear from the report whether Yu was eventually admitted to a mental hospital or whether her parents decided to continue to confine her at home.[24] In another case, Kim Chong-ho, the twenty-two-year-old son of Kim Yong-seon, used a kitchen knife to murder his infant sister. After obtaining his diagnosis of mental illness the previous year, his parents had instructed Kim to not wander outside the home and had kept him under close surveillance. However, one day while the entire family was out doing their laundry, he stabbed his sister to death and then tried to bury her. Before he could commit suicide, the police arrested him and confined him at the local precinct. It is not clear whether the police admitted the suspect to a mental hospital.[25] Another story reported that Kim Seong-nyo, the wife of Cho Gap-je, had tragically drowned her two-year-old son near her sister-in-law's house and had then been caught by her husband using a hoe to bury her son. Cho had "gone crazy" several years ago and was known among neighbors to beg for food, but no one would have guessed that she would be capable of committing such an atrocious crime. And in still another case, a thirty-year-old man named Yang Gyu-seop, who had done very well in school and had gotten admitted to a college in Tokyo, became despondent and, after being diagnosed with mental illness, was sequestered in his family's house and placed under strict surveillance. Despite all their precautions, however, he one day suddenly stabbed his father with a pair of scissors.[26]

Acts of violence by the mentally ill that targeted people outside the family were even more alarming because they were so unpredictable and could affect anyone. For example, in one report a patient who was seeking treatment for his mental illness unexpectedly attacked a doctor and his wife with an ax.[27] According to the *Joseon ilbo,* a *jeongsin byeongja* (mentally ill person) ruthlessly stabbed three adults and six young children with a dagger in broad daylight.[28] Similarly, a young man brandishing a sickle went on a killing rampage, injuring fifteen bystanders and killing four people, including a woman about to give birth.[29]

Adding to the public's fears was the sense that, as one writer warned, "there is no telling when the mentally ill will experience a *jaebal* (relapse)." For example, all of Bong Yun's neighbors knew that his son suffered from mental illness and often exhibited fits of rage. One day, when Bong was berating his son in the yard, the son suddenly turned violent and cracked Bong's skull, killing him instantaneously. He would later be apprehended by the police and incarcerated at the station.[30]

Perhaps the most riveting stories reported in the press in the late 1920s and early 1930s involved dangerous mental patients on the loose, raising the specter of more grisly attacks. "A lack of supervision of the mentally ill," one commentator argued, was contributing to more patients' escapes from East Ward Number Eight.[31] Yi Chang-deok, a twenty-three-year-old patient, became the second person in 1924 to dig his way out of the ward.[32] One of the many intense manhunts reported in the press concerned Yi Chu-ri, a thirty-five-year-old mentally ill man from North Gyeongsang Province who first cut the throats of a tavern owner and his wife and injured several other people in Ulsan, South Gyeongsang Province, and then killed his wife by a one single blow to her throat with a sharp sickle. As the reporter for the *Joseon ilbo* observed, "Simply seeing all the blood splattered over the corpse would make anyone shudder." The police in Cheongha (North Gyeongsang Province) and assisting police from Gokgang, Singwang, Songra, and Sangok rounded up six hundred people to create a dragnet around the forest where the criminal was hiding. Yi was finally caught while trying to steal sweet potatoes and melons from a field and was taken into custody by the police, temporarily easing a lot of tension in the various townships. After two days of investigation he was deemed mentally ill despite his claims he was *jeongsang* (normal).[33]

These stories based on police reports were influential in shaping the general public's knowledge and attitudes regarding mental illness, and to some extent they provided important public information. But they were woefully deficient in providing information on how to deal with the afflicted. Further, they fueled the public's fears and contributed to the erroneous belief that all mentally ill people and indeed all aberrant behaviors were dangerous.

EXPLANATIONS OF MENTAL ILLNESS IN THE PRESS

The press reported three possible primary causes of mental illness. First, it began to popularize the medical model and portray at least some forms of mental illnesses as springing from a hereditary "defect" and being innate (*seoncheonjeok*), in contrast to infectious diseases such as smallpox or malaria, which attacked the weak and the strong indiscriminately.[34] One writer, for example, proclaimed that "genetic" mental illness was the "scariest mental illness."[35] Drawing on Social Darwinism, which circulated widely in the nineteenth and early twentieth centuries, eugenics, or the "science of good breeding," sought to prevent social misfits from breeding future generation of recidivists, imbeciles, and the feeble-minded. Preparations for marriage now took on a new meaning. The newspapers warned that it was imperative to conduct a thorough investigation of one's spouse's upbringing and health history, including all past illnesses and diseases. One doctor warned prospective couples that instead of judging someone "on the basis of external appearance" they should carefully examine their partner's genetic inheritance, which was "innately acquired" and "impossible to correct."[36] Failure to identify these traits would doom future descendants if "bad genes" introduced into a family produced a generation of "imbeciles."[37]

Although medical theorists lacked organic proof, morbid heredity became their explanation for functional aberrations of the nervous system, which they claimed would only worsen with each succeeding generation and would cause progressive decline not only within families but within the population as a whole.[38] Korean doctors warned that the accumulation of bad hereditary traits over several generations would fall on one unlucky individual. One social commentator asserted that keeping bad genes out of a family was particularly important because they could affect the looks or behavior of children, who would "never get fully healed [*wankwae*]."[39] The insane were dangerous to their neighbors and even more to themselves, and the majority would eventually commit suicide.

The second most common explanation for mental illness lay in understanding *hucheonjeok* (acquired or external) factors contributing to mental illness.[40] According to the *Joseon ilbo*, "In the past, the understanding was simply that a malevolent ghost had driven the person to lunacy." Now, however, the public expected more "modern" explanations rooted in such everyday problems as "a failure in love, family discord, failure in business, or difficulty with one's livelihood."[41]

More broadly, social problems spawned by demographic change (mass migration), changing family patterns, urbanization, and rapid industrialization were also blamed for potentially generating mental illness in some people. One article in the *Donga ilbo* pointed to civilization (*munhwa*) as primarily responsible for the increase in the number of people suffering from mental illness in Korea. Urban dwellers were more likely to succumb to nervous disorders than their compatriots in the countryside because of the pace of modern civilization, "all the happenings in the city," "the intensity in the struggle for existence," the temptations of city life, and "extravagant living."[42] The *Maeil sinbo* reported the example of a young "country bride" who could not adjust to urban culture. She allegedly ran around the main thoroughfares of Gyeongseong (Seoul) fully naked, causing a major commotion, screaming and dancing in a crazy frenzy. The restlessness, speed, and constant change of life in modern Seoul had made this girl mad.[43]

Many people whose nerves were stretched to a breaking point by the pressures and temptations of modern civilized living had the less severe disorder of neurasthenia, a term coined in 1869 by the American neurologist George Beard to describe a "morbid condition of the exhaustion of the nervous system."[44] Neurasthenia was seen by contemporaries as a disease common among male intellectuals, professionals, and urban workers because of their busy lifestyles. Writers described it as chronic fatigue but also the incapacity to deal with a modern and fast-changing world. It was characterized best by the *flâneur* Gubo who wanders aimlessly around Seoul in Bak Tae-won's novel *A Day in the Life of Gubo the Novelist*.[45] Some newspaper articles suggested that neurasthenics were especially likely to fall into the immoral living conditions and pursuits that were common in cities, such as drinking, fornication, and vagrancy, and could thus contract syphilis or become alcoholics.[46]

A third cause of mental illness discussed in the press was the effects of seasonal and climate variations on the nerves. According to one article, it was always after a quiet period in winter that "a lot of people go mad," especially "when the day gets longer."[47] Warmer weather was said to exacerbate psychiatric symptoms and to trigger previously "sane" people to commit violent crimes.[48] It was possible, another article noted, for "average" people to go insane during this period because "their bodies find it hard to adjust to the sudden [climatic] changes."[49] One writer suggested that "it's during the humid *jangma* [monsoon season] that a lot of people run away from their homes."[50] As Michael Staub notes in a different context, epidemiological research throughout the first half of the twentieth century continued to provide compelling evidence that environmental factors posed a risk in the etiology of mental illness.[51] Dr. Matsumura, who was employed at the psychiatry ward at Tokyo Imperial University, warned parents that during the spring season rates of mental illness surged among children. He noted that children's symptoms were similar to those of adults and that parents would have to be vigilant at this time because "once the brain stops functioning, one will be impaired for life."[52]

The press provided numerous reports of large groups of mentally ill people roaming the streets during the warmer months. The Jongno police precinct in Seoul, for instance, reported having to deal with a dozen or so mentally ill residents who raised a ruckus by singing and dancing at the station. Those whose guardians were identified were lucky enough to be returned to their homes; however, "those whose addresses could not be verified had to be kept in the station's cell."[53] In another case on April 8, 1934, the *Joseon ilbo* reported that twenty people with mental illness had left their homes unexpectedly and thronged the streets of Pyeongyang, singing and dancing in joy to welcome the spring. Although they raised a huge commotion, "most of them seemed rather docile and behaved like infants." However, what concerned the public were the six or seven "dangerous" people who randomly charged into people's homes and smashed their furniture. The Pyeongyang police precinct expressed frustration about trying to identify and incarcerate these lunatics.[54]

Some writers linked such seasonal changes to periodic outbreaks, among men and women, of sudden or excessive passions to engage in "immoral acts" that they connected to venereal disease (presumably tertiary syphilis).[55] "It is no different in other [civilized] countries like America and Europe," one social commentator observed; "during the warm spring season" mental illness was triggered by underlying venereal disease.[56] However, another writer reminded his readers that lax moral behavior, such as illicit *chijeong gwan-gye* (sexual liaisons) or overindulgence in sex, sprang from an individual's genetic predisposition.[57] In a more gendered analysis of the root of this problem, an editorial in the *Donga ilbo* blamed prostitution: capitalist society created "genetic defects" by sanctioning the buying and selling of sex, a permissive attitude that would encourage sexual laxity generally and "would lure many young girls to become harlots." "It is because of this 'unnatural and artificial' occupation that women's nerves get damaged," the editorial concluded, and "because of the sensitive nature of the business it is obvious why so many [prostitutes] are suffering from mental illness."[58]

Whereas warm spring or summer weather seemed to make people passionate and active, colder temperatures were said to make people melancholic and listless. According to one writer in the *Maeil sinbo,* the "cool winds during the fall season" made people *senchimental* ("sentimental," or melancholic), and the Jongno police station reported having to deal with fifty crazy people seeking assistance for their mental distress.[59]

According to the colonial press, men and women experienced mental illness in very different ways. The timing of the first appearance of mental illness was one example of difference: according to one writer, one could detect symptoms among men a little before or after their forties, but many women were said to experience symptoms starting in their twenties.[60] Antisocial and hypochondriac behaviors were considered to be typically male, whereas melancholia and hysteria were considered to be female. No longer seen as a possession by spirits, hysteria was deemed a real neurological disease and was a well-established diagnostic category in Japan.[61] One hundred and sixteen Korean women were admitted to the Government-General Hospital's psychiatric ward with this diagnosis between the years 1914 and 1928.[62] Most of them were clinically identified as neurotic, psychotic, or frigid and were subjected to a wide range of specialized treatments specific to their reproductive organs.[63] In contrast to the description of their male counterparts, the press employed a morally disapproving tone to write about hysteric women; invoking old male prejudices, writers focused on causes and cures related to sexuality. In some respects the titillating description of female mental illness exposed to the male gaze gave the articles a voyeuristic character. An exemplary case was a lurid exposé in the popular journal *Byeolgeongon* (Another World) in 1929 by a doctor who divulged confidential information about his single twenty-one-year-old "virgin" female patient who was suffering from some serious emotional problems.

Ms. Cho, a resident of Gwanghun-dong (central Seoul), had visited this doctor several years earlier to seek professional diagnosis and treatment. She had never been sick since childhood and considered herself healthy. However, her symptoms included bouts of mild migraines, insomnia, nightmares, over-excitement, and excessive mood swings. Her condition deteriorated as she experienced anxiety and could no longer suppress these emotions. The doctor sensed that perhaps she was suffering from some urban disorder like *sin-gyeongsoeyak* (neurasthenia), a kind of weakness of the nerves, or an acute case of *hiseuteri* (hysteria). Unable to come up with a certain diagnosis, he asked the patient to come in for treatment. But for several days, despite receiving every medical treatment available to her, including acupuncture, the patient kept complaining about the same symptoms. Eventually the doctor concluded that marriage was the cure for her mental disorder. Using an intermediary service, the patient found a spouse, and once she was married all of her symptoms disappeared. The doctor claimed that she became much healthier and gained a lot of weight.[64] This male expert's explanation of female mental disorders was clearly grounded in a culture that advocated marriage and by inference, sexual intercourse, as a cure for all female maladies, especially hysteria.

Biological explanations that linked mental illness to the female reproductive organs posited that a woman's mind became weakened, and that she consequently became more likely to commit crimes of passion, during puberty and pregnancy, around menstruation, after childbirth, and around menopause. One riveting article described a new mother who ripped out her infant's eyes with her bare hands. The police noted that the woman's husband was not living with her and concluded that she was suffering from postpartum mental illness.[65] In another case, a thirty-year-old mother was also reported as suffering from postpartum disorders when, according to the Ulsan police, she allegedly pushed four of her children into the river.[66]

SUICIDE

Between 1910 and 1942, the Government-General of Korea reported a total of 54,053 completed suicides among Koreans.[67] Such alarming statistics as well as sensational stories in the press fostered a sense of crisis among Koreans. Views of the problem were diverse, reflecting the competing agendas that shaped the discourse. The colonial authorities viewed the rise in suicide rates in Korea as an indicator that their project of modernization was working. Suicides were simply a by-product of the transformations that Korea needed to undergo. That is why the colonial government's documents rarely ever grappled with solutions to prevent suicides. The Korean press, on the other hand, treated suicides as emblematic of the tragic consequences of colonial modernity, which transformed Korean mores (especially in the area of marriage and family) and economic circumstances. At the same time, perhaps paradoxically, it also utilized suicide to deliver internal critiques of traditional Korean society. In this sense, the press also gradually adopted and internalized the medical framework employed by the colonial state and medical experts to explain the social problems of the day. Indeed, the pathologization of deviant behavior as due to neurological disorders contributed to a broader discourse on suicide as a measure of social health, which placed people's lives under increasing scrutiny.

Suicide in Traditional Korea

In the 1920s, a new popular notion emerged that Korean society was being plagued by an "epidemic" of suicides. The Korean press blamed various facets of modern life—internal migration, rapid industrialization and urbanization, the end of a rigid class system, moral decadence, and other social stressors—as fostering a new type of pathological behavior that traditional remedies could no longer control. This marked a shift from the traditional Korean understanding of suicide as having both a political and a social meaning. In political terms, the word *jagyeol* (individual suicide) signified an ultimate act of honor or atonement for a crime whereby the state granted a corrupt official, a captured enemy officer, or a *banyeok joein* (an enemy of the state) the option to kill himself to avoid facing public humiliation. It was customary for the accused to declare his or her loyalty to the king before drinking lethal poison.

Joseon wangjo sillok (The annals of the Joseon kings) also describes suicides that were more "social" in nature. It mentions some 435 suicide cases during the Joseon period (1392–1910) that allegedly resulted from a wide range of motives: an ignominious political defeat, unrequited love, *ulhwa* (accumulated stress in social life), *bun* (feelings of anger due to failure), *eogul* (feelings of social injustice), regret, and failure to live up to certain moral expectations.[68] While hardly any official sources explicitly examine individual cases among commoners, the *Hyeongsa panryejip simnirok* (Criminal case studies, trial documents for the king), which were published between 1776 and 1800 during King Jeongjo's reign, shed light on possible motives for suicide among commoners in the late Joseon period. For example, in 1781, Bak Seong-je, a commoner who lived in Yangyang, Gangwon Province, was falsely accused of stealing and endured a painful leg-screw torture. Overcome by shame and aggrieved over his inability to defend himself, he decided to hang himself. In another case in 1784, two neighbors were rumored to have fought over enlistment in the *sogogun*, a special unit for commoners.[69] Yu Yeo-nin felt embarrassed and angry after quarreling with his neighbor and hanged himself.[70] While these two cases might not be representative of all suicides during this period, this volume suggests that *bunsa* (killing oneself because of indignation) was the most common reason why commoners killed themselves.[71] Given the paucity of sources, one can only surmise that honorable deaths or politically motivated suicides received attention in the public realm while the majority of suicides remained unreported or were kept a family secret.

There was yet another form of "sanctioned" suicides: the system of state canonization of widows (*yeollyeo-jeon*), which promoted the Confucian view of morality, popularized the practice of widow suicide during the Joseon dynasty. While the *Joseon wangjo sillok* mentions a total of 326 individual cases, Bak Jong-seong suggests a much higher figure if one includes other official records. According to Bak, a total of 694 faithful young widows followed their husbands to death.[72] Perhaps the most well-known cases of mass suicides by widows took place during Toyotomi Hideyoshi's seven-year depredation of Joseon, when 356 women killed themselves to preserve their chastity and were later honored posthumously for their "virtuous acts."[73] While these official sources might suggest that the imposition of a set of moral and social obligations (e.g., chastity ideology, the three obediences, the five human relationships) on society induced people to commit suicide, there may have been other triggers. For instance, stories told in folk culture and represented in *talchum* (masked dance) and *pansori* (traditional epic songs) stressed that unjust social situations, commonly precipitated by violence, discrimination, isolation, poverty, an overbearing mother-in-law, or infidelity, could lead people to take their own lives—circumstances that would be scrutinized in great detail for the first time by writers in the following period.

Suicide and the Japanese Colonial State

As mentioned in the previous chapter, in an era of growing empiricism the power of the medical gaze provided unprecedented possibilities for a professional group of medical "experts" to intervene and exclusively administer services prophylactically as well as to sequester populations in institutions in the name of social security. Likewise, national figures on the social conditions, in particular birth and death rates, crime, and suicide, began to be published annually by the Government-General, providing a useful index for gauging the "well-being" of society. According to the historian Junko Kitanaka, by the late nineteenth century biomedicine in Japan had already won legitimacy over folk power and the local networks of healing, successfully eradicating a wide range of contagious diseases like cholera while improving sanitation and hygiene.[74] These "modern technologies of power," which ranged from medical examinations to diagnostic practices, began to influence how Koreans thought about suicide, especially as the press adopted medicalized language and concepts.[75]

A year after conducting its first national census, the Government-General published a detailed fifteen-year report on the demographic trends on the peninsula entitled "Population Phenomena of Korea in 1926," which included a section on suicide rates in the colony.[76] Categorized by race, age, and gender, police suicide reports and tallied annual figures also identified personal motives for committing suicide, which included mental illness; chronic illness; livelihood difficulties; crimes of passion or jealousy; shame about crimes committed in the past; discord with relatives; fears about being caught for a criminal act; worries about the future; business losses; difficulties in repaying a debt; disciplinary action by an employer, a father, or some other elder; immoral debauchery; an extramarital affair; anxiety over pregnancy; concerns of the elderly (physical frailty and worries over a loss of freedom); anxiety over marriage; and despondency about a deformity.[77] These figures by the

Government-General's office show a gradual increase in the rate of "recorded" suicides—from 474 in 1910 to 1,065 in 1920 to 1,536 in 1925. The incidence of suicide was reported to be the highest during the spring and early summer, which seemed to corroborate with newspaper reports.[78] The report also singled out men in their thirties as the most vulnerable among all age groups.[79]

The report did not offer any concrete recommendations or solutions to help avert suicide in the colony, for that was not Japan's concern. Instead, investigators took a macro approach to examine these demographic trends, claiming that suicide was a "social phenomenon" whose rates were inevitably going to increase as Korea developed into a more modern civilization. They hypothesized that the industrialization and modernization of Korean society caused more suicides, and they especially noted higher rates of suicide among urban dwellers, echoing the views of nineteenth-century moral statisticians in Europe such as Jean-Etienne Esquirol and Adolphe Quetelet.[80] According to Esquirol, suicide had subverted traditional forms of deference because man no longer had the authority to "direct his passion and govern his actions" and was left "defenseless against the suffering of life's predicaments, against internal anguish, against the vicissitudes of fortune, against outbursts of passion."[81] For the colonial authorities, these statistics demonstrated that their project of uprooting Koreans from their passive, traditional ways was indeed on the road to success.

The colonial state co-opted the police and medical community to deal with suicide. The police were requested to analyze the victim's suicide note and to interrogate family members in order to create their own diagnostic labels and classifications. As in the Weimar Republic, where "social prejudices and clichés about suicide held by the criminal police and the public certainly played a great role in determining whether a given death was classified as murder or suicide," the police also drew on public opinion to determine if the victim had been suffering from some type of mental disorder.[82] They treated failed suicide as a criminal act, often subjecting the survivor to interrogation. In cases of unnatural deaths (*byeonsa*) or a discovery of an unidentified corpse, a doctor always accompanied a policeman to the scene of the crime. When the doctor provided his expert opinion that the cause of the death was a suicide, the police would contact a family member and arrange for the transfer of the body and permission to proceed with the burial.[83] However, if the police or doctor suspected foul play or considered it a homicide, the authorities conducted an autopsy as part of the investigation process.[84] For example, on October 29, 1929, the *Donga ilbo* reported that a railroad employee had discovered a corpse floating on the Han River. During the autopsy, the police discovered a suicide note in the victim's pocket, which identified the man as Hwang In-su, a thirty-eight-year-old man who had become despondent after being laid off from work. After interviewing the victim's friend Gyeong Su-yeong, the police informed the press that a series of setbacks including the contraction of pulmonary tuberculosis and the loss of his job had prompted Hwang to hurl himself into the Han River.[85]

The Government-General required all of its police precincts to tally the number of completed suicides, along with each victim's age, race, gender, and cause of death. It did not, however, include failed suicides. According to their annual reports, the most common method of suicide was by hanging, followed by drowning, consuming poison, and hurling oneself onto a passing train.[86] Sodium hydroxide, also called lye or caustic soda, a popular whitening detergent introduced to Korea by the Japanese, was the most common poison used, followed by rat poison, morphine, bitters, soy sauce, corrosive sublimate, petroleum, blowfish eggs, brine, and a lethal medicine called "Nice."[87] Women often chose methods that did not involve physical violence, such as hanging, drowning, and taking poison, while their male counterparts opted for more violent methods, such as stabbing oneself or jumping off a cliff. The press commonly attributed men's use of more violent methods to men's greater aggression.

Suicide in Popular Discourse

With the easing of publication laws in the aftermath of the March First Movement in 1919, suicide featured quite regularly in the popular press, which had multiple agendas for exploiting the public's morbid fascination with violence and tragedy and catching their attention with dramatic headlines.[88] One role the press sought to play was to modernize its readers' understanding of suicide, eschewing traditional explanations. It also exposed readers to new medico-legal terms like *yeomsejuui* (tedium vitae), *chijeong* (crimes of passion), and *jeongsin isang* (mental disorder) to explain the crisis of selfhood in the modern age.[89] Fictional writers, who often serialized many of their stories in the newspapers, contributed to this effort, often experimenting with new genres like realism to define a wide range of "modern" emotions (i.e., amorous passion, unrequited love, despondency). This is not to suggest that people did not experience these emotions earlier; however, in the newspapers and in popular fiction they were linked to problems of modern life.

Moreover, these stories grappled with the price for pursuing individual happiness at the expense of the family. Indeed, the ideals of romantic love and fulfillment were quite different than a decade earlier when the long-standing Neo-Confucian ethos of preserving one's chastity or family honor was the conventional trope in any narrative discourse.[90] If the state endorsed the idea that social forces larger than individuals were the catalysts for suicide, writers focused on the everyday life and the changing consciousness of the people, especially themes of self-discovery and the free-willed individual.

The press also focused on specific suicide cases committed in public spaces that gained particular notoriety. On October 7, 1917, city planners at the Government-General Office celebrated the completion of the Han River Footbridge that linked Yongsan to Noryangjin. But despite great fanfare by the state, the bridge had suddenly had become the venue of choice for suicides, tarnishing the glory of the colonial authorities for its engineering achievements.[91] The popular saying "I am going to the Han River" also signified something pathological, evoking feelings of sadness and despair, captured brilliantly by the poet Kim Gi-rim in his short poem in the epigraph to this chapter.[92] The reports of daily suicides in the press prompted the Yongsan Young Men's Association to hold a *siagwi,* a special Buddhist rite that offers food to hungry ghosts, to appease the homeless spirits.[93] Unable to curb the growing number of suicides on the bridge, the Yongsan precinct even sponsored an event offering a prize to the person who could come up with the most catchy suicide prevention slogan. Out of the potpourri of entries—ranging from the poetic to the religious—"Wait a minute and restrain yourself" received the highest number of votes. To promote this campaign further, the state, frustrated by the negative publicity that the bridge brought to its reputation, opened a counseling-cum-employment center next to the bridge.[94] Despite this publicity stunt, suicides continued to increase. This prompted the Yongsan precinct to solicit funds from a Japanese expatriate, who offered 10,000 *won* to help defray the costs of installing lamps, railings on both sides, netting, and a full-time watchman. However, despite these efforts by the state and individuals, the number of suicides on the bridge kept increasing every year.[95]

By the 1920s, the press was increasingly reporting that urban diseases such as neurasthenia and hysteria were contributing to suicide among the urban population. One Korean specialist asserted that neurasthenics were all "suffering from *jeongsin soran* (mental disturbance)," which could trigger them to commit suicide.[96] The press and the police began to accept such explanations and to frame suicides in medical terms. For instance, the *Donga ilbo* reported that on May 12, 1928, Choe Seong-mun, a twenty-seven-year-old student who was enrolled at Rikkyo University in Tokyo, threw himself off a boat and drowned in the choppy waters near the Genkai-nada in northern Kyūshū. Police contacted his family in Busan and concluded that he not only was despondent about his paralyzed right leg but had been suffering from neurasthenia, which had compelled him to quit his studies and return to Korea.[97] In another case, the newspaper reported that Mr. Kotō, a Japanese expatriate who worked as a manager at a certain joint-stock bank in Daegu, had recently gotten despondent over some life disappointments and had decided to drink lethal poison. The police concluded that Kotō had also been suffering from neurasthenia.[98] There were also reports of young men like Mun Sang-min, a former twenty-year-old factory worker, who had to return to Korea from Japan after developing an extreme case of neurasthenia. Unable to find work and despondent, Mun hurled himself into the sea off the coast of North Jeolla Province.[99] Not surprisingly, the pharmaceutical companies jumped on the bandwagon, taking out large advertisements in the newspapers, promising readers effective cures to neurasthenia and other "urban" scourges.[100]

Hysteria was another biomedical diagnosis that the press often linked to suicidal behavior. The press featured a number of stories of about women who had developed this illness with tragic results. For example, a certain Yang Seung-hyeok claimed that he had had a loving relationship with his twenty-two-year-old wife, Kim A-chin, and their son until she got diagnosed with hysteria; then she started to frequently express a desire to die. One evening, a family member caught her drinking lye and rushed her over to Jeonchi Hospital for emergency treatment.[101] In another case, the *Donga ilbo* reported that "Tomo," the twenty-four-year-old wife of Mr. Fujimoto, who lived in Sakurai i-chome (the Japanese quarters), had become despondent in the previous year and was suffering from an acute case of hysteria. She refused to take a walk outside, did not talk to anyone, and only glared at the mountains. She told her husband that she was no longer enjoying life and wanted to die. Determined to kill herself, Tomo used a kitchen knife to slash her neck and then tried in vain to hang herself. She then jumped into an outhouse's cesspit to drown herself and was discovered by Fujimoto, who quickly called a doctor and had Tomo admitted to the Government-General Hospital for treatment.[102]

But the press also sought to understand suicide in terms of the new environmental triggers in modern society; these were linked directly to the process of colonial modernization that influenced Koreans' economic condition. Articles cited the stresses of modern life—*bigwan* (feelings of despondency) and *saenghwalgo* (livelihood difficulties)—as the primary causes for suicide in colonial Korea.[103] Contemporaries warned that rapid industrialization, which had triggered out-migration from the countryside to the urban centers, had already transformed into an acute social crisis as traditional social relations were quickly unraveling. Indeed, as Émile Durkheim noted in his observation of the political, social, and economic upheavals in France that started with the French Revolution, "In stable times, the individual willingly adheres to the standards imposed to his society—at least if he respects regulations and is docile to the collective authority" and that if he "has a wholesome moral constitution, he feels that it is not well to ask more."[104] However, as more people faced isolation and anxiety with the breakdown of traditional social structures and class expectations, which often resulted from a lack of normlessness and social regulation, they experienced a sense of anomie (in the Durkheimian sense) that could induce suicidal tendencies.[105]

The press profiled the rise of a new group at risk for suicide—namely the *rumpen* or unemployed intellectuals who drifted around in the urban centers without a sense of belonging or community. After the March First Movement, Im Gi-sun, a twenty-one-year-old man who lived a life of paranoia after escaping arrest, became increasingly frustrated about his inability to express his thoughts freely. Despondent about his life, he penned a suicide note describing his brushes with the law and the reasons for his involvement in the youth movement, which had frustrated his parents' wishes and led him to neglect his studies.[106] Another intellectual, Kim Chae-dong, claimed that he felt despondent after studying abroad in Tokyo for years yet still being unable to secure a job; this resulted in mounting debts and an attempt to take his life.[107] Given high expectations and intense desires concerning admission to a top high school or university, the press also reported an increase in the number of suicide cases among students over failing the entrance examination, getting caught cheating, doing poorly in school, or feeling pressure to drop out because of financial problems at home.[108] For example, Min Byeong-ho, an eighteen-year-old student who had recently been admitted to a higher common school in Seoul, became despondent after his parents told him that they could no longer afford to pay for his tuition. Having lost all hope for living, Min attempted to commit suicide by jumping off the Han River Bridge.[109]

The press also blamed failures in entrepreneurial ventures as a relatively new trigger for suicide. Fueled by dreams of striking it rich, waves of people from the countryside migrated to the cities to find better employment or to start up a business. After making a large windfall profit in the speculation of rice, a certain Yun Gi-seon suddenly suffered a reversal of fortune and lost his entire twenty-year savings in one risky bid. Overwhelmed by his losses, Yun decided to commit suicide.[110] The news that Kim Cheong-min, a well-known businessman who was the director of the Samhwa Youth Association and a distinguished member of the Board of Trade, had committed suicide by drowning shocked the community in Jinnampo.[111] In another case, the entrepreneur Yi Hwa-il, who had invested his entire life savings in the beef and pork business, could no longer manage his operations; after giving up his house to his creditors he became very despondent and decided to commit suicide.[112] No Bong-ha also became a victim to creditors, forfeiting his home in hopes of saving his rice business; this blow caused his optimism to turn to a "bitter resentment toward the world" that prompted him to eat the poisonous eggs of a blowfish and end his miserable life.[113]

But it was not simply failed entrepreneurs, intellectuals, or students who were allegedly at risk: the press argued that modernization also had a calamitous effect on the lower classes, as the gap between the rich and poor was widening further.[114] For instance, Kim Yong-gwan, a thirty-year-old employee at the Pyeongyang Eastern Rice Mill, stole a sack of rice from the warehouse while the owner was away out of pure desperation. The humiliation of being caught and chided by a member of the owner's family led to deep embarrassment and anguish before he used a cross-shaped object to slit his stomach.[115] In another case, Won Bok-deok, the twenty-five-year-old wife of Yi Chan-gol, decided to throw herself in front of a speeding train after getting berated for stealing some bean leaves from her neighbor's field.[116] Although desperate straits had driven both Kim and Won to steal, it was their moral "conscience" that compelled them to commit suicide.[117]

A study of Gyeonggi Province conducted by the *Donga ilbo* in 1927 identified poverty as the root cause of livelihood difficulties.[118] Individual cases in North Pyeongan Province, North Chungcheon Province, and the city of Taegu reflected similar findings.[119] Suicide was seen as a symptom of a wider crisis as unscrupulous landlords continued to charge higher rents, often stripping farmers of their tenancy rights. As Karl Polyani notes of the social and political upheavals that took place in England during the rise of the market economy, "This was the full institutionalization of labor as a commodity in that workers now had only themselves to sell in order to survive. The right to live outside the wage system no longer existed as the 'social net' disappeared in favor of allowing the market, not the state, to allow wages to find their proper level."[120] In this "great transformation," the economy became "disembedded" from social institutions, land and labor were commodified, and subsistence activities became devalued or destroyed.[121] The problems of Kim Se-bin, a thirty-three-year-old tenant farmer from North Pyeongan Province, resulted from an insurmountable debt he owed to his landlord. Despondent about losing his tenancy rights, Kim decided to commit suicide by swallowing opium.[122] Water shortage and poor yields coupled by anxieties over debt were cited most commonly as the cause for suicides in the countryside. This was reflected in the literature as well. In Cho Myeong-hui's short story "Nongchon saramdeul" (Rural people), Won-bo, an honest and diligent farmer, gets into a scuffle with the son of Kim Cham-bong, a gendarme, over water for his parched fields and ends up serving time in jail. Not only does he lose his wife to Kim Cham-bong's son, but he loses his tenancy rights to an evil landlord after another bad drought. In desperation, he tries to steal from the landlord's house, gets arrested, and ends up hanging himself in the holding cell at the local precinct.[123] Likewise, in Na Do-hyang's "Mullae bang-a" (Watermill), Yi Bang-won, a male servant, feels betrayed after learning that Sin Cha-gyu, the master of the household, has had sex with his wife. After serving time in jail, he is released and tries to return to his wife. Angered by her rejection, he decides to kill her and then commits suicide.[124]

The *Donga ilbo* placed the blame for this destructive poverty squarely on the colonial authorities: for instance, it described a slash-and-burn farmer in North Hamgyeong Province who could no longer make a livelihood because of the Government-General's new forest ordinance.[125] The press argued that impoverished families ended up resorting to prostitution in order to survive. For example, in Hong Chang-un's case, his inability to provide from his family compelled his wife, Yi Yeong-nyeo, to sell her body for food. Unable to forgive himself, Hong became despondent and committed suicide by drinking lye.[126] In another case, Choe Jeong-eop sold Seo Bo-pae, his seventeen-year-old wife, to his roommate Byeon Seo-ho for 150 *won* because he was in dire financial straits. However, when Seo's parents tried to take their daughter back home, an angry Byeon filed a complaint with the police, a development that triggered Seo's mother to commit suicide "out of exasperation."[127] In another tragic story, a mother in her thirties, despite every exertion, felt "disgraced" that she could no longer feed her family and decided to commit suicide.[128] Another woman jumped to her death because she was unable to support her ailing husband.[129] Literary representations such as Yeom

Sang-seop's short story "Isim" (Disloyalty) became common: in this story, Chun-gyeong is sold into prostitution by her alcoholic husband. Unable to get out of this grim world, she starves herself and then swallows sleeping pills.[130]

The press reported countless stories not only of individuals but also of entire families who committed suicide to escape poverty.[131] With no social safety net in the large urban centers, the elderly were also vulnerable and found it very difficult to adjust to drastic economic and social changes. The elderly allegedly also committed suicide because of harsh treatment by their "unfilial children," loss of self-esteem, inability to deal with chronic illness, despondency over not having children, and resentment over a spouse or child's squandering of the family's fortunes.[132]

Related to livelihood difficulties as a motive for suicide was the motive of terminal or chronic illness. For the first time, the press sought to link suicidal tendencies to the "chronicity" (*manseong*) of physical illness.[133] After she had her finger amputated because of boils at a hospital in Hwanghae Province, Ms. Yi, the twenty-four-year-old wife of Kim Hwa-nyeong, suffered yet another setback when her right wrist had to be amputated. Unable to work and pressed with livelihood difficulties, Ms. Yi, who was already several months pregnant, hurled herself into the river with her two-year-old son. In another case, Ms. Cho, the wife of Kim Chun-san, became despondent after contracting venereal disease from her husband. Not only had she lost her youth to this disease, but she regretted not marrying the man whom she loved. With her beloved child strapped to her back, she took her life.[134] Still another article reported that Song Sang-ok, a sixty-seven-year-old man in North Pyeongan Province had apparently lived a comfortable life until he was diagnosed with chronic stomach disorder and respiratory disease. But the intense pain began to affect his nerves and eventually led him to drown himself in a pond near his home.[135] And in another instance the *Donga ilbo* reported that Kim Seong-chae, a forty-eight-year-old man, had decided to hang himself after his sufferings from a chronic illness, according to the police, "had made Kim go crazy."[136] While in these instances it was easy to identify the motive for suicide, no one could accurately predict when the afflicted would experience the final "break." For example, Kim Ung-su, a twenty-five-year-old man, had become despondent about the world. Although his family members were vigilant and made sure he was not left unattended because of his "mental illness," one day Kim "suddenly" slashed his stomach with a knife, splitting his intestines, and died from the wounds.[137]

Contemporaries argued that people with *nanchi* (incurable illnesses)—such as tuberculosis, measles, hemorrhoids, leprosy, syphilis, or epilepsy—were a burden to their families, who were driven to the edge while caring for the afflicted.[138] The financial burden of a family member's illness was yet another cause of suicidal despair. For example, despondent about not being able to scrape enough money to pay for his father's medical bills, Kim Chang-su, a twenty-seven-year-old who worked as a branch officer at a Japanese joint-stock company in Dongdaemun, drank too much alcohol, "which affected his nerves." He became crazy and hanged himself from a pine tree.[139]

While the press blamed natural causes, the colonial state, or the pressures of modernity for some suicides, it also took issue with the traditional family, which contemporary reformers viewed as the source of many social evils. Reformers especially targeted early marriage, arranged marriage, male infidelity, abusive mothers-in-law, domestic violence, the buying and selling of wives, profligate husbands squandering family fortunes, and divorce, practices that compelled women in particular to take their own lives.[140] As will be shown below, in some cases suicide was a "weapon of the weak," a form of protest.[141] Whereas newspapers cited alcoholism, gambling, and economic problems as more typical suicide motives for men, they most frequently cited family problems as a suicide motive for women. And for women they were more likely to portray suicides as desperate acts arising from a sense of helplessness and inferiority in situations that they had little power to remedy.

Efforts to abolish early marriage during the Gabo Reforms of 1894 and then the amendment of the Government-General Civil Code (Ordinance No. 13) in 1922, which fixed the minimum age for marriage at seventeen for boys and fifteen for girls, had no visible impact in the countryside. The frequency of suicides by young girls became the cause célèbre to put an end to the oppressive practice of early child marriage. For example, a fifteen-year-old girl from Uiju County who became a *minmyeoneuri* (young daughter-in-law-to-be) to a twenty-four-year-old man when she was eleven years old could no longer handle the sexual demands of her husband and fled to another village to work as a maid. She was captured by her husband and taken back home. Unwilling to live in bondage, she took her own life by jumping off a railroad bridge.[142]

In other cases, the despotic behavior of a mother-in-law who joined her son in abusing her young daughter-in-law was to blame. For example, Yi Seong-nyo, an eighteen-year-old who had been forced to get married when she was only thirteen, decided to commit suicide rather than endure abuse from her "heartless" husband and her overly critical mother-in-law.[143]

The *gobu galdeung* (daughter-in-law and mother in-law conflict) was perhaps the relationship most commonly recognized as a serious problem affecting family dynamics. Incessant nagging, meddling, and taunts by overzealous mothers-in-law often provoked young daughters-in-law to commit suicide. For example, Sim Un, a twenty-two-year-old, became despondent over her mother-in-law's daily verbal harassment about not being able to get pregnant and decided to take her life.[144] In another case, a young girl consumed caustic soda and committed suicide because "she could no longer deal with her mother-in-law's harsh treatment."[145] And in still another, the request of Ms. Ju, the nineteen-year-old wife of Gung Jong-o, a farmer in North Pyeongan Province, to visit her parents during the peak of the harvest season met with a harsh reprimand by her mother-in-law. After being berated about her insensitivity and the timing of her request, Ms. Ju became despondent and decided to hang herself on a mulberry tree.[146]

The press also highlighted cases of tyrannical fathers-in-law and male siblings who abused women in the household. In one case, of Lee, the twenty-year-old wife of Choe Ho-nam, decided to end her misery by drinking lye rather than endure the abuse by the men in her family.[147] In Kim Dong-in's story "Jeonjeja" (The despot), Sun-ae, the protagonist, can no longer endure the tyranny of the men in her household (husband, father, and younger brother) and decides to commit suicide.[148]

Such reports suggest that women had little recourse to address their grievances and had to resort to extreme measures to escape their unbearable circumstances. In some of these situations, a woman would resort to impassioned self-dramatization as the only way to win sympathy, as when Yi Seung-hyeok's wife Kim A-gwi consumed several spoons of lye and "concerned family members discovered her and took her to XXX hospital."[149] In others, a woman was described as storing up unexpressed anger that eventually erupted in a dramatic act of protest. Suicide could publicly challenge the authority of the family, as when a wife verbally confronted her husband or her overbearing mother-in-law and then committed suicide. For example, Bak Bong-deok, the twenty-one-year-old wife of Yi Hon-gyeong, after a heated argument with her mother-in-law and sister-in-law, decided to commit suicide by dramatically throwing herself down a well.[150] In other cases, it was the exasperated mother-in-law who drank poison to humiliate her daughter-in-law publicly.[151] In the most tragic cases, mothers would carry their children on their backs and plunge into the river or well.[152]

Marital discord, especially acts of infidelity, was commonly cited as a cause of suicide. Kim Gye-saeng, the feature writer for a women's column in the *Donga ilbo,* discussed the recent suicide of Han Gyeong-suk, a mother of a two-year-old boy who was several months pregnant. This columnist suspected that a letter she had received several days earlier had been written by Han; the anonymous writer explained in detail her decision to end her life rather than grant her cheating husband a divorce. Kim emphatically explained to her readers that any woman would get teary-eyed after reading Han's letter and suggested that "a lot of women would want to do the same thing and end their lives." Moreover, she felt that "this deep-rooted masculine culture of drinking and frequenting taverns" gave Korean women no alternative but to suppress their *bun* (anger) and *eogul* (feelings of injustice). However, Kim noted that "women have a pretty good amount of self-esteem (*ja-a*) and can end their suffering if they really want to."[153] In other words, a woman could "choose" to die if she wanted to and "sever the ties that [bound her] to others."[154]

While the majority of cases of extramarital affairs involved a philandering husband, the press also reported cases of jealous husbands who suspected their wives of infidelity.[155] Such cases became a staple of popular literature. In Kim Dong-in's short story "Baettaragi" (Following the boat), a possessive and abusive husband who is overly blinded by jealousy and rage suspects that his wife is having an affair with his younger brother. Hoping to please his wife, he purchases a mirror for *chuseok* (the Harvest Moon Festival) and heads home to find his younger brother and his wife in the living room looking rather disheveled and loosely dressed. Despite their pleas that they were looking for a rat, he pummels both of them with his fists and tells his wife to "go and drown your dirty body." The brother later discovers a rat in the room and later his dead wife on the shore of the Daedong River. He holds a simple funeral for her and becomes a seaman in hopes of seeking mercy from his deceased wife and reuniting with his brother.[156] In this story, the act of suicide can also be read as a protest "whereby the victim ceases at last to be a victim by taking control of [her] fate."[157]

The growing rate of family dissolution, especially in the urban centers, concerned contemporaries because of its links to suicide. While many women wanted to end their unhappy marriages and to pursue their own happiness, husbands often ignored their pleas and refused to go to court to file divorce papers. In the case of Kim Tae-un, a forty-six-year-old man from Gongju whose wife tried to seek a divorce, he became very violent and killed her. After realizing what he had done, he tried to commit suicide by drinking lye and was discovered by a passerby and admitted to Jahye Hospital in serious condition.[158] In another case, Ms. Kim, the eighteen-year-old wife of Choe Hui-seon, became despondent over "her loveless marriage" and returned to her natal home. After being told that she was a *chulga oein* (a married daughter is no longer part of her natal family), Choe decided to throw herself in front of a speeding train rather than return to her husband.[159] Women had very little legal recourse against their husbands. For example, Choe Won-sil's attempts to salvage her marriage fell on deaf ears as her husband demanded a divorce and her return to her parental home. After being rebuffed by her own parents, Choe became despondent and decided to jump off a bridge and drown herself in the river rather than return to her husband.[160]

As a result of changing ideas about sexual freedom and desires, stories of misguided love affairs and suicide pacts appeared frequently in the press, triggering a "Werther effect" in the 1920s and early 1930s as copycat suicides suddenly became a fad of the times.[161] According to Bak Chong-seong's analysis of Government-General statistics, a total of 490 people successfully committed love suicides between 1910 and 1942.[162] The suicide note left by the twenty-eight-year-old doctor No Byeong-un gives us some clues about why young couples were committing suicide. On September 27, 1933, the *Joseon ilbo* reported that a woman had hurled herself from the Han River Bridge. The public would find out the following day that the victim was Bong-ja (aka Kim Gap-su), a twenty-year-old café waitress who was the lover of No Byeong-un, a doctor at Keijō (Gyeongseong) Imperial University Hospital, and a married man and father. After suffering from the indignity of taunts by No's legal wife, Kim had decided to commit suicide. What made this story even more sensational was Dr. No's suicide the following day when he hurled himself into the Han River. The press portrayed No's motive as "a cheap price for death" and questioned his mental state. Why would someone who was destined for fame and glory ruin his life and marriage for a woman who "waited tables on her knees"? The formula "R (No) + K (Kim) = RK = L (Life), R − K = D (Death)" provided by Dr. No in his suicide note suggests that the two were seriously in love.[163]

Arranged marriage was often cited in the press as a motive among young couples who committed *jeongsa* (amorous love suicide), especially when one of them was being held hostage to the whims of the family. Yun Seong, a twenty-year-old man, and his eighteen-year-old sweetheart, Jeong Un-seok, were involved in a blissful relationship when Jeong's parents informed the former that they had long ago arranged for their daughter's marriage to another man. In response, the star-crossed lovers tried to commit suicide by drinking lye, but only Yun succeeded; his lover Un-seok found herself alone in an intensive care ward at Jahye Hospital. The romantic and desperate elements of such suicides captured the imagination of writers such as Kim Gi-jin. In his short story "Jeolmeun isangjuuija ui jugeum" (The death of the youthful idealist), Deok-ho, a literary artist who can barely make ends meet, becomes very despondent about life under Japanese colonial rule. After hearing the shocking news that Yeong-ae, the woman he loves dearly, is going to get married to another man, he decides to commit suicide.[164]

The press also reported stories of unrequited love, particularly among the *gisaeng* and their paramours. In one incident, Go Na-myeon, a twenty-two-year-old *gisaeng*, decided to poison herself after the parents of her lover, Choe Byeong-ho, refused to accept her because of her low social status.[165] In a more dramatic case, the *gisaeng* Kim Myeong-hwa, who had fallen in love with one of her clients, decided to drink poison in front of her lover when his parents rejected her as a form of protest against the inequities of class-based love.[166] Writers also granted greater agency to lower-class women in their fictions when they confronted prejudices based on class or simply selfish actions of their clients. For instance, in Hyeon Jin-geon's short story "Geulibeun heulgil nun" (Yearning for his scowling eyes), the protagonist falls in love with Chae-seon, a *gisaeng*, and accumulates major debts from purchasing expensive gifts for her. Driven into a corner, he decides that the two should commit suicide by consuming opium together. However, Chae-seon experiences a moment of clarity about her own fate, which is not tied to her lover's financial woes, and resolves not to swallow the opium. The protagonist, feeling pangs of conscience, attempts to remove the opium from Chae-seon's mouth to save her life, only to realize that she has no intention of dying with him. Shocked at this unexpected "betrayal," he stares at Chae-seon in anger as he dies slowly from the lethal effects of the poison.[167] In this twist ending, the suicide highlights the raw narcissism of a privileged protagonist who is willing to take a life besides his own to justify his actions. Of course, there were also instances in literature where the author punished women for their self-indulgence. For example, in both Na Do-hyang's "Chulhak" (Expulsion from school) and Yeom Sang-seop's "Jeya" (New Year's Eve) the female protagonists are accused of living dissolute lifestyles, are treated as moral degenerates by society, and write confessional letters before they commit suicide.[168] In general, there was a tone of moral reproach against suicides that were committed for the sake of pure vanity without a thought for the family or Korean society as a whole.

Some press accounts of suicides that followed some internal family crisis pointed only to individuals who might have prevented the tragedies. For instance, in 1922, the press reported the case of Yun Chi-ik, whose husband had not sent a single letter to her after he went abroad to study in the United States. She allegedly became mentally ill because of this cold absence of communication and drowned herself in a small pond near her home.[169] In another report, Yi Gyeong-su, a forty-nine-year-old man from Suwon, committed suicide when his profligate son squandered all of the family assets and when Yi's daughter-in-law, who was at her wits' end, left Yi's son, taking her son with her and moving to her maternal uncle's house. Because of these traumatic events, Yi "became mentally ill" and decided to hang himself.[170]

PUBLIC PERCEPTIONS OF A CRISIS IN MENTAL HEALTH CARE

Two reports published in the *Joseon ilbo* illustrate the dilemma faced by many families of people with severe mental illness in colonial Korea. In the first case, the *Joseon ilbo* reported that Gwon Gap-swae's beautiful twenty-year-old wife, Jo Seo-yeo, had committed suicide. She had a troubled past and had suffered when she was young but had been doing well as an adult. However, a month earlier, Jo had become mentally ill. Her family tried to watch her, but she did not like to stay at home, and they had to be quite vigilant whenever she went outside. On the evening of March 21, she visited a shaman and had her perform a *gut* (exorcism). Afterwards she claimed that "she felt refreshed and healed from the illness." So when she urged her family to let her go out, they felt at ease and let her leave home unattended. However, that evening Jo went to the pine forest and hanged herself.[171]

In another case, the *Joseon ilbo* interviewed a family who had decided to have an unwanted family member, Song Chang-seop, admitted to the Government-General Hospital for mental illness. There he was quite violent and caused trouble for the nurses because he would have angry outbursts and break windows. On August 15, 1926, the Dongdaemun police station notified Song's sister that he was going to be discharged. Shocked by this sudden news, she asked the police to hold him for a couple days so that other family members from the countryside could fetch him from Seoul. But several days later, when she went to the Government-General Hospital, she was told that her brother had been "cured" and had already been released on August 14. Family members searched for Song all over Seoul but could not find him. In her interview with the *Joseon ilbo,* Song's sister asked how someone as insane as her brother could suddenly be "healed completely"—it was hard to believe. Moreover, why was the family not told that he had run away, and why would the hospital discharge someone so dangerous? These kinds of stories did not bode well for family members like Song, who were not only dismayed by the sloppiness of the hospital but suspicious about committing afflicted family members to a facility that cared very little about the welfare of the insane.[172]

Many press reports suggest that the treatments offered at the various hospitals were not effective. For example, Sanda, the forty-one-year-old wife of Mr. Yamada, had been admitted to a hospital and had received treatment for mental illness. Less than a year after her release, however, she had suffered another relapse and died tragically by hurling herself in front of a speeding train.[173] In another case, Kang Gil-yeol, a thirty-five-year-old from Pyeongyang who had just been discharged from Gihol Hospital after receiving treatment for his mental disorders, headed to a high cliff near the Daedong River and hurled himself down a ravine, spattering his brains all over the rocks.[174]

Families' fears that their mentally ill kin were a danger to themselves and perhaps the public were reflected in the press: when an afflicted member escaped from home, families routinely reported his or her disappearance to the police in an attempt to protect the mentally ill person and others. For example, when Eom Ju-jeong, a twenty-seven-year-old man who was kept under strict surveillance by his family "because of his erratic behavior," found a way to escape from his home after threatening to kill himself, his family members rushed to the police. However, six days after his escape even a police dragnet had failed to find Eom, leading to much public anxiety. In Yangdeok County in North Pyeongan Province, Yi Bong-hwa, the wife of Yi Yi-jeong, went to the local precinct station to report her husband missing. She told the authorities that he had been suffering from some kind of mental illness and had been missing for several days. After searching the county, the police discovered Yi, who had hanged himself in a pine forest, and after an autopsy they called Bong-hwa to claim his body.[175]

The press expressed sympathy for family members on whom fell the burden of caring for the mentally ill. It often highlighted the plight of spouses, who were the most vulnerable to acts of violence or becoming victims themselves. While there was the option to commit an individual to the hospital, fears of social stigma, which could potentially jeopardize marriage prospects, compelled many to conceal their ill family members behind closed doors. This practice affected married women more than men because of gender expectations that a wife remain at home. One Kim Bok-sil, for example, decided to drink lye to escape the torment of living with her mentally ill husband and oppressive in-laws who refused to release her.[176] Other wives met a violent death at the hands of their ill husbands: Yi Sil-dan, a twenty-one-year-old wife, was stabbed in the chest with a kitchen knife because her husband became angry that she had become cold toward him; before the murder, he had expressed his fears that she was going to get married to someone else.[177] Some wives seized on their husbands' absence as an opportunity to commit suicide: Yun Jeong-sun, for example, drank lye during a time when her mentally ill husband was out of the house. Although a family member discovered Yun and rushed her to Severance Hospital, she died later that evening.[178]

Even if the doctor did not consider the patient to be a menace to society, the family would still be responsible for nursing (*ganho*) him or her. Further, although admitting an unwanted family member to the hospital did provide temporary respite, the vast majority of ordinary Koreans had very few medical options other than confinement at home. For example, in 1922, out of 294,687 patients admitted to the Government-General Hospital only 346 (0.12 percent) were mentally ill patients. In 1924, the figures increased slightly to 528 (0.19 percent), and by 1937, out of the 604,563, only 1,069 mentally ill patients (0.18 percent) were admitted to the hospital and the majority of the patients were treated as outpatients.[179] As noted in chapter 2, the costs of hospitalization were so high as to be unaffordable for most Koreans.

As this chapter has shown, the emergence of *jeongsinbyeong* (mental illness) as a new nosological category during the 1920s contributed to a wide range of social and institutional discourses. The medical community introduced new diagnoses of mental pathologies and abnormalities and gave new scientific labels to the ailments described in Korean folk culture. The state employed these constructions in their records of their dealings with deviant individuals. The popular press traced mental disorders to a variety of presumed causes, from hereditary defects and biological maladies to stresses such as social and economic pressures and injustices and the disorienting changes of modernity. The new discourses of insanity reflected social prejudices that led to identifying certain maladies like hysteria and neurasthenia in gendered terms. As these discourses became increasingly embedded in everyday life, they prompted a fear of stigma and also a "desire" to absolve oneself of the duty to care for those diagnosed as "mentally ill."

Care for the mentally ill was costly and inadequate, but sensational newspaper stories of crime, suicide, and bizarre behavior did little to solve this problem and only invited suspicion, prejudice, and discrimination. Whether the press described mental problems as innate or acquired, it portrayed the mentally ill as "different," potentially dangerous to themselves or others, and in need of custodial care. Traditional representations, understandings, and categories of madness were inflected by the modern disciplinary constructions of mental illness and were taken up by ordinary Koreans in varied, contradictory, and even confused ways.

Stories of people committing suicide also entered the public discussion for the first time in the 1920s as newspapers started to collate and analyze statistical evidence offered by the Government-General Office. Contemporaries drew on various assumptions as they tried to rationalize the motives for self-destruction. The Korean press treated suicide as a social phenomenon, a tragic by-product of colonialism and flawed modernity, which had radically transformed existing social mores and economic conditions. At the same time, it paradoxically used suicide to critique institutions like the traditional family. Meanwhile, the colonial state saw no cause for alarm in increasing suicide rates and argued that Korea, like Japan and other "civilized nations," had to pay a price to become "modern" and that suicide was one of the destructive aspects of civilization. At the level of governance, these statistics were considered useful indices for gauging the "moral well-being" of Korean society. Using the census, the state could analyze which people were committing suicide and what their motives were. If the press used these statistics and police reports to critique modernity's dizzying pace and corrupt values, it also advocated for more medical intervention to prevent family tragedies. Ironically, such intervention would come at a steep price for Koreans in that it would introduce greater interference and surveillance by the colonial state apparatus.

Finally, as new medical truths came to be formulated about mental illness, the emerging field of psychology provided a language to frame suicides in pathological terms. As Ian Marsh has noted, "Attempts to understand suicide and to prevent its occurrence have an obvious rationale, but the assumptions embedded within these approaches and their effects (in terms of both intended and unintended consequences) have not themselves been the subject of any sustained critical analysis." Specifically, such pathologizing strips the act of suicide of other potential meanings, including those of "protest or resistance."[180] Yet in the popular press and in vernacular fiction a growing popular awareness of suicide as a socially created pathology and an eagerness to explain it within such conceptual frames led to the expression of an alternative to the biomedical discourse that helped to shape the meaning of suicide in colonial Korea.

Conclusion

A METHOD TO THE MADNESS

> If you are not like everybody else, then you are abnormal, if you are abnormal, then you are sick. These are three categories, not being like everybody else, not being normal and being sick are in fact very different but have been reduced to the same thing.
>
> MICHEL FOUCAULT, "Je suis un artificier" (2004)

> To create new ways of classifying people is also to change how we can think of ourselves, to change our sense of self-worth, even how we remember the past. This in turn generates a looping effect, because people of the kind behave differently and so are different. That is to say the kind changes, and so there is new causal knowledge to be gained and, perhaps, old causal knowledge to be jettisoned.
>
> IAN HACKING, "The Looping Effects of Human Kinds"

IN 2005, THE *SIN DONGA*, a current events monthly magazine and a subsidiary of the *Donga ilbo* (East Asia Daily), published a series of *gidam* or bizarre stories and scandals that appeared in popular newspapers and magazines during the 1930s in Gyeongseong (Seoul).[1] Compiled and narrated by Jeon Bong-gwan (a scholar of Korean literature at KAIST), the stories revolve around scandals that do not fit easily into conventional historical narratives. Jeon proposes that these "sensational" stories were not exceptional but represented common everyday occurrences for most people living in colonial society. But rather than ask whether they are representative, it might be more fruitful to view them as moments that leave imprints in the fabric of everydayness. In fact, Maurice Blanchot has observed that "everyday life becomes vivid in moments of effervescence—those we call revolution [or in this cases, sensational]—when existence is public through and through."[2] As this study has shown, new practices and understandings of mental illness had to be learned vis-à-vis the old, which were ingrained in people's lives. Sensational stories in the press about mental illness can provide a glimpse of the tenuous relationship between indigeneity and modernity as well as the internal contradictions and limits of Japanese colonialism.[3]

Against this backdrop, Jeon's first feature story of the 1930s examines a sensational murder case that elucidates many of the themes covered in this book, tracing the inscriptions and erasures of different ideas and practices superimposed on each other in a palimpsest. It reveals the different layers that colonial psychiatric practice had to contend with—the resiliency of folk beliefs, Korean naturalistic medicine, traditional emotional regimes, and syncretistic understandings of modern medicine.

On May 16, 1933, the Seodaemun district police station in Gyeongseong (Seoul) received an urgent dispatch around 7:30 a.m. to a grisly crime scene: the decapitated head of an infant had been found near a landfill next to the Korea Industrial Bank. Swarms of onlookers and reporters from the press descended on the crime scene, trampling on possible footprints left in the mud before the policemen arrived to cordon off the area. Kimura, the chief officer of the Seodaemun police, and Yoda, a district attorney from the Seoul bureau, also rushed to the crime scene with their attendants. While sentries guarded the area, the lead detective, Nomura, ordered a photographer to take pictures of the evidence: a piece of a torn skirt, a paper bag, and a worn-out hand towel used to wrap the severed head. Traces of blood drops beyond the tracks suggested that the perpetrator had already fled toward Mapo and was headed to the vicinity of the French legations.[4] The gruesome discovery and horrific nature of the crime made for riveting and sensational headlines. What had inspired such an evil crime? Was this an act of a *beomin* (criminal) or someone who suffered from *jeongsin isang* (a mental disorder)? Unlike crimes of past eras, this case involved new interpretations of information about the incident as well as experts— psychiatrists, medical coroner, and detectives—trained to solve this kind of crime. Although the daily newspapers occasionally published stories of violent crimes, this particular psychological murder case spawned three main narratives that reflected the conflict between traditional and modern understandings of crime and mental health. Reporters who provided daily coverage of the investigation scrutinized the so-called experts and their procedures.

CONCLUSION · 143

The first narrative centered on rumors circulating in the teahouses, cafés, and the streets that someone with an incurable disease had committed the crime to obtain a traditional cure. Rumors cast the suspected perpetrator as an epileptic, a leper, or an individual suffering from an abscess.[5] People speculated that the culprit had discarded the head after boiling the brain and eating the marrow. The practice of kidnapping children for their organs to use as remedies was not new in the history of folk medicine.[6] In fact, in the 1920s the press launched a series of articles calling for the abolishment of these superstitious practices—a social reform that the colonial state also sought to implement. It cited gruesome examples to bolster its case: in 1922, for instance, the *Donga ilbo* reported that a woman had killed her two-year-old daughter so she could extract the blood from the child's intestines to save her ailing husband.[7] Regarding the case of the decapitated baby, one reporter claimed to have overheard some lunchtime chatter that the criminal was actually a beggar or vagrant who had kidnapped and sold the victim to an ill person. Others claimed that since no parent had reported a missing child to the police, the victim had probably already been sold by the birth family for some heinous purpose. Stories of poor families selling their children into slavery or prostitution to pay off a debt or simply to reduce the number of household members were ubiquitous.[8] It is impossible to discern the veracity of these tales, but it is clear that both the press and the state exploited such salacious tales of greed and desperation to pursue their reform agendas and to contest indigenous forms of healing.

The second narrative, employing gendered prejudices, framed the story as one of a woman acting out of vengeance. Drawing on cultural notions about women's supposed weakness and irrationality, some argued that this was a crime of a jealous concubine or wife. In other words, the eruption of *han* (resentment) had led to an irrational crime. It was routine for the press to report tragic tales of women jumping into wells, callous wives killing their husbands, and heartless mothers murdering their children: the violation of gendered norms, whether real or imagined, led to public condemnation. The story of a headless infant and the presumption that a female culprit had committed the crime had become entirely credible. The public had only to look to the new statistics: according to the social investigator Kudō Takeki's study of female convicts, for example, seventy-two women who were sentenced to prison in 1930 had been charged with infanticide. All of the murdered children were illegitimate, and 94 percent of the women confessed to killing their child out of shame.[9]

A third narrative suggested that the perpetrator suffered from *jeongsin jilhwan* (mental disease) and was roaming the streets of Seoul kidnapping and killing young children. The medical discourse of psychiatry offered the denizens of Seoul a new kind of language to frame and quantify a new social pathology of madness. There were plenty of cases for the press to explore. As chapter 4 has noted, bizarre cases of pyromaniacs, kleptomaniacs, exhibitionists, homicidal maniacs, and the like started to appear frequently in the press starting in the 1920s. These heightened anxiety about the threat that the *jeongsin byeongja* (mentally ill)—who seemed to lurk on every street corner—posed to the social order.[10] The idea that the suspect—cast by the media as a dangerous psychopath—had escaped from a mental hospital evoked tremendous anxiety. This was in part due to the changing meaning of mental illness and institutions of treatment in Korea.

As this study has related, the colonial state officially opened its first psychiatric ward for mental patients at the Government-General Hospital (Chōsen sōtokufu iin / Chongdokbu uiwon) on April 11, 1913. In 1915, the Government-General started to allocate 150,000 *won* to the ward for the treatment of the mentally ill; by 1921 the ward had expanded to twenty-one rooms with forty-four patients.[11] Despite these facilities, colonial authorities immediately confronted several challenges. As in Japan, the traditional practice of concealing the mentally ill behind closed doors made it difficult for the colonial state to document and incarcerate them. Quite apart from their desire to preserve family honor, Koreans were naturally suspicious about committing afflicted family members to a facility operated by the colonial state.

Indeed, during the Joseon period (1392–1910), responding to "madness" with institutionalization was rare and exceptional. Indigenous beliefs and practices remained widespread among both sufferers and would-be healers. Shamanism approached these problems in supernatural terms: it did not distinguish the cause of mental illness as unique from that of other illness. Assuming a fatalistic worldview, the shaman prescribed similar treatments for all illnesses, which involved prayers, vigils, exorcism, or fasting; suitable rites were accordingly made to fit the needs of the afflicted. Despite the inroads of modern medicine, some Koreans continued to turn to shamanism, for it continued to be an everyday religion of the home, and, for the most part, the burden of caring for the afflicted fell on the family, who kept them at home. Of course, some of the afflicted were not so fortunate to rely on family support and found themselves wandering the streets. To allow the family member to go out in public entailed great social shame. Whereas in the past certain illnesses such as *sinbyeong* had garnered respect when a *mudang* emerged from her sufferings, behaviors associated with these "afflictions"—the loss of self-control, involuntary trembling, frenzied dancing, and so forth—now came be viewed in medical terms as "symptoms" of mental illness. Even some who converted to Christianity or accepted treatment from medical practitioners stubbornly held syncretistic views about mental ailments. Commoners continued to regarded mental disturbances as simply one of the many forms of human misery (such as famine, disease, and early death) that threatened the health and happiness of society. The *michin yeoja* (crazy woman) with a flower in her hair yanking at the laces of her *hanbok* (traditional dress) and other morally disreputable people like invalids or vagrants who roamed the countryside were all an integral part of the social landscape.

Practitioners of traditional Chinese-influenced Korean medicine emphasized natural rather than supernatural causes of disturbances of the body. Cultural understandings about the nature of affliction and its healing centered on the body, which healers viewed as a system of interrelated elements that were in constant interaction with the environment and the spirit world. Hence, healers who sought the causes of inappropriate and dangerous behaviors tried to understand what had upset the body's natural equilibrium. A treatment would entail a thorough examination of the major visceral organs for some kind of functional disorder and the restoration of the imbalance between yin and yang that had thrown the individual into a state of disease. In this respect, traditional medicine understood mental illness as a somatic disease like any other, the manifestation of a brain and body gone awry. In both this approach and the approach of indigenous Korean shamanism, the idea of isolating and managing the afflicted separately did not exist, and such traditional treatments did provide a source of comfort and consolation, regardless of whether they provided a cure.

Institutionalization of the mentally ill came with its own set of challenges. A study by a former medical school student in the *Joseon ilbo* in 1926 shed light on the costs and bureaucratic procedures of institutionalization as well as popular ambivalence about the actual benefits of "modern medicine." In terms of expense, a trip to the hospital alone could cost Koreans their entire daily income. The inability to pay for medical services meant that the ill person often went untreated. Equally intimidating was the bureaucratic red tape that involved the intrusion of the state authorities. To enter a government facility, one had to secure an introduction from an official at the police station or from some other influential person. In addition, the hospital required all in-patients to sign a "consent form" to allow the authorities to perform an autopsy in the event of death or to use the cadaver as "research material" if death occurred during surgery or treatment. This relinquishment of power over the dead was unacceptable in a culture that valued elaborate death rituals and revered the departure of souls. Rumors of hospitals cremating patients who had died from some contagious diseases and the interring of corpses during epidemic disease campaigns for testing certainly added to the mistrust of the authorities.[12] Compounding these anxieties were rumors that hospitals admitted patients only for their organs—perhaps another version of stories about organ theft for the use of ritual healers.[13] Such concerns shaped patients' and families' decisions about hospitals.

As noted in chapter 2 (table 1), statistics on admission rates in the annual reports of the Government-General Hospital indicate that by 1921 outpatients were beginning to outnumber in-patients. By 1927, out of 576 patients admitted to the mental ward, only 128 or roughly 22 percent were inpatients and more than half of these were diagnosed with dementia praecox, a diagnostic category invented by the German psychiatrist Emil Kraepelin that was considered one of the most serious degenerative disorders.[14] These figures reveal that only the most desperate chose institutionalization of family members.

By the 1920s, new nosological terms started to emerge in print culture in tandem with the birth of the clinic. Companies began to market medical products specifically for the *heoyakja* (mentally feeble) as well as to treat over eighty different urban scourges such as tuberculosis and syphilis. Advertisements of pharmaceutical companies like Rondon or Re-ben began appearing in all sizes—as small as a business card to as large as a quarter-page spread. These introduced the urban public to a whole gamut of nervous and degenerative conditions classified by etiology and pathogenesis. They advertisements included professional endorsements by doctors and a detailed description of various illnesses' symptoms and *manseong* (chronicity). Pharmaceutical advertising thus increased the currency of a biomedical approach to mental disorders in the general public.

The process of medicalization also affected the policing institutions that sought clues about the mental state of the perpetrators of crimes. The detectives in the case of the headless infant conducted their investigation like doctors diagnosing a patient, employing idioms of objectivity and scientific rationality rather than relying on old taxonomies. Ignoring the chatter in the streets as lurid rumors, the police, fully confident of their objective and scientific techniques and army of experts, arranged for the severed head to be sent to the morgue at the Keijō (Gyeongseong) Imperial University Medical School for a postmortem examination. Several years earlier, the medical school had started to offer courses in forensic science and Kraepelinian German psychiatry, and now such institutions had as much an educational as a clinical role. Dr. Kunihusa, a professor in the medical jurisprudence division (*hōigakubu*) who was trained in diagnostic clinical pathology, conducted the autopsy. After inspecting the infant's teeth and hair, he announced that the victim was a one-year-old male. On the basis of blood splatter and lesions, the crime had to have been committed within one to ten hours prior to its discovery.

Following the data from Kunihusa's autopsy reports, Officer Kimura, who was trained in criminology, announced that the investigation would focus on the hard evidence—the piece of a torn skirt, the paper bag, and the used towel. While Kimura suspected that this crime might have been motivated by a personal grudge or an illicit love relationship, he rejected folk explanations as unprofessional. He claimed that the crime could not have been a random act of violence committed by a madman, given the criminal's dexterity with the knife and the methodical cover-up of the evidence.[15]

With the mobilization of the entire police force in Gyeongseong (Seoul), Kimura felt confident that a citywide dragnet would catch the suspect in no time. Since the annexation of Korea, the colonial government had prided itself on the maintenance of public peace with its efficient police and stringent legal system. By 1926, the colony had a four-tier police system; a police department at the highest level of organization, thirteen bureaus at the provincial level, 250 police stations at the county and municipality levels, and more than 2,500 substations at the township level.[16] As an important part of their function, the colonial police in Korea not only monitored public health through their Sanitation and Public Health Section (otherwise known as the hygiene police) but also oversaw rice production, inspected passengers on sea vessels and trains, and assisted in various social projects, from conducting studies on indigenous practices to compiling the nation's vital statistics. The statistical studies had the aim of "establish[ing] the general truths of the population." As part of their responsibilities, the police worked to stamp out unorthodox popular practices and superstitions (*misin tapa*) in the name of health and the maintenance of public order.[17] As the legal historian Chulwoo Lee observes, "The dense presence and extensive functioning of the police were symptoms of the 'excessive attention' that Hyman Kublan underlines as a unique characteristic of Japanese colonial rule." This "entailed a refined system of collecting and storing information on the idea that the state could and ought to engineer society in ways to guarantee order and achieve material progress, the two greatest gifts of civilization that the Japanese claimed they were bringing to the colonial population."[18]

Drawing on these detailed studies as well as census reports, the police investigated every family register in the area for clues to the brutal beheading of the infant. This was made possible by several earlier state initiatives. When sanitary activities of the Ministry of Internal Affairs were transferred in 1911 to the police and the Infectious Disease Prevention Act was promulgated in 1915, the new "hygiene police" conducted a variety of household surveys to oversee epidemic prevention programs that included implementing quarantine and vaccination campaigns against cholera, typhoid fever, and smallpox as well as urban scourges like tuberculosis and syphilis in the familiar idiom of public health.[19]

The justification of public health campaigns could mobilize large numbers of officers and traditional medical doctors in the name of public security, and allowed the police to be quite intrusive in intervening in the everyday lives of Koreans. Indeed police were armed with "virtually unlimited power to regulate people's behavior," whether through household visits or vaccination or quarantine campaigns. For instance, from 1912 on they were able to carry out individual house inspections using humiliating and coercive means to force those suspected of carrying an infectious disease to undergo a standard fecal examination.[20] More appositely to the beheaded infant case, those with illegitimate children or families who had lost or adopted children had to report to the detention house (*yuchijang*) for questioning. On May 18, the police extended their investigation and examined the records of recent deaths of infants in the area and instructed officers to inter all the bodies at the local cemeteries.

The police investigation would be hampered by its "scientific" understanding of crime and its deliberate exclusion of folk explanations for possible motivations. Frustrated over their inability to find any leads, the Seodaemun police took a cue from the newspapers and dispatched officers dressed as beggars, day laborers, and morphine addicts to infiltrate the ghetto on the outskirts of town where all the *hacheungmin* (underclass) lived. The police suspected that someone from this large floating population of vagrant workers would know the perpetrator of this crime. As the police started to round up individuals, a suspect who looked like a day laborer attempted to discard a knapsack and flee toward the hills, only to be apprehended. But instead of finding a headless corpse in his knapsack, the police discovered only a dead dog that had been stolen from a neighbor to be consumed. Unable to find any leads, the police began to round up all the lepers, beggars, and vagrants—often viewed as the usual suspects—in Seoul for interrogation. In one day, the Dongdaemun station alone arrested ninety suspects.[21]

The list of possible suspects also extended to other somewhat less marginal social figures such as widows, mistresses, and stepmothers, who were deemed by the authorities as emotionally unstable. The police assumed that certain types of women had a greater propensity to suffer from depression, elevated mood swings, and delusions that could trigger them to commit such a heinous crime. The Seodaemun police rounded up an average of six suspects a day and put them in detention without due process. By the sixteenth day of the investigation, the Seodaemun police had arrested more than one hundred suspects and had detained thirty of them in a holding cell.[22]

On June 1, seventeen days into the investigation, the police finally gave credence to the folk rumors about the crime and focused on a shaman, her family, and a vagrant who called himself Ppeokkugi. The evidence seemed overwhelming; not only did they live near the French legations where the last drops of the trail of blood had been discovered, but a police dog had detected a cloth at the shaman's house that looked very suspicious. Within a week of confinement, Ppeokgugi confessed to have committed the crime. According to Ppeokgugi, a moneylender by the name of Bak Chung-hwa had been suffering from a malignant abscess on his back. His wife, Yi Seong-nyeo, a professional shaman, sought out Ppeokgugi, who was an employee at a wine shop at that time and asked him to purchase a child and bring the boiled marrow to her so that she could feed her ailing husband. As noted in the first chapter, it would be typical for Koreans to consult a *mudang* (shaman), a culturally sanctioned way of experiencing and understanding various illness, including mental disorders. Ppeokgugi claimed that he had found a child of a poor family in Anam-ri and had promised to raise him, only to murder him for the desired marrow. Unfortunately, after Bak had consumed the marrow, his condition worsened and died after spending a night in the hospital.

After documenting Ppeokgugi's confession, the police thoroughly searched Bak's house and discovered a dress with blood stains, children's clothing, and a liver of some kind. However, they could not extract a confession from the shaman, who claimed that the blood stains on her dress were from her period and that the children's clothes were basic accessories for the *gut* (exorcism) that she performed. More importantly, according to hospital records Bak died on May 12, four days prior to the discovery of the severed head. Desperate to frame the shaman, the police dispatched officers to the hills of Geunhwa where Ppeokkugi claimed to have buried the body, only to find a corpse of a thirty-year-old man who had committed suicide over a failed business.[23]

After a second interview with Ppeokgugi, the police learned that the man was what Koreans deemed a *jugwang* (alcohol crazy) and was famous for his disorderly conduct. He had had several brushes with the law, had been convicted of burglary and disorderly conduct, and had spent some time in prison.[24] One can see how the "looping effect," mentioned in the epigraph above by Ian Hacking, worked in the case of Ppeokkugi. In colonial Korea, police stations at the municipality level and substations at the townships often transferred convicts like Ppeokkugi with a history of antisocial behavior to the Government-General Hospital's mental ward in Seoul for treatment. For example, according to the annual reports in 1913, municipal and township police stations sent ninety-nine criminals convicted of larceny, violent fights, swindling, loitering, lewd behavior, indecent exposure, and destroying public property, to name a few offenses, to Seoul for rehabilitation. The hospitals experimented with softer forms of treatment such as behavioral/moral training and even offered social programs like knitting and crocheting for female convicts and horticulture and stock farming for male offenders respectively. For patients with more chronic disorders, the doctors experimented with somatic treatment, often sedating them with saline injections, barbiturates, chloral hydrate, or bromides. By the 1930, hospitals started to apply electroshock as well as cardiazol shock therapy and conducted transorbital lobotomies on certain patients. Drawing on a wide range of explanatory models—biological and social—the police concluded that Ppeokkugi was a *jeongsin byeongja* (mentally ill person) and connected his mental disturbances to the effects of alcohol and his upbringing.[25] According to Hacking, such classifications (e.g., alcoholic) affect humans because they are not objects and are conscious of the ways in which they are classified: "Once a human kind gets classified and becomes an object for knowledge, control, healing, punishment and so forth, this kind will tend to react and respond to such treatment."[26]

Although the police had been misled in this case, they decided—against their usual practice—to heed folk rumors once again to solve the crime. On June 5, twenty-one days into the investigation, the police received a tip from an anonymous source that a man in Ahyeon-ri had secretly buried his daughter, who had died of meningitis. Ten officers from the Seodaemun police accompanied Han Chan-gu (the father of the deceased girl), his brother Han Seong-u, and his housemate Baek Gu-seok and his wife to the cemetery. The police immediately arrested the four on the spot after discovering that Han Gi-ok (the deceased daughter—the forensic expert was wrong about the infant being male) had no head.[27]

After a second autopsy at the Keijō (Gyeongseong) Imperial University Hospital, Professor Kunihusa announced that the head and body were a match and that the heavy downpour had probably compromised the bloodstain evidence. That afternoon, Baek Gu-seok confessed to police that his child was an epileptic and that he had asked his friend Yun Myeong-ju to sever Han Gi-ok's head and obtain the marrow from her brain to cure his epileptic son. After a short trial, a judge sentenced Baek to four years, while his accomplice Yun received three years for the desecration of a tomb and injuring a corpse. Ppeokkugi was deemed mentally ill, released from prison, and not prosecuted.[28]

The case of the headless infant provides us with a glimpse of indigenous beliefs and folk practices and the social responses to it. First and foremost, the authorities were prone to dismiss culturally significant symbols and local arrangements for the management and treatment of those with mental disorders and physical ailments as part of the unreasonable world of magic and superstition. Instead of trying to understand the culture-bound maladies inscribed on this palimpsest of Korean culture, the police organized their investigation around modern (Western and medical) conceptualizations of mental illness. This involved the introduction of experts into a judicial procedure that was based on detailed scientific knowledge and routine intervention.

Second, this case sheds light on the emerging field of colonial psychiatry, which had incorporated wholesale Emil Kraepelin's descriptive taxonomy. It offered a medical language to categorize the hysteric widow, the jealous concubine, the frigid stepmother, the recidivist criminal, the imbecile beggar, and the vagrant as pathological types. Psychiatry also sought to secure boundaries of "normal behavior." The new diagnostic labels reflected preexisting moral and gender assumptions. Moreover, the language of criminology framed mental illness as a threat to public safety, moving the mentally ill from the sphere of "care work" and treatment to that of incarceration and police discipline. Indeed, disturbing behaviors that might once have been associated with spiritual or moral failings were now increasingly defined in the press by the early 1920s as symptoms of a *singyeong* (nervous) disorder.

As Japanese authorities resorted to modern forms of surveillance, Koreans found themselves forced to respond to the new definitions of "normality" and the state's attempts to regulate public health in ways that often reflected the political tensions between the colonized and colonizers. At one level, maintaining healthy, mentally sound subjects involved a new apparatus of power (medicine, psychiatry, and criminology) and its corresponding institutions (hospital, asylum, and prison), which, as seen in this case, did not always achieve their intended results. Ironically, neither forensic evidence nor psychiatric criminology (both touted as modern and scientific methods) helped to solve the case of the headless infant; rather, it was popular rumors that helped redirect the police first to Ppeokgugi and then to Baek Gu-seok and his accomplice Yun Myeong-ju.

Finally, as this book has illustrated, the development of psychiatry in colonial Korea, in particular its standards and norms of pathology, therapeutic techniques, and institutional regimes, could not replace traditional practices overnight because of the incommensurability of lay knowledge and state management. But the power of the medical gaze provided unprecedented possibilities for a group of psychiatrists to professionalize their discipline in the medical field. In fact, the shift from treating patients in medical establishments as subjects of care to treating them as objects of scientific study would have a lasting impact on the relationship between medicine and mental illness. During the colonial period Koreans became wary of "medical interventions," viewing the clinic and methods of psychiatrists as tools of the Japanese colonial state—a lasting legacy that would have profound consequences for the course of psychiatry in Korea.

NOTES

INTRODUCTION

The chapter's two epigraphs are from Susan Sontag, *Illness as Metaphor and AIDS and Its Metaphors* (New York: Picador, 2001), 3, and Erving Goffman, *Stigma: Notes on the Management of Spoiled Identity* (New York: Prentice-Hall, 1963), 2–3, respectively.

1. Yi Seok-u, "Sikeomeoke, uri gaseumdo tadeureogatta" [Our chests were also charred black], *Chosun ilbo,* February 12, 2008, http://news.chosun.com/site/data/html_dir/2008/02/12/2008021200166.html.

2. Jennifer Veale, "Can Korea Protect Its Historical Sites?" *TIME,* February 13, 2008, http://content.time.com/time/world/article/0,8599,1712836,00.html.

3. Kyong-Whan Ahn, "Korean Legal System and the Human Rights of Persons with Mental Disorders: Current State and Challenges," *Journal of Korean Law* 7, no. 1 (2007): 4.

4. World Health Organization and Ministry of Health and Welfare, Republic of Korea, "WHO-AIMS Report on Mental Health System in Republic of Korea: A Report of the Assessment of the Mental Health System Using the World Health Organization Assessment Instrument for Mental Health Systems, Seoul, Republic of Korea, 2006," 2007, www.who.int/mental_health/evidence/korea_who_aims_report.pdf, 26.

5. K. Ahn, "Korean Legal System," 5–8.

6. Richard J. Dalton, "Korean's Refugee Status Upheld in Historic Case," *Vancouver Sun,* June 20, 2009, www.canada.com/story.html?id=82b296e4-8e87-4a3e-9760-d671e5400f84.

7. Organisation for Economic Co-operation and Development, "Korea's Increase in Suicides and Psychiatric Bed Numbers Is Worrying, Says OECD," 2011, www.oecd.org/els/health-systems/MMHC-Country-Press-Note-Korea.pdf.

8. Bogeon bokjibu [Ministry of Health and Welfare], press release on Cho Maeng-je's report, February 15, 2012. According to this report, 26.5 percent of Koreans are likely to suffer from mental illness during their lifetime.

9. Ibid. See also "1 in 6 Koreans Has Mental Illness," *Korea Herald,* February 15, 2012, www.koreaherald.com/view.php?ud=20120215001185.

10. Ibid., 3. The study also reported that 15.6 percent of the population had experienced suicidal thoughts and that 3.3 had planned to commit suicide.

11. "Hanguk jasallyul heubyeonyul·uiryobi jeunggayul OECD choego" [Increase in Korea's suicide rates, smoking rates, medical expenses; the highest among OECD nations], *Yonhap News,* July 2, 2014, www.yonhapnews.co.kr/society/2014/07/02/0706000000AKR20140702089300017.HTML.

12. Kyung Lah, "South Korean Ferry Victims' Families Ask, 'How Are We Going to Live Now?'" CNN, April 20, 2014, www.cnn.com/2014/04/19/world/asia/south-korea-grieving-parents/; Young-Ha Kim, "South Korea's Struggle with Suicide," *New York Times,* April 2, 2014, www.nytimes.com/2014/04/03/opinion/south-koreas-struggle-with-suicide.html?_r=0.

13. "Mapodaegyo 'saengmyeongui dari', haeoe gwanggoje seokgwon," [Mapo Bridge's 'Bridge of Life' sweeps overseas advertising awards], *News1,* May 13, 2013, http://news1.kr/articles/1130132. Citing its failure to curb suicide rates, the Seoul Metropolitan Government announced on September 1, 2015, that it would remove all the panels from the Mapo Bridge and pledged to come up with a new suicide prevention program in the near future. Yi Syu-tim, "Manhi himdeulguna, jal jinaeji? Mapodaegyo 'saengmyeongui dari,' jasalbangji yeokhyogwa nollan e cheolgeo hwakjeong" [You must be really be under a lot of duress, are you doing all right? The Mapo Bridge's Bridge of Life: A reverse effect on suicide prevention; a dispute over removing the [panels on the] bridge], September 1, 2015, www.datanews.co.kr/news/article.html?no=82639.

14. Y. Kim, "South Korea's Struggle." Unemployment and divorce can trigger clinical depression, a common factor in suicides. See Mihee Nam et al., "U uljeung, jasal geurigo hanguksahoe" [Depression, suicide, and Korean society], *Journal of the Korean Medical Association* 54, no. 4 (April 2011): 358–61.

15. Y. Kim, "South Korea's Struggle."

16. Bogeon bokjibu [Ministry of Health and Welfare], press release on Cho Maeng-je's report, February 15, 2012, 15. See also "Suicide Epidemic Sweeping Korea," *Chosun ilbo,* March 10, 2014, http://english.chosun.com/site/data/html_dir/2014/03/10/2014031001758.html; Y. Kim, "South Korea's Struggle."

17. American Psychiatric Association, *Diagnostic and Statistical Manual of Mental Disorders, Fifth Edition (DSM-5)* (Arlington, VA: American Psychiatric Association, 2013), 749–50.

18. "Yi Teuk buchin-jobumo sumjinchae balgyeon . . . 'jasal' vs 'gyotongsago' saineun?" [Yi Teuk's father and grandparents found dead: Suicide or traffic accident the cause?], *Donga ilbo,* January 7, 2014, http://news.donga.com/BestClick/3/all/20140107/60008746/1.

19. Mark McDonald, "Stressed and Depressed, Koreans Avoid Therapy," *New York Times,* July 6, 2011.

20. Tomi Gomory, David Cohen, and Stuart A. Kirk, "Madness or Mental Illness? Revisiting Historians of Psychiatry," *Current Psychology* 32 (2013): 1.

21. Ibid.

22. Ibid., 6.

23. Albert Deutsch, *The Mentally Ill in America: A History of Their Care and Treatment from Colonial Times* (New York: Columbia University Press, 1967), 1–2, 495.

24. Quoted in Kenneth Weiss, "Albert Deutsch, 1905–1961," *American Journal of Psychiatry* 168, no. 3 (2011): 252.

25. Edward Shorter, *A History of Psychiatry: From the Era of the Asylum to the Age of Prozac* (New York: Wiley, 1997), vii.

26. Ibid.

27. Ibid., viii.

28. Ibid., 313.

29. Michel Foucault, *Madness and Civilization: A History of Insanity in the Age of Reason* (London: Vintage, 1988); Erving Goffman, *Asylums: Essays on the Social Situations of Mental Patients and Other Inmates* (Oxford: Doubleday, 1961); R. D. Laing, *The Divided Self: An Existential Study in Sanity and Madness* (Harmondsworth: Penguin, 1960); Thomas Szasz, *The Myth of Mental Illness* (1961; repr., New York: Harper and Row, 1974).

30. Szasz, *Myth of Mental Illness*, ix.

31. Eric J. Dammann, "The Myth of Mental Illness: Continuing Controversies and Their Implications for Mental Health Professionals," *Clinical Psychological Review* 17, no. 7 (1997): 733.

32. Szasz, *Myth of Mental Illness*, 48–49.

33. See, e.g., Laura Hirshbein, "Sex and Gender in Psychiatry: A View from History," *Journal of Medical Humanities* 31 (2010): 155–70.

34. Thomas Szasz, "The Myth of Mental Illness," *American Psychologist* 15 (1960): 116.

35. Thomas Szasz, *Coercion as Cure: A Critical History of Psychiatry* (New Brunswick, NJ: Transaction, 2009). But while some have appreciated the cultural contexualization, others, like Karen Nakamura, have cautioned that the antipsychiatry literature has ignored the realities of certain mental disorders that "can be very physically and psychically painful and can also lead to significant self-harming behavior." Karen Nakamura, *A Disability of the Soul: An Ethnography of Schizophrenia and Mental Illness in Contemporary Japan* (Ithaca, NY: Cornell University Press, 2013), 36. Similarly, Ronald Pies has contended that patients suffering from severe impairments of the brain (such as a drunk driver or a hallucinating LSD user) do not act intentionally and cannot be held responsible for their bad behavior. Ronald Pies, "On Myths and Countermyths: More on Szaszian Fallacies," *Archives of General Psychiatry* 36 (1979): 139–44.

36. Foucault, *Madness and Civilization*, 46.

37. Mark S. Micale and Roy Porter, *Discovering the History of Psychiatry* (New York: Oxford University Press, 1994), 7–8.

38. German E. Berrios, *The History of Mental Symptoms: Descriptive Psychopathology since the Nineteenth Century* (Cambridge: Cambridge University Press,

1996); Allan Horowitz, *Creating Mental Illness* (Chicago: University of Chicago Press, 2002).

39. Nakamura, *Disability of the Soul*, 35.

40. Roy Porter, *Madness: A Brief History* (New York: Oxford University Press, 2002).

41. Frantz Fanon, *Black Skin, White Masks*, trans. Constance Farrington (New York: Grove Press, 1994); Richard C. Keller, *Colonial Madness: Psychiatry in French North Africa* (Chicago: University of Chicago Press, 2007); Waltraud Ernst, *Mad Tales from the Raj: The European Insane in British India* (London: Routledge, 1991); Jonathan Sadowsky, *Imperial Bedlam: Institutions of Madness in Colonial Southwest Nigeria* (Berkeley: University of California Press, 1999).

42. Nancy Scheper-Hughes, *Saints, Scholars, and Schizophrenics: Mental Illness in Rural Ireland* (Berkeley: University of California Press, 1979), 189–90.

43. Arthur Kleinman, *Rethinking Psychiatry: Cultural Category to Personal Experience* (New York: Free Press, 1988), 14–15.

44. Yi Bu-yeong, Kim Gwang-il, and Min Seong-gil have authored more than a dozen books and numerous articles on topics ranging from shamanism to *hwabyeong* (fire illness), folktales, and mental health. See, for example, Yi Bu-yeong, "Iljeha jeongsin gwa jinryowa geu byeoncheon: Joseon chongdokbu uiwon ui jeongsingwa jinryo reul (1913–1928) jungsimeuro" [Psychiatric care and its change under the Japanese government in Korea with special reference to the clinical activities at the Colonial Governmental Hospital, 1913–28], *Uisahak* 3, no. 2 (1994): 147–69; Jeong Won-yong, Yi Na-mi, and Yi Bu-yeong, "Seoyang jeongsinuihak ui doip gwa geu byeoncheon gwajeong (2) ilje gangjeomgi ui jeongsin uihak gyoyuk, 1910–1945" [The introduction of Western psychiatry into Korea (II): Psychiatric education in Korea during the forced Japanese annexation of Korea, 1910–1945], *Uisahak* 15 (December 2006): 157–87; Min Seong-gil, *Hwabyeong yeongu* [The study of *hwabyeong*] (Seoul: Emel keomyunikeisyeon, 2009); Kim Gwang-il, "Syameonijeumui jeongsin bunseokhakjeok gochal" [A psychoanalytical consideration of shamanism], *Singyeong jeongsin uihak* 11, no. 2 (1972): 57–65; Kim Gwang-il, "Hanguk mingan jeongsinuihak" [Folk psychiatry in Korea], *Singyeong jeongsin uihak* 11, no. 2 (1972): 85–98.

45. Yi Na-mi, "Seoyang jeongsinuihagui doip gwa geu byeoncheon gwajeong: 17-segi buteo iljechogi kkaji" [The introduction of Western psychiatry and the process of change: From the seventeenth century to the early part of Japanese colonial rule] (PhD diss., Seoul National University, 1994); Jeong Won-yong, "Geundae seoyang jeongsinuihagui jeongaewa byeoncheongwajeong—1920-nyeondae chobuteo 8. 15 gwangbok ijeonkkaji" [The development and process of transition of modern Western psychiatry from 1920 to August 15 [1945] (preindependence)] (PhD diss., Seoul National University, 1996).

46. Yeo In-seok, "Sebeuranseu jeongsingwa ui seollip gwajeong gwa indojuuijeok chiryo jeontong ui hyeongseong: Maekraren gwa i jungcheol ui hwaldongeul jungsimeuro" [The establishment of Severance Union Medical College's psychiatry department and the formation of a humanistic approach: Focusing on McLaren and

Yi Jung-cheol], *Uisahak* 17, no. 1 (June 2008): 57–74; Min Seong-gil, *Malsseumi yuksini doeeo: Maekraren gyosuui saeng aewa sasang* [The Word became flesh: Dr. McLaren's life and thought] (Seoul: Yeonsedaehakgyo daehak chulpanmunhwawon, 2013).

47. Yi Su-yeong, *Seksyueolliti wa gwanggi* [Madness and sexuality] (Seoul: Geurinbi, 2008); Jeong Chang-gwon, *Yeoksa sok jangaein eun eotteoke sarasseulkka* [How did people with disabilities in Korean history live?] (Seoul: Geulhangari, 2011).

48. Jieun Lee, Amy Wachholtz, and Keum-Hyeong Choi, "A Review of the Korean Cultural Syndrome *Hwa-Byung*: Suggestions for Theory and Intervention," *Asia Taepyeongyang Sangdam Yeongu* 4, no. 1 (January 2014): 49, www.ncbi.nlm.nih.gov/pmc/articles/PMC4232959/; Soyoung Suh, "Stories to Be Told: Korean Doctors between *Hwa-byung* (Fire-Illness) and Depression, 1970–2011," *Culture, Medicine and Psychiatry* 37, no. 1 (March 2013): 81–104, ww.ncbi.nlm.nih.gov/pmc/articles/PMC3585958/.

1. FORMS OF MADNESS

The chapter epigraphs are from Paul U. Unschuld and Herman Tessenow, *Huang Di nei jing su wen: Nature, Knowledge, Imagery in an Ancient Chinese Medical Text* (Berkeley: University of California Press, 2003), 229, and Murayama Chijun, *Chōsen no kishin* [Ghosts of Korea] (Seoul: Chōsen Sōtokufu, 1929), 261–65.

1. Heo Jun, *Wonbon dong-ui bogam* [Treasured mirror of Eastern medicine: Original] (Seoul: Namsangdang, 1987), 103.

2. Ibid.

3. Antonetta Bruno, *The Gates of Words: Language in the Rituals of Korean Shamans* (Leiden: CNWS, 2002).

4. Boudewijn Walraven, "National Pantheon, Regional Deities, Persona, Spirits? *Mushindo, Sŏngsu*, and the Nature of Korean Shamanism," *Asian Ethnology* 68, no. 1 (2009): 58.

5. Ibid.

6. Sung Deuk Oak, "Healing and Exorcism: American Encounters with Shamanism in Early Modern Korea," *Asian Ethnology* 69, no. 1 (2010): 95–128.

7. Keh-Ming Lin, "Traditional Chinese Medical Beliefs and Their Relevance for Mental Illness and Psychiatry," in *Normal and Abnormal Behavior in Chinese Culture*, ed. Arthur Kleinman and Tsung-yi Lin (Boston: D. Reidel, 1981), 96.

8. Dongwon Shin, "How Commoners Became Consumers of Naturalistic Medicine in Korea, 1600–1800," *East Asian Science, Technology, and Society: An International Journal* 4 (2010): 275–301.

9. Ibid.

10. Kim Dae-won, "18-segi mingan uiryo ui seongjang" [The growth of private medicine in the eighteenth century] (MA thesis, Seoul National University, 1998), 48–49.

11. Ibid.

12. Sarah Dillon defines the palimpsest as a "multi-layered record" created through a process of layering. See Sarah Dillon, *The Palimpsest: Literature, Criticism, Theory* (London: Continuum, 2007), 3.

13. Roy Porter, *Madness: A Brief History* (New York: Oxford University Press, 2002), 10.

14. George Heber Jones, "The Spirit Worship of the Koreans," *Transactions of the Korea Branch of the Royal Asiatic Society* 2 (1901): 58.

15. Oak, "Healing and Exorcism," 97.

16. Bou-Yong Rhi, "Psychotherapeutic Aspects of Shamanism with Special Reference to Korean *Mudang*," *Mental Health Research* 8 (1989): 40–55.

17. Merose Hwang, "The *Mudang*: Gendered Discourses on Shamanism in Colonial Korea" (PhD diss.: University of Toronto, 2009).

18. David Kelly Lambuth, "Korean Devils and Christian Missionaries," *Independent* 63 (July-December 1907): 287–88.

19. J. Robert Moose, *Village Life in Korea* (Nashville, TN: Publishing House of the M.E. Church, 1911), 191–92.

20. Homer B. Hulbert, *The Passing of Korea* (New York: Doubleday, Page, 1906), 196.

21. Andrew Scull, *Madness in Civilization: A Cultural History of Insanity* (Princeton, NJ: Princeton University Press, 2015), 67.

22. E. Taylor Atkins, *Primitive Selves: Koreana in the Japanese Colonial Gaze* (Berkeley: University of California Press, 1910), 65–66; See also Boudewijn Walraven, "The Natives Next-Door: Ethnology in Colonial Korea," in *Anthropology and Colonialism in Asia and Oceania,* ed. Jan van Bremen and Akitoshi Shimizu (Richmond, Surrey: Curzon, 1999), 214–44.

23. Atkins, *Primitive Selves*, 66.

24. Kilsŭng Choe, "War and Ethnology/Folklore in Colonial Korea; The Case of Akiba Takashi," in *Wartime Anthropology in Asia and the Pacific,* ed. Shimizu Akitoshi and Jan van Bremen (Osaka: National Museum of Ethnology, 2003), 169–87. See also Stefan Tanaka, *Japan's Orient: Rendering Pasts into History* (Berkeley: University of California Press, 1995).

25. Atkins, *Primitive Selves*, 74.

26. Kim Hui-yeong, "Murayama Jijun-i bon Jeonnam ui mugyeok sinang" [Shamanistic practices of Jeonnam seen by Murayama Chijun], unpublished manuscript, 2011, Jeonnam Daehakgyo Honamhak Yeonguwon, 1–15.

27. Yi Neung-hwa, "Joseon musokgo" [Records of Korean shamanism]. *Gyemong* 19 (1927): 1–85.

28. Theodore Jun Yoo, *The Politics of Gender in Colonial Korea: Labor, Education, and Health, 1910–1945* (Berkeley: University of California Press, 2008), 81–93.

29. Oak, "Healing and Exorcism."

30. Ibid., 99.

31. Boudewijn Walraven, *Songs of the Shaman: The Ritual Chants of the Korean Mudang* (London: Kegan Paul International, 1994).

32. Laurel Kendall, "Korean Shamanism: Women's Rites and a Chinese Comparison," *Senri Ethnological Studies* 11 (1984): 58.

33. Hyun-key Kim Hogarth, *Korean Shamanism and Cultural Nationalism* (Seoul: Jimoondang, 1999), 4–5.

34. Rhi, "Psychotherapeutic Aspects," 41–42. According to Eli Barr Landis, who was a missionary doctor working for the Korean Mission of the Church of England in the 1890s, the "initiation illness" followed several steps that included possession by spirits, dreams of "peach trees, a rainbow, a dragon, or man in armor," oracles and reception of messages from "heaven, earth, and lightning," flower offerings, acquisition of a dead "sorceress's clothes," followed by an exorcism and acquisition of rice from neighbors, the inscription of names on a tablet to garner blessings, and finally "going to other houses to exorcise them." Quoted in Oak, "Healing and Exorcism," 106.

35. Mircea Eliade, *Rites and Symbols of Initiation: The Mysteries of Birth and Rebirth*, trans. William Trask (New York: Spring, 1998), 81–102.

36. Hogarth, *Korean Shamanism*, 6.

37. Chōsen sōtokufu keimu sōkanfu, *Chōsen eisei fūshūroku* [A record of Korean's hygiene customs], ed. and comp. Sin Jong-won and Han Ji-won (1915; repr., Seoul: Miksogwon, 2013), 119.

38. Kwang-il Kim, "*Kut* and the Treatment of Mental Disorder," in *Shamanism: The Spirit World of Korea*, ed. Richard W. I. Guisso and Chai-shin Yu (Berkeley, CA: Asian Humanities Press, 1988), 134. See also Chongho Kim, *Korean Shamanism: The Cultural Paradox* (Aldershot: Ashgate, 2003), 18–19.

39. Murayama Chijun, *Chōsen no kishin* [Ghosts of Korea] (Seoul: Chōsen Sōtokufu, 1929), 226, 262.

40. K. Kim, "*Kut*," 41–42.

41. Boudewijn Walraven, "Shamans, the Family, and Women," in *Religions of Korea in Practice*, ed. Robert E. Buswell Jr. (Princeton, NJ: Princeton University Press, 2007), 306; Boudewijn Walraven, "Our Shamanic Past: The Korean Government, Shamans and Shamanism," *Copenhagen Papers* 8, no. 93 (1993): 5–25; Youngsook Kim Harvey, "The Korean *Mudang* as a Household Therapist," in *Culture-Bound Syndromes, Ethnopsychiatry and Alternative Therapies*, ed. William P. Lebra (Honolulu: University of Hawaii Press, 1976), 189–98.

42. Walraven, "Shamans." Lay people, who experienced more oppression and traumatic events in their lives, turned to cathartic play as well to sublimate their anger through performances in various folk genres. See chapter 3 below and Sung Kil Min, "*Hwabyung* in Korea: Culture and Dynamic Analysis," *World Cultural Psychiatry Research Review* 4, no. 1 (2009): 12–15.

43. John A. Grim, "*Chaesu Kut*: A Korean Shamanistic Performance," *Asian Folklore Studies* 43 (1984): 237.

44. Bou-Yong Rhi, "Psychological Aspects of Korean Shamanism," *Korea Journal* 10, no. 9 (1970): 18.

45. K. Kim, "*Kut*," 137–38.

46. Murayama cited in Yi Bu-yeong, *Hanguk ui syameonijeum gwa bunseok simnihak* [Korean shamanism and analytical psychology] (Paju: Hangilsa, 2012), 282.

47. Frantz G. Alexander and Sheldon T. Selesnick, *The History of Psychiatry: An Evaluation of Psychiatric Thought and Practice from Prehistoric Times to the Present* (New York: Harper and Row, 1966), 19.
48. Yi Bu-yeong, *Hanguk ui syameonijeum gwa bunseok simrihak*, 266–67.
49. *Joseon ilbo*, January 11, 1935.
50. Murayama Chijun, *Chōsen no kishin*, 267–68.
51. Jeong Gu-yeong, "Singyeong gwa chukgwi ui sangjing" [Symbolisms of enchanted lands and exorcism], *Wolgan Joseon*, May 2007, http://monthly.chosun.com/client/news/viw.asp?ctod=&nNewsNumb=200705100069.
52. Kim Ui-suk, *Hanguk minsokjeui wa eumyangohaeng* [Korean rites and ceremonies and the yin-yang and five elements] (Seoul: Jipmundang, 1993), 101.
53. Homer B. Hulbert, *The Korea Review* 2 (Seoul: Methodist Publishing House, 1902), 3.
54. Marilyn Ivy, *Discourses of the Vanishing: Modernity, Phantasm, Japan* (Chicago: University of Chicago Press, 1995), 169–70; Christine Pratt, *An Encyclopedia of Shamanism*, vol. 1 (New York: Rosen, 2007), 258.
55. Sin Do-won, *Hoyeolja joseoneul seupgyeokhada* [Cholera invades Joseon] (Seoul: Yeoksa bipyeongsa, 2004), 151.
56. Murayama, *Chōsen no kishin*, 262, 266.
57. Ibid., 229; see also Chōsen sōtokufu keimu sōkanfu, *Chōsen eisei fūshūroku*, 118–20.
58. Yi Bu-yeong, *Hanguk ui syameonijeum gwa bunseok simnihak*, 268.
59. *Joseon ilbo*, January 11, 1935.
60. *Gyeongseong ilbo*, December 9, 1912.
61. *Gyeongseong ilbo*, April 1, 1917.
62. Quoted in Hwang, "*Mudang*," 110.
63. Quoted in Han Ji-won, *Joseon chongdokbu uiryo minsokjireul tonghae bon wisaeng pungseup yeongu* [A study of the Government-General of Joseon's medical ethnography on hygienic customs] (Seoul: Minsokwon, 2013), 96.
64. Oak, "Healing and Exorcism," 111–19.
65. Ibid., 115, citing Lambuth, "Korean Devils," 287–88.
66. Ibid., 118, citing Donald N. Clark, *Living Dangerously in Korea* (Norwalk, CT: EastBridge, 2001), 39.
67. Ibid., 114, citing *K'urisudoin hoebo* [Christian Advocate], May 23, 1900.
68. Ibid., 117.
69. Lin, "Traditional Chinese Medical Beliefs," 102–3.
70. Yi Dong-geon, *Dong-ui imsang singyeong jeongsingwa* [Eastern medicine clinical neuropsychiatry] (Seoul: Seowodang, 1994), 70.
71. Paul Ulrich Unschuld and Herman Tessenow, *Huang Di nei jing su wen: An Annotated Translation of Huangdi's Inner Classic—Basic Questions*, vol. 1 (Berkeley: University of California Press, 2011), 683.
72. Elisa Rossi, *Shen: Psycho-Emotional Aspects of Chinese Medicine*, trans. Laura Caretto (London: Churchill Livingstone, 2007), 128.
73. Yi Dong-geon, *Dong-ui imsang singyeong jeongsingwa*, 9–86.

74. Zhang Congzheng's Gong Xie Pai (Attack and Drain School) recommended attacking external pathogens through sweating, emesis, or purgation. Other canonic texts cited by Korean physicians included Zhang Zhongjin's *Jingui yaolue* [Essential medical treasures of the golden chamber], a classic clinical treatise on internal disorders; Ge Hong's *Zhouhou jiuzufang* [Handbook of prescriptions for emergency]; Yang Yonghe's *Jishengfang* [A book of formulas to promote well-being]; and Zhang Jinyue's *Jingyue quanshu* [The collected works of Jingyue]. For more, see Kim Jong-u, *Jeungryero bon jeongsin hanuihak* [Records of neuropsychiatry in Oriental medicine] (Seoul: Jimmundang, 2006), 25–40.

75. Sun Simiao's *Beiji Qiangjin yaofang* [Essential prescriptions worth a thousand pieces of gold] highlighted one hundred pathogenic factors that could cause *diankuang* disorders. In *Suwen xuanji yuanbing shi* [Exploration of the mechanism of Illness based on Suwen], Liu Wansu, a key figure behind the Cooling School, advocated a theory around pathogenic fire and how an excess, often in the form of anger, in the kidney or liver could manifest into *kuang*. For more, see Rossi, *Shen*, 136; Kim Jong-u, *Jeungryero bon jeongsin hanuihak*, 25–33.

76. Kim Jong-u, *Jeungryero bon jeongsin hanuihak*, 25–33.

77. Rossi, *Shen*, 128; also see Lee Dong-geon, *Dong-ui imsang singyeong jeongsingwa*, 189–90.

78. The four-step diagnosis involved observation, auscultation and olfaction, interrogation, and palpitation.

79. Yeo Hyeon-suk et al., *Hanguk uihaksa* [The history of medicine in Korea] (Seoul: KMA Uiryo jeongchaek yeonguso, 2012), 93–113.

80. Heo Jun drew on both Li Gao and Zhu Zhenzheng, who represented the northern and southern schools respectively.

81. Yi Dong-geon, *Dong-ui imsang singyeong jeongsingwa*, 52–53.

82. Ibid.

83. Kim Tae-hyeon, "Dong-ui bogam sinmun jeon-gan cheobang ui jeonsa e daehan yeongu" [The literature review on procedure of historical changes on herb medicines in the chapter 'Sinmun jeon-gan' of *Dong-ui bogam*], *Journal of Oriental Neuropsychiatry* 23, no. 3 (2012): 175–90.

84. Don Baker, "Oriental Medicine in Korea," in *Medicine across Cultures: History and Practice of Medicine in Non-Western Cultures,* ed. Helaine Selin (New York: Kluwer Academic Publishers, 2003), 144–45.

85. Yi Pu-yong (Yi Bu-yeong), "Illness and Healing in the Three Kingdoms Period: A Symbolic Interpretation," *Korea Journal* 21, no. 12 (1981): 10–11.

86. Hong Sun-hyang, "Hanguk yeoksa e girokdoen jeongsin jilhwan e gwanhan yeongu" [A study of mental disorders reported in Korean history], *Singyeong jeongsin uihak* 20, no. 2 (1981): 185–94; Dae-ho Kim and Hae-won Lee, "Post-traumatic Stress Disorder and Trauma-Related Conditions in Korean History: Literature Review of Six Cases," *Psychiatry Investigation* 2, no. 2 (2005): 18–21.

87. Martina Deuchler, "Neo-Confucianism in Action: Agnation and Ancestor Worship in Early Yi Korea," in *Religion and Ritual in Korean Society,* ed. Laurel Kendall and Griffin Dix (Berkeley, CA: Institute of East Asian Studies, 1988), 39.

88. Jeong Chang-gwon, *Yeoksa sok jangaeineun eotteoke sarasseulkka?* [How did people with disabilities live in the past?] (Seoul: Geunghangari, 2011), 206–9.

89. Martina Deuchler, *The Confucian Transformation of Korea: A Study of Society and Ideology* (Cambridge, MA: Council on East Asian Studies, Harvard University, 1992), 143.

90. Jeong Chang-gwon, *Yeoksa sok jangaeineun eotteoke sarasseulkka*, 96–98.

91. Ibid., 140–41.

92. Ibid., 84–85.

93. Yonglin Jiang, *The Mandate of Heaven and the Great Ming Code* (Seattle: University of Washington Press, 2011), 59–61.

94. Jeong Chang-gwon, *Yeoksa sok jangaeineun eotteoke sarasseulkka*, 210.

95. Ibid., 52–53.

96. Yeo Hyeon-suk et al., *Hanguk uihaksa*, 86.

97. Jeong Chang-gwon, *Yeoksa sok jangaeineun eotteoke sarasseulkka*, 210–11.

98. Ibid., 211.

99. Ibid., 341–43.

100. Ibid., 53.

101. Ibid., 335–60.

102. Ibid., 363–65.

103. Edward Willet Wagner, *The Literati Purges: Political Conflict in Early Yi Korea* (Cambridge, MA: East Asian Research Center, Harvard University, 1974), 56.

104. Jahyun Kim Haboush, *The Memoirs of Lady Hyegyŏng: The Autobiographical Writings of a Crown Princess of Eighteenth-Century Korea* (Berkeley, University of California Press, 1996), 22–30.

105. Min Seong-gil, *Hwabyeong yeongu* [Study of *Hwabyeong*] (Seoul: ML, 2009), 9.

106. Ibid., 39.

107. Other common somatic symptoms included a pounding heart, sighing, disordered sleep, bodily pains, and anorexia.

108. Min Seong-gil, *Hwabyeong yeongu*, 19–20.

109. Haboush, *Memoirs of Lady Hyegyŏng*, 281.

110. Eli Barr Landis, "Notes on the Exorcism of Spirits in Korea," *Chinese Review* 21, no. 6 (1895): 404.

111. To be sure, there were other physicians like Yi Je-ma (1838–1900) who advocated new healing techniques and prescriptions based on his idea of *Sasang uihak*, or the four physiological constitutions (*taeyang, taeeum, soyang,* and *soem*).

112. Yi Na-mi, *Seoyang jeongsinuihagui doipgwa geu byeoncheon gwajeong: 17-segi buteo iljechogi kkaji* [The introduction of Western psychiatry and the process of change: From the seventeenth century to the early part of Japanese colonial rule] (PhD diss., Seoul National University, 1994), 16–47.

113. *Hanseong sunbo*, June 4, 1884.

2. MADNESS IS...

The chapter epigraphs are from Michel Foucault, *Madness and Civilization: A History of Insanity in the Age of Reason,* trans. Richard Howard (New York: Vintage, 1988), 250; C.I. McLaren, "The Problem of Insanity and the Responsibility of the Church," *Korean Mission Field* 18, no. 7 (1922): 138; and Emil Kraepelin, *Psychiatrie: Ein Lehrbuch fur Studirende und Aerzte. Funfte, vollstandig umgearbeitete Auflage* (Leipzig, 1896), v, quoted in Richard Noll, *The Encyclopedia of Schizophrenia and Other Psychotic Disorders,* 3rd ed. (New York: Facts on File, 2007), xiv.

1. Chae Man-sik, "Michin ideul ui nara, dongpalho sil jamipgi isang namnyeo sasip yeoin" [The land of crazy people, my report, sneaking into the East Eight Ward, forty or so odd men and women], *Byeolgeongon* 6, no. 4 (April 1931).

2. *Donga ilbo,* August 31, 1938.

3. Hashimoto Akira, *Seishin byōsha to shitaku kanchi* [Mental illness and home confinement] (Tokyo: Rikka Shupan, 2011), 17–52.

4. Government of Japan, "The Code of Criminal Procedure," accessed May 8, 2006, www.oecd.org/site/adboecdanti-corruptioninitiative/46814489.pdf.

5. Akihito Suzuki, "Were Asylums Men's Places? Male Excess in the Asylum Population in Japan in the Early Twentieth Century," in *Psychiatric Cultures Compared: Psychiatry and Mental Health Care in the Twentieth Century,* ed. Marijke Gijswijt-Hofstra et al. (Amsterdam: Amsterdam University Press, 2005), 296–97.

6. Ibid.

7. Janice Matsumura, "Mental Health as Public Peace: Kaneko Junji and the Promotion of Psychiatry in Modern Japan," *Modern Asian Studies* 38, no. 4 (October 2004): 903–4.

8. Amy Vladeck Heinrich, *Fragments of Rainbows: The Life of the Poetry of Saitō Mokichi* (New York: Columbia University Press, 1983), 46. See also Shigeki Kuzuhara, "History of Neurology and Education and Neurology in Japan," *KNA-JNS Joint Symposium* 3 (May 2009): 968; Naboru Ishida, "Correspondence," *American Journal of Insanity* 73 (1916–17): 744–48. In 1935 the society renamed itself as the Japanese Society of Psychiatry and Neurology.

9. Suzuki, "Were Asylums Men's Places?," 299–30.

10. See Yi Man-yeol, *Hanguk gidokgyo uiryosa* [The history of Christian medicine work in Korea] (Seoul: Akanet, 2003).

11. Ho Young Lee, "Past, Present and Future of Korean Psychiatry," *Psychiatry Investigation* 1, no. 1 (2004): 13–19.

12. Horace Grant Underwood, *The Call of Korea: Political—Social—Religious* (London: Fleming H. Revell, 1908), 100. See also Allen's own account of his achievement, quoted in "Medical Work in Korea," *Foreign Missionary* 45 (October 1886): 215–16.

13. Underwood, *Call of Korea,* 264–65.

14. Horace N. Allen, "Medical Work in Korea," *Foreign Missionary* 44 (July 1885): 75.

15. Yeo In-seok, "Sebeuranseu jeongsingwa ui seollip gwajeong gwa indojuuijeok chiryo jeontong ui hyeongseong: Maekraren gwa i jungcheol ui hwaldongeul jungsimeuro" [The establishment of Severance Union Medical College's psychiatry department and the formation of a humanistic approach: Focusing on McLaren and Yi Jung-cheol], *Uisahak* 17, no. 1 (June 2008): 58.

16. Yi Yeong-a, "Seongyo uisa allen (Horace N. Allen) ui uiryo hwaldonggwa joseon-in ui mom e daehan insik gochal" [A study of Horace N. Allen's medicine and recognition of the Korean body], *Uisahak* 20, no. 1 (2011): 307.

17. Horace Newton Allen, *Things Korean: A Collection of Sketches and Anecdotes, Missionary and Diplomatic* (New York: F. H. Revell, 1908), 202–5.

18. Oliver R. Avison, *Annual Report of the Imperial Korean Hospital* (Seoul: Methodist Publishing House, 1901), 3.

19. Ibid., 13.

20. Annette Hye Kyung Son, "Modernization of the System of Traditional Korean Medicine, 1876–1990," *Health Policy* 4, no. 3 (June 1998): 265.

21. Jeong Won-yong, "Geundae seoyang jeongsinuihagui jeongaewa byeoncheongwajeong—1920-nyeondae chobuteo 8. 15 gwangbok ijeonkkaji" [The development and process of transition of modern Western psychiatry from 1920 to August 15 [1945] (preindependence)] (PhD diss., Seoul National University, 1996), 26–28.

22. Charles F. Bernheisel, *The Apostolic Church as Reproduced in Korea* (New York: Board of Foreign Missions of the Presbyterian Church in the United States, 1912), 9.

23. Sung Deuk Oak, "Healing and Exorcism: Christian Encounters with Shamanism in Early Modern Korea," *Asian Ethnology* 69, no. 1 (2010): 96.

24. Son, "Modernization of the System," 264.

25. Kanekawa Hideo, *Nihon no seishin iryoshi: Meiji kara Showa shoki kara* [A history of medical psychiatry: From Meiji to the early Showa] (Tokyo: Seikyūsha, 2012), 91–95.

26. *Chōsen sōtokufu kanpō* [Official Gazette of the Government-General of Korea], March 28, 1912.

27. H. Lee, "Past, Present and Future," 14.

28. Lee Bu-yeong, "Iljeha jeongsingwa jinryowa geu byeoncheon: Joseon chongdokbu uiwon ui jeongsingwa jinryo (1913–1928) reul jungsimeuro" [Psychiatric care and its change under the Japanese government in Korea with special reference to the clinical activities at the Colonial Governmental Hospital, 1913–28], *Uisahak* 3, no. 2 (1994): 150–51.

29. *Chōsen sōtokufu iin* 2 (1912–13): 4–6.

30. Yi Bu-yeong, "Iljeha jeongsin gwa jinryowa geu byeoncheon," 151–52.

31. Ibid.

32. Yoshiharu Honda et al., "A Pioneer in Occupational Therapy at Mental Hospitals in Local Cities: Approaches at Shichiyama Hospital at the Beginning of Taisho Era," *Seishin shinkeigaku zasshi* 111, no. 9 (2009): 1047–54.

33. *Chōsen sōtokufu iin* 3 (1914–15): 475–76.

34. *Chōsen sōtokufu iin* 6 (1918): 257–58.
35. Ibid.
36. *Chōsen sōtokufu iin* 9 (1922): 119.
37. *Joseon ilbo,* April 15, 1923.
38. Yi Bu-yeong, "Iljeha jeongsin gwa jinryowa geu byeoncheon," 158–59.
39. *Maeil sinbo,* October 3, 1919.
40. *Maeil sinbo,* October 3, 1919; *Donga ilbo,* April 25, 1920; August 8, 1923; December 8, 1924; January 9, 1925; *Sidae ilbo,* June 26, 1926; June 3, 1927; *Jungoe ilbo,* May 18, 1927; *Joseon ilbo,* April 15, 1923.
41. *Maeil sinbo,* October 3, 1919; *Donga ilbo,* April 25, 1920; August 8, 1923; December 8, 1924; January 9, 1925; *Sidae ilbo,* June 26, 1926; June 3, 1927; *Jungoe ilbo,* May 18, 1927; *Joseon ilbo,* April 15, 1923.
42. *Donga ilbo,* June 3, 1927.
43. *Donga ilbo,* January 9, 1925.
44. *Joseon ilbo,* August 26, 1921; September 9, 1934; January 11, 1935.
45. *Donga ilbo,* August 8, 1924; *Joseon ilbo,* April 15, 1923.
46. *Joseon ilbo,* April 15, 1923.
47. J. D. VanBuskirk, "Severance," *Korean Mission Field* 21, no. 10 (1925): 203.
48. Min Seong-gil, *Malsseumi yuksini doeeo: Maekraren gyosuui saeng aewa sasang* [The World became flesh: Dr. McLaren's life and thought] (Seoul: Yeonsedaehakgyo daehak chulpanmunhwawon, 2013), 1–81.
49. C. I. McLaren, "An Hypothesis Concerning the Relationship between Body and Mind," *Australasian Journal of Psychology and Philosophy* 6, no. 3 (1928): 272–82.
50. Ibid.
51. C. I. McLaren, "My Beliefs," *Korean Mission Field* 28, no. 4 (1932): 75–77.
52. C. I. McLaren, "Care of the Insane," *Korea Mission Field* 35, no. 3 (1939): 62.
53. C. I. McLaren, "Things Both New and Old in Psychological Medicine," *Chinese Medical Journal* 46, no. 3 (1932): 913–26.
54. McLaren, "Hypothesis."
55. Ibid.
56. Esmond W. New, *A Doctor in Korea: The Story of Charles McLaren, M.D.* (Sydney: Australian Presbyterian Board of Missions, 1958), 35.
57. C. I. McLaren, "Lessons from the Neurological Clinic," *Korea Mission Field* 21, no. 10 (1925): 214.
58. John M. Reisman, *A History of Clinical Psychology* (New York: Ardent Media, 1976), 126–27; McLaren was also exposed to Carl Jung's analytical psychology. See McLaren, "My Beliefs."
59. McLaren, "My Beliefs."
60. Ibid.
61. McLaren, "Things Both New and Old."
62. McLaren, "Lessons," 214.
63. C. I. McLaren, "Saturday Morning in a Hospital in Korea," *Korea Mission Field* 28, no. 3 (1932): 45–49.

64. J. D. VanBurskirk, "Present Problems," *Korea Mission Field* 21, no. 10 (1925): 206.

65. Ibid., 204.

66. C. I. McLaren, "Saturday Morning," 45–49.

67. Ibid.

68. Andrew Gosling, *Jessie's Korea: A Guide to the McLaren-Human Collection in the National Library of Australia* (Canberra: National Library of Australia, 2007), 11.

69. New, *Doctor in Korea*, 34.

70. Ibid., 45.

71. D. H. Ahn and B. Y. Rhi, "Community Leaders' Reaction to Mental Disorders," *Seoul Journal of Psychiatry* 11, no. 4 (1986): 281–93.

72. In 1926, only 5 out of the 57 faculty members and 47 out of the 150 incoming students were Korean.

73. Jeong Won-yong, Yi Na-mi, and Yi Bu-yeong, "Seoyang jeongsinuihak ui doip gwa geu byeoncheon gwajeong (2) ilje gangjeomgi ui jeongsin uihak gyoyuk, 1910–1945" [The introduction of Western psychiatry into Korea (II): Psychiatric education in Korea during the forced Japanese annexation of Korea, 1910–1945)], *Uisahak* 15 (December 2006): 171.

74. Yi Bu-yeong, "Hanguk geundae cheongsin uihak ui yeoksajeok jomyeong: Ilje eseo hanguk dongran ijeon kkaji" [Historical review of modern Korean psychiatry: From the colonial period up to the Korean War], symposium celebrating the tenth-year anniversary of Seoul National University Hospital, *Seoul uidae jeongsin uihak* 14, no. 1 (1989): 5.

75. Ibid., 6.

76. Yi Chung-ho, *Ilje amheukgi uisa gyoyuksa* [A history of medical education during the dark period under Japanese colonial rule] (Seoul: Gukhak jaryowon, 2011), 182.

77. Liu Shi-yung, "An Overview of Public Health Development in Japan-Ruled Taiwan," in *Death at the Opposite Ends of the Eurasian Continent: Mortality Trends in Taiwan and the Netherlands, 1850–1945*, ed. Theo Engelen, John R. Shepherd, and Yang Wen-shan (Amsterdam: Amsterdam University Press, 2011), 165–82. Hoi-eun Kim notes that almost 1,200 Japanese medical students went abroad to study medicine in Germany after Meiji Japan adopted German medicine as its official model in 1869. See also Hoi-eun Kim, *Doctors of Empire: Medical and Cultural Encounters between Imperial Germany and Meiji Japan* (Toronto: University of Toronto Press, 2014).

78. H. Lee, "Past, Present and Future," 13.

79. Kanekawa Hideo, "Keijō teikoku daigaku shinkei-ka seishinka kyōshitsu no tō gakkai ni okeru gakujutsu happyō" [Academic presentation on neurology and psychiatry at the annual meeting at Keijō Imperial University], *Seishin shinkeigaku zasshi* 114, no. 10 (2012): 1180–86.

80. James R. Bartholomew, *The Formation of Science in Japan: Building a Research Tradition* (New Haven, CT: Yale University Press, 1989), 68.

81. Yu Hyeong-sik, *Hanguk geundae uihak yeongusa* [Research on the history of modern Korean medicine] (Seoul: Hanguk uihakwon, 2011), 437–41.

82. Jeong Won-yeong, Yi Nami, and Yi Buyeong, "Seoyang jeongsinuihak ui doip gwa geu byeoncheon gwajeong (2)," 179–81.

83. Kyoichi Kondo, "The Origin of Morita Therapy," in *Culture-Bound Syndromes, Ethnopsychiatry and Alternate Therapies*, vol. 4 of *Mental Health Research in Asia and Pacific*, ed. William P. Lebra (Honolulu: University Press of Hawaii, 1976), 250–58; Kei Nakamura, "The Formation and Development of Morita Therapy," in *Two Millennia of Psychiatry in West and East*, ed. Toshihiko Hamanaka and German E. Berrios (Tokyo: Gakuju Shoin, 2003), 125–29.

84. *Donga ilbo*, October 22, 1922.

85. Seoul daehakgyo byeongwon yeoksa munhwa senteo, *Sajin gwa hamkke boneun hanguk geunhyeondae uiryo munhwasa* [A pictorial history of modern medicine in Korea] (Seoul: Ungjin jisik hangseu, 2009), 141.

86. Jeong Won-yong, "Geundae seoyang jeongsinuihagui jeon-gaewa byeoncheongwajeong," 169.

87. Eric J. Engstrom, *Clinical Psychiatry in Imperial Germany: A History of Psychiatric Practice* (Ithaca, NY: Cornell University Press, 2003), 97.

88. Jeong Won-yong, "Geundae seoyang jeongsinuihagui jeongaewa byeoncheongwajeong," 168–69.

89. *Donga ilbo*, December 8, 1924.

90. *Donga ilbo*, January 31, 1928.

91. Yi Chung-ho, *Ilje amheukgi uisa gyoyuksa*, 268–69.

92. Akihito Suzuki, "Global Theory, Local Practice: Shock Therapies in Japanese Psychiatry, 1920–1945," in *Transnational Psychiatries: Social and Cultural Histories of Psychiatry in Comparative Perspective, c. 1800–2000*, ed. Waltraud Ernst and Thomas Mueller (Cambridge: Cambridge Scholars, 2010), 116–42.

93. Seoul daehakgyo byeongwon yeoksa munhwa senteo, *Hanguk geunhyeondae uiryo munhwasa*, 244–45.

94. Bou-Yong Rhi (Yi Bu-yeong), "The Roots of Korean Psychiatry and Its Development before and after World War II," in Hamanaka and Berrios, *Two Millennia*, 95.

95. Kim Gi-ju, "Sorokdo jahyeuiwon nahwanja jeongchaegui seonggyeok" [The character of the leper policy of Jahye Hospital on Sorok Island], *Yeoksahak yeongu* 44 (2011): 234–35.

96. Jeong Won-yong, "Geundae seoyang jeongsinuihagui jeongaewa byeoncheongwajeong," 160.

97. *Sidae ilbo*, June 26, 1926.

98. *Donga ilbo*, July 5, 1926.

99. *Donga ilbo*, August 12, 1926.

100. *Donga ilbo*, January 31, 1928.

101. *Donga ilbo*, January 25, 1929.

102. For an interesting discussion on social prophylaxis and public enlightenment, see Engstrom, *Clinical Psychiatry*.

103. C. I. McLaren, "The Necessary Connection between Healing of the Body and Healing of the Soul," *Korean Mission Field* 10, no. 7 (1914): 211–12.

3. A TOUCH OF MADNESS

The chapter epigraphs are from Arlie R. Hochschild, "Emotion Work, Feeling Rules, and Social Structures," *American Journal of Sociology* 25, no. 3 (1979): 551, and Erving Goffman, *Interaction Ritual: Essays on Face-to-Face Behavior* (New York: Anchor Books, 1967), 5.

1. Jan E. Stets and Jonathan H. Turner, "The Sociology of Emotions," in *Handbook of Emotions*, ed. Michael Lewis, Jeannette M. Haviland-Jones, and Lisa Feldman Barrett, 3rd ed. (London: Guilford Press, 2008), 32.

2. In "A Society That Drives You to Drink" (1921), "A Lucky Day" (1924), and "Fire" (1925), Hyeon Jin-geon offers a depressingly bleak yet realistic representation of colonial society, rendering his characters as marionettes whose movements are largely determined by socioeconomic forces beyond their control. See Hyeon Jin-geon, *Unsu joeun nal* [A lucky day], Hanguk munhak jeonjip 34 (Seoul: Munhak gwa jiseongsa, 2010).

3. William M. Reddy, *The Navigation of Feeling* (Cambridge: Cambridge University Press, 2001), 129.

4. Vieda Skultans, "The Appropriation of Suffering: Psychiatric Practice in the Post-Soviet Clinic," *Theory, Culture and Society* 24, no. 3 (2007): 27–48.

5. For recent groundbreaking scholarship on this topic, see Eugenia Lean, *Public Passions: The Trial of Shi Jianqiao and the Rise of Popular Sympathy in Republican China* (Berkeley: University of California Press, 2007); Elizabeth J. Perry, "Moving the Masses: Emotional Work in the Chinese Revolution," *Mobilization: An International Journal* 7, no. 2 (2002): 111–28; David Matsumoto, *Unmasking Japan: Myths and Realities about the Emotions of the Japanese* (Stanford, CA: Stanford University Press, 1996); Takeo Doi, *The Anatomy of Dependence* (Tokyo: Kondansha, 1973) and *The Anatomy of Self* (Tokyo: Kondansha, 1985).

6. Jan Plamper, "The History of Emotions: An Interview with William Reddy, Barbara Rosenwein, and Peter Stearns," *History and Theory* 49 (May 2010): 237; Mark D. Steinberg and Valeria Sobol, *Interpreting Emotions in Russia and Eastern Europe* (Dekalb: Northern Illinois University Press, 2011), 3; Patricia Tincineto Clough with Jean Halley, eds., *The Affective Turn: Theorizing the Social* (Durham, NC: Duke University Press, 2007), 16.

7. Paul Ekman, *Emotion in the Human Face: Guide-Lines for Research and Integration of Findings* (Oxford: Pergamon Press, 1972); Paul Ekman and Richard J. Davidson, eds., *The Nature of Emotion: Fundamental Questions* (London: Oxford University Press, 1994).

8. Ekman, *Emotion*.

9. Alice M. Isen and Gregory Andrade Diamond, "Affect and Automaticity," in *Unintended Thoughts: Limits of Awareness, Intention, and Control*, ed. James S. Uleman and John A. Bargh (New York: Guilford Press, 1989), 124–49.

10. Clifford Geertz, *The Interpretation of Cultures* (London: Fontana Press, 1973); Catherine Lutz and Geoffrey M. White, "The Anthropology of Emotions," *Annual Review of Anthropology* 15 (1986): 417.

11. Michelle Z. Rosaldo, "Toward an Anthropology of Self and Feeling," in *Culture Theory: Essays on Mind, Self, and Emotion,* ed. Richard A. Shweder and Robert A. LeVine (Cambridge: Cambridge University Press, 1984), 147.

12. Ibid., 35; Dylan Evans, *Emotions: A Very Short Introduction* (London: Oxford University Press, 2001), 11.

13. Reddy, *Navigation of Feeling*, 42; See also Catherine A. Lutz and Lila Abu-Lughod, eds., *Language and the Politics of Emotions* (London: Cambridge University Press, 1990).

14. Robert A. Schneider, ed., "AHR Conversation: The Historical Study of Emotions," *American Historical Review* 117, no. 5 (2012): 1487–1531. The participants included Nicole Eustace, Eugenia Lean, Julie Livingston, Jan Plamper, William M. Reddy, and Barbara H. Rosenwein.

15. Ibid., 1490.

16. Lean, *Public Passions.*

17. Peter N. Stearns and Carol Z. Stearns, "Emotionology: Clarifying the History of Emotions and Emotional Standards," *American Historical Review* 90, no. 4 (1985): 813.

18. Ibid.

19. Reddy, *Navigation of Feeling,* 129,

20. Ibid.

21. Plamper, "History of Emotions," 242.

22. Barbara Rosenwein, review of *The Navigation of Feeling*, by William M. Reddy, *American Historical Review* 107, no. 4 (October 2002): 1181.

23. Plamper, "History of Emotions," 253.

24. Ibid., 254.

25. Yi Kwang-su [Yi Gwang-su], "What Is Literature?," trans. Jooyeon Rhee, *Azalea: Journal of Korean Literature and Culture* 4, no. 1 (2011): 295.

26. Yi Kwang-su [Yi Gwang-su], "The Value of Literature," trans. Jooyeon Rhee, *Azalea: Journal of Korean Literature and Culture* 4, no. 1 (2011): 288.

27. Michael D. Shin, "Interior Landscapes: Yi Kwangsu's 'The Heartless' and the Origins of Modern Literature," in *Colonial Modernity in Korea,* ed. Gi-wook Shin and Michael Robinson (Cambridge, MA: Harvard Asia Center, 1999), 257.

28. Yi Kwang-su, "What Is Literature?," 299–300.

29. Ibid.

30. Edward Y. J. Chung, *The Neo-Confucianism of Yi T'oegye and Yi Yulgok: A Reappraisal of the "Four-Seven" Thesis and Its Practical Implications for Self-Cultivation* (Albany: State University of New York Press, 1995), 37.

31. Ibid., 176.

32. Yoon Joon Choi, *Dialogue and Antithesis: A Philosophical Study on the Significance of Herman Dooyeweerd's Transcendental Critique* (Philadelphia: Hermit Kingdom Press, 2006), 308.

33. Michael C. Kalton, with Oak Sook C. Kim et al., *The Four-Seven Debate: An Annotated Translation of the Most Famous Controversy in Korean Neo-Confucian Thought* (Albany: State University of New York Press, 1994); E. Chung, *Neo-Confucianism*.

34. Wei-ming Tu, "Probing the 'Three-Bonds' and the 'Five-Relationships' in Confucian Humanism," in *Confucianism and the Family*, ed. Walter H. Slote and George A. DeVos (New York: SUNY Press, 1998), 127.

35. Bruce Cumings, *Korea's Place in the Sun* (New York: W. W. Norton, 1997), 13.

36. Martina Deuchler, "The Tradition: Women during the Yi Dynasty," in *Virtues in Conflict: Tradition and the Korean Woman Today*, ed. Sandra Mattielli (Seoul: Royal Asiatic Society, Korea Branch, 1977), 2.

37. Kim Seong-gyu, *Jeong iran mueosinga* [What is this *jeong*?] (Seoul: Chekbose, 2013), 53. While *jeong* includes basic feelings such as affection, love, and sympathy, it governs how Koreans interact with each other, which also involves a general awareness of one's place in the social structure. For more, see Christopher K. Chung and Samson Cho, "Conceptualization of *Jeong* and Dynamics of *Hwabyung*," *Psychiatry Investigation* 3, no. 1 (2006): 47; Stets and Turner, "Sociology of Emotions," 32; Choe Sang-jin and Kim Gi-beom, *Munhwa simnihak hangugin ui simni bunseok* [Cultural psychology: Analyzing the psychological state of Koreans] (Seoul: Jisiksaneopsa, 2011), 53.

38. C. Chung and Cho, "Conceptualization of *Jeong*," 48.

39. Ibid.

40. Choe Sang-jin and Kim Gi-beom, *Munhwa simnihak hangugin ui simri bunseok*, 56.

41. Ibid.

42. Stets and Turner, "Sociology of Emotions," 36.

43. Kim Seong-gyu, *Jeong iran mueosinga*, 53.

44. Sang-Chin Choi and Gyuseong Han, "Shimcheong Psychology: A Case of an Emotional State for Cultural Psychology," *International Journal for Dialogical Science* 3, no. 1 (Fall 2008): 205–24.

45. Choe Sang-jin and Kim Gi-beom, *Munhwa simnihak hangugin ui simni bunseok*, 71–77.

46. Erving Goffman, *The Presentation of Self in Everyday Life* (New York: Pelican Books, 1990), 22–27.

47. Arlie Russell Hochschild, "The Sociology of Emotion as a Way of Seeing," in *Emotions in Social Life: Critical Themes and Contemporary Issues*, ed. Gillian Bendelow and Simon J. Williams (London: Routledge, 2005), 6–7.

48. Goffman, *Presentation of Self*, 30.

49. Erving Goffman, "On Face-Work: An Analysis of Ritual Elements in Social Interaction," in *Language, Culture and Society: A Book of Readings*, ed. Ben G. Blount (Cambridge: Winthrop, 1974), 224.

50. Reddy, *Navigation of Feeling*, 129.

51. According to Helen Flam, shame is best understood as being "triggered in us by others when they want to achieve our compliance." See Helen Flam, "Emotions' Map: A Research Agenda," in *Emotions and Social Movements*, ed. Helen Flam and Debra King (London: Routledge, 2005), 22.

52. Matsumoto, *Unmasking Japan*, 10.

53. Reddy, *Navigation of Feeling*, 129.

54. John Lie's excellent monograph chronicles the broad historical, sociological, political, and economic forces that have shaped the cultural expression of *han* (resentment) in the past half century in South Korea. See John Lie, *Han Unbound: The Political Economy of South Korea* (Stanford, CA: Stanford University Press, 2000).

55. Choe Sang-jin and Kim Gi-beom, *Munhwa simnihak hangugin ui simni bunseok*, 116.

56. Geertz, *Interpretation of Cultures*, 93.

57. Reddy, *Navigation of Feeling*, 129.

58. Mikhail Bakhtin, *Rabelais and His World*, trans. Helene Iwolsky (Bloomington: Indiana University Press, 1984), 1–27; Jeon Gyeong-uk, *Hanguk gamyeongeuk: Geu yeoksawa wonri* [Korean mask drama: History and structural principles] (Seoul: Yeolhwadong, 1998), 1–48.

59. Kim Hŭnggyu, "Pansori," in *A History of Korean Literature*, ed. Peter Lee (Cambridge: Cambridge University Press, 2003), 288.

60. Kim Hŭnggyu, "Chosŏn Fiction in Chinese," in Lee, *History of Korean Literature*, 267, 275.

61. Kim Hŭnggyu and Peter Lee, "Chosŏn Fiction in Korea," in Lee, *History of Korean Literature*, 274.

62. Kim Hŭnggyu, "Folk Drama," in Lee, *History of Korean Literature*, 304–6.

63. Ibid., 307–8.

64. Ibid., 312. Puppet plays like *Pak Ch'ŏmji* (Cheomji) also used satire laced with sexual innuendo to critique those with moral or religious authority.

65. Jeon Gyeong-uk, *Hanguk gamyeongeuk*, 1–48.

66. For example, in September 1915, the Government-General of Chōsen hosted the Gyeongseong gongjin hoe (the Keijō Industrial Exhibition), which was attended by more than 450,000 people and featured a gallery exposing Koreans to the existence of microorganisms not seen by the naked eye. The display also showcased the advances of modern medicine and civilization through scientific instruments like the microscope, portable examination kits, and other medical tools that could detect with accuracy germs that caused infectious diseases such as tuberculosis, gonorrhea, dysentery, the black plague, cholera, and pneumonia. See Choe Gyu-jin, *Geundaereul boneun chang 20* [Twenty windows on modernity] (Seoul: Seohaemunjip, 2007), 118.

67. Nancy Tomes, "Epidemic Entertainments: Disease and Popular Culture in Early-Twentieth Century America," *American Literary History* 14, no. 2 (Winter 2002): 629.

68. *Joseon ilbo*, May 18, 1934.

69. Erving Goffman, *Stigma: Notes on the Management of Spoiled Identity* (New York: Prentice-Hall, 1963), 3.

70. Richard C. Keller, *Colonial Madness: Psychiatry in French North Africa* (Chicago: University of Chicago Press, 2007), 55.

71. Ibid.

72. See Liah Greenfeld, *Mind, Modernity, Madness: The Impact of Culture on Human Experience* (Cambridge, MA: Harvard University Press, 2013); Louis A. Sass, *Madness and Modernism: Insanity in the Light of Modern Art, Literature, and Thought* (Cambridge, MA: Harvard University Press, 1994); Vieda Skultans, *English Madness: Ideas on Insanity, 1580–1890* (Piscataway, NJ: Routledge and Kegan Paul, 1979); Allen Thiher, *Revels in Madness: Insanity in Medicine and Literature* (Ann Arbor: University of Michigan Press, 1999).

73. James C. Scott, *Domination and the Arts of Resistance: Hidden Transcripts* (New Haven, CT: Yale University Press, 1992).

74. Schneider, "AHR Conversation," 1490.

75. Ellie Choi, "Introduction to 'From Tokyo to Seoul' (Tonggyŏng eso Kyŏngsŏng kkaji, 1917) and 'Record of Travels in the Diamond Mounts' (Kumgangsan yugi, 1922)," *Azaelea: Journal of Korean Literature and Culture* 4 (2011): 330.

76. Eve Kosofsky Sedgwick preferred the term *male homosocial desire* to another of its cognates, *homoeroticism*. As Jason Edwards observes, "As a phrase, 'male homosocial desire' might, like 'homoerotic,' contain and foreground the idea of *desire,* rather than say, *identification,* within relations between men." See Jason Edwards, *Eve Kosofsky Sedgwick* (New York: Routledge, 2009), 37; Eve Kosofsky Sedgwick, *Between Men: English Literature and Male Homosocial Desire* (New York: Columbia University Press, 1985); Eve Kosofsky Sedwick, *Epistemology of the Close*t (Berkeley: University of California Press, 1990).

77. Yi Kwang-su, "Maybe Love (Ai ka, 1909)," trans. John Whittier Treat, *Azalea: Journal of Korean Literature and Culture* 4, no. 1 (2011): 321–27.

78. John Whittier Treat, "Introduction to Yi Kwang-su's 'Maybe Love' (Ai ka, 1909)," *Azalea: Journal of Korean Literature and Culture* 4, no. 1 (2011): 315–20; Yi Kwang-su, "Maybe Love," 321–27.

79. Soonsik Kim, *Colonial and Postcolonial Discourse in the Novels of Yom Sangsop, Chinua Achebe, and Salman Rushdie* (New York: Peter Lang, 2004), 36.

80. Yeom Sang-seop, *Pyobonsil ui cheong gaeguri* [The green frog in the specimen room] (Seoul: Sodam chulpansa, 1995).

81. Uchang Kim, "Extravagance and Authenticity: Romantic Love and the Self in Early Modern Korean Literature," *Korea Journal* 39, no. 4 (Winter 1999): 81.

82. Peter Lee, introduction to Lee, *Modern Korean Literature*, 49.

83. Henry Em, "Yi Sang's 'Wings' Read as an Anti-colonial Allegory," *muae: a journal of transcultural production* 1 (1995): 105.

84. Ibid., 107.

85. Yi Sang, "Nalgae" [Wings], trans. Walter K. Lew and Youngju Ryu, in *Modern Korean Fiction: An Anthology,* ed. Bruce Fulton and Youngmin Kwon (New York: Columbia University Press, 2005), 83.

86. Em, "Yi Sang's 'Wings,'" 109.

87. Hyeon Jin-geon Jungdanpyeonseon, "Sarip jeongsin byeongwonjang" [The director of the private mental hospital], in *Unsu joeun nal*, 193.

88. Ibid., 199.

89. Ibid., 202.

90. Ibid., 203.

91. Hyeon Jin-geon, "Bul" [Fire], in *Unsu joeun nal*, 173–83.

92. Hyŏn Chin-gŏn (Hyeon Jin-geon), "Fire," in *Flowers of Fire: Twentieth-Century Stories*, ed. Peter Lee (Honolulu: University of Hawaii Press, 1974), 8–9. Subsequent citations from this story are to this translation and are given parenthetically in the text.

93. Ahn Byung sup, "Humor in Korean Cinema," *East-West Film Journal* 2, no. 1 (December 1989): 90–98.

94. One *ri* is equivalent to five hundred meters.

95. Arlie R. Hochschild, *The Managed Heart: Commercialization of Human Feeling* (Berkeley: University of California Press, 2003), 27.

96. Kim Jong-won and Jeong Jung-heon, *Uri yeonghwa 100-nyeon* [100 years of Korean film] (Seoul: Hyeonamsa, 2000), 112–21.

97. Jo Hae-mun, *Na Un-gyu* (Seoul: Hangilsa, 1997), 160.

98. Ibid., 147–71.

99. *Joseon ilbo*, October 1, 1926.

100. Ibid.

4. MADNESS AS A SOCIAL EPIDEMIC

The chapter's two epigraphs are from Kim Gi-rim's "Hangang indogyo" [Han River Footbridge], in *Kim Gi-rim jeonjip* [The complete works of Kim Gi-rim], vol. 1 (Seoul: Namseoldang, 1988), 101, and Émile Durkheim's *On Suicide*, trans. Robin Buss (New York: Penguin Books, 2006), 19.

1. *Donga ilbo*, June 27, 1925.

2. *Joseon ilbo*, January 16, 1923; *Donga ilbo*, December 18, 1930.

3. *Donga ilbo*, December 6, 1930.

4. *Maeil sinbo*, May 1, 1932.

5. *Joseon ilbo*, May 3, 1928.

6. *Maeil sinbo*, September 1, 1932.

7. *Maeil sinbo*, September 3, 1932.

8. Yi Bang-hyeon, "Ilje sidae sinmun e natanan jeongsin jilhwanja sahoe pyosang" [The social representation of people with mental disorders who appeared in newspaper articles during Japanese colonial rule] (PhD diss., Ewha Womans University, 2010), ix–x.

9. *Donga ilbo*, July 5, 1926.

10. *Joseon ilbo*, May 6, 1933.

11. *Maeil sinbo*, May 31, 1935.

12. *Donga ilbo,* April 28, 1934.
13. *Joseon ilbo,* December 21, 1934.
14. *Joseon ilbo,* April 9, 1937.
15. *Donga ilbo,* December 5, 1928.
16. *Maeil sinbo,* August 2, 1936.
17. *Maeil sinbo,* October 6, 1937.
18. *Maeil sinbo,* November 12, 1933.
19. *Donga ilbo,* May 7, 1928.
20. *Joseon ilbo,* March 31, 1928.
21. *Donga ilbo,* November 23, 1926.
22. *Donga ilbo,* January 9, 1925.
23. *Maeil sinbo,* May 18, 1933; September 11, 1935; February 26, 1936; January 13, 1938; *Donga ilbo,* February 5, 1932.
24. *Donga ilbo,* October 23, 1925.
25. *Donga ilbo,* November 16, 1925.
26. *Donga ilbo,* October 23, 1925.
27. *Donga ilbo,* February 9, 1934.
28. *Joseon ilbo,* July 7, 1929.
29. *Donga ilbo,* September 15, 1931.
30. *Donga ilbo,* July 26, 1931.
31. *Joseon ilbo,* May 13, 1927.
32. *Joseon ilbo,* April 17, 1924.
33. *Joseon ilbo,* December 19, 1927.
34. For the colonial authorities, the susceptibility to and prevalence of communicable and contagious diseases like cholera, tuberculosis, and leprosy (also called Hansen's disease) in the urban centers became more urgent as enforcing sanitation and hygiene in the colony became a top priority. With very few doctors trained in Western medicine, the state relied on a pervasive police force to monitor the Infectious Disease Prevention Act enacted in 1915, to administer all vaccination campaigns, to impose quarantine measures on ships and trains, to inspect restaurants, and to carry out "house inspections," often collecting samples of feces and urine from household members. See Yun-jae Park, "Sanitizing Korea: Anti-cholera Activities of the Police in Early Colonial Korea," *Seoul Journal of Korean Studies* 23, no. 2 (2010): 151–71.
35. *Maeil sinbo,* September 26, 1930.
36. *Donga ilbo,* December 16, 1930.
37. *Joseon ilbo,* July 8, 1939.
38. Emil Kraepelin and Allen Ross Diefendorf, *Clinical Psychiatry: A Textbook for Students and Physicians* (New York: Macmillan, 1915), 115–16.
39. *Joseon ilbo,* April 12, 1935.
40. *Maeil sinbo,* September 26, 1930.
41. *Joseon ilbo,* April 12, 1925.
42. *Donga ilbo,* December 16, 1930.
43. *Maeil sinbo,* July 13, 1934.

44. George Beard, "Neurasthenia or Nervous Exhaustion," *Boston Medical and Surgical Journal* 3, no. 13 (April 1869): 217–18.

45. Bak Tae-won, *Soseolga Gubossi ui iril* [A day in the life of Gubo the novelist] (Seoul: Munhakgwajiseongsa, 2005). See also Jo Yi-dam, *Gubossiwa deobureo gyeong-seong eul gada* [Accompanying Gubo around Seoul] (Seoul: Baram Gudu, 2005).

46. *Joseon ilbo,* April 12, 1935; *Joseon ilbo,* July 8, 1939.

47. *Donga ilbo,* April 22, 1924; *Maeil sinbo,* September 26, 1930.

48. *Donga ilbo,* August 14, 1933.

49. *Maeil sinbo,* March 26, 1930.

50. *Maeil sinbo,* June 8, 1926.

51. Michael Staub, *Madness Is Civilization* (Chicago: University of Chicago Press, 2011), 15.

52. *Donga ilbo,* March 25, 1933.

53. *Joseon ilbo,* June 21, 1926.

54. *Joseon ilbo,* April 8, 1934.

55. *Joseon ilbo,* April 12, 1935.

56. *Maeil sinbo,* April 1, 1932.

57. *Maeil sinbo,* October 11, 1930; October 15, 1932.

58. *Donga ilbo,* December 14, 1930.

59. *Maeil sinbo,* September 21, 1935.

60. *Joseon ilbo,* March 13, 1932.

61. Junko Kitanaka, *Depression in Japan: Psychiatric Cures for a Society in Distress* (Princeton, NJ: Princeton University Press, 2012), 57–65. See also Susan Burns, "Constructing the National Body: Public Health and the Nation in Nineteenth-Century Japan," in *Nation Work: Asian Elites and National Identities,* ed. Timothy Brook and Andre Schmid (Ann Arbor: University of Michigan Press, 2000), 17–49.

62. Yi Bu-yeong, "Iljeha jeongsin gwa jinryowa geu byeoncheon: Joseon chongdokbu uiwon ui jeongsingwa jinryo reul (1913–1928) jungsimeuro" [Psychiatric care and its change under the Japanese government in Korea with special reference to the clinical activities at the Colonial Governmental Hospital, 1913–28], *Uisahak* 3, no. 2 (1994): 163.

63. For a discussion of hysteria more generally, see Phyllis Chesler, *Women and Madness,* 3rd ed. (New York: Four Walls Eight Windows, 1997), 93.

64. "Jinchalsil eseo bon nocheonyeo wa 'hiseutaeri': neomu neujeun kyeolhon ui hae" [Seen from a doctor's office: An old maid and hysteria; the dangers of getting too old], *Byeolgeongon* 19 (February 1, 1929).

65. *Donga ilbo,* January 30, 1926.

66. *Maeil sinbo,* September 4, 1941.

67. Bak Jong-seong, *Sarang hada jukda: Jeongsa ui jeongchihak* [To love, to die: The politics of love suicides] (Seoul: Ingan sarang, 2012), 156–57.

68. Ibid., 83–85; Jeong Gu-seong, *Joseon ui memento mori: Joseon i beorin jadeul ui jugeum eul gieok hara* [Memento mori: Remembering the deaths of those who were discarded by the Joseon dynasty] (Seoul: Aepeulbuksu, 2010), 1–15; Min Seong-

gil, *Hwabyeong yeongu* [A study of fire illness] (Seoul: Emel keomyunikeisyeon, 2009), 16–18.

69. Unlike the *mobyeong* (paid recruits of the central army), the *sogogun* were privately funded local militias composed mainly of commoners and *nobi* (slaves).

70. Na Yeong-in, "Jasal gwa chŏngsin jilhwan, geurigo joseon ui geundaehwa" [Suicide and mental illness, and Korea's modernization], *Seoul Daehak Sinmun*, March 17, 2012.

71. Ibid.

72. Bak Jong-seong, *Sarang hada jukda*, 83–87.

73. The number of "filial sons" and loyal subjects was 78; that of women who committed suicide to preserve their chastity was 356. See Compilation for the History of Korean Women, *Women of Korea: A History from Ancient Times to 1845*, trans. Yun-Chung Kim (Seoul: Ewha Womans University Press, 1976), 104–5.

74. Kitanaka, *Depression in Japan*, 41.

75. Ian Marsh, *Suicide: Foucault, History and Truth* (Cambridge: Cambridge University Press, 2010), 220.

76. Chōsen Sōtokufu, *Chōsen jinkō genshō* [Population phenomena of Korea] (Keijō, 1926), 422–30.

77. Ibid.

78. *Donga ilbo*, June 27, 1925.

79. Chōsen Sōtokufu, *Chōsen jinkō genshō*, 442–430.

80. Howard Kushner, "Suicide, Gender and the Fear of Modernity in Nineteenth-Century Medical and Social Thought," *Journal of Social History* 26, no. 3 (Spring 1993): 464.

81. Ibid.

82. Christian Goeschel, *Suicide in Nazi Germany* (Oxford: Oxford University Press, 2009), 47.

83. *Donga ilbo*, December 31, 1924.

84. *Donga ilbo*, August 18, 1927.

85. *Donga ilbo*, October 29, 1929.

86. *Donga ilbo*, May 6, 1923.

87. *Donga ilbo*, November 14, 1921; December 28, 1921; May 13, 1922; June 18, 1923; September 24, 1923; October 26, 1923; October 30, 1923; April 28, 1925; November 12, 1928.

88. For examples of sensational headlines such as "Is It Homicide or Suicide?," see *Donga ilbo*, February 22, 1924; February 25, 1924; August 3, 1924; September 3, 1925.

89. While utilizing newspapers can be problematic because of sensational yellow journalism, rumor-mongering, and lack of consistent verification of data, newspapers supplement official information with the kinds of reports of individual cases that are graphic and opinion-shaping.

90. Yi Yeong-a, "1920 nyeondae soseol ui 'jasal' hyeongsanghwa yangsang yeongu" [A study on the figurative methods and meanings of 'suicide' in 1920s novels], *Hanguk hyeondae munhak yeongu* 33 (April 2011): 207–48.

91. *Donga ilbo*, July 2, 1920.

92. Kim Gi-rim, "Hangang indogyo" [Han River Footbridge], in *Kim Gi-rim jeonjip* [The complete works of Kim Gi-rim], vol. 1 (Seoul: Namseoldang, 1988), 101.

93. *Donga ilbo,* July 28, 1921.

94. *Donga ilbo,* May 16, 1922.

95. *Donga ilbo,* August 18, 1923.

96. *Donga ilbo,* March 1, 1925.

97. *Donga ilbo,* May 12, 1928.

98. *Donga ilbo,* October 27, 1927.

99. *Donga ilbo,* May 28, 1923.

100. One pill company peddled a popular medicine (*machisu*) by promising that it was very effective in curing neurasthenia. See *Donga ilbo,* May 18, 1923.

101. *Donga ilbo,* October 5, 1926.

102. *Donga ilbo,* June 19, 1922.

103. *Donga ilbo,* August 5, 1926.

104. Quoted in Lisa Lieberman, *Leaving You: The Cultural Meaning of Suicide* (Chicago: Ivan R. Dee, 2003), 34–35.

105. Émile Durkheim, *The Division of Labor in Society,* trans. W. D. Halls (New York: Free Press, 1984), 201–12.

106. *Donga ilbo,* June 20, 1923.

107. *Donga ilbo* May 15, 1921.

108. *Jung-oe ilbo,* November 14, 1929; *Sidae ilbo,* May 15, 1924; *Donga ilbo,* March 8, 1922; February 25, 1924; November 18, 1924; April 13, 1925; July 30, 1926; February 22, 1927; March 17, 1928; March 25, 1928.

109. *Donga ilbo,* May 15, 1924.

110. *Donga ilbo,* January 4, 1925.

111. *Donga ilbo,* July 22, 1920.

112. *Donga ilbo,* July 3, 1924.

113. *Donga ilbo,* June 18, 1923.

114. *Donga ilbo,* June 4, 1924.

115. *Donga ilbo,* December 15, 1925.

116. *Donga ilbo,* August 25, 1925.

117. Ibid.

118. *Donga ilbo,* April 10, 1923; June 15, 1923; March 1, 1925; June 9, 1927.

119. *Donga ilbo,* April 13, 1925; July 7, 1927; October 10, 1928, March 4, 1929.

120. Fred Block and Margaret Somers, "Beyond the Economic Fallacy: The Holistic Social Science of Karl Polanyi," in *Visions and Methods in Historical Sociology,* ed. Theda Skocpol (Cambridge: Cambridge University Press, 1984), 56.

121. Ibid.

122. *Donga ilbo,* April 23, 1928.

123. Cho Myeong-hui, "Nongchon saramdeul" [Rural people], *Hyeondae Pyeongron,* November 1926, www.seelotus.com/gojeon/hyeon-dae/soseol/bonmun/-%EC%A1%B0%EB%AA%85%ED%9D%AC-%EB%86%8D%EC%B4%8C%EC%82%AC%EB%9E%8C%EB%93%A4.htm. See also Yi Yeong-a, "1920 nyeondae soseol ui 'jasal' hyeongsanghwa yangsang yeongu."

124. Na Do-hyang, "Mullae bang-a" [Watermill], *Joseon mundan*, September 1925, http://snsj7537.com.ne.kr/ssol/380.htm. See also Yi Yeong-a, "1920 nyeondae soseol ui 'jasal' hyeongsanghwa yangsang yeongu."

125. *Donga ilbo,* June 1, 1925.

126. *Donga ilbo,* August 23, 1924.

127. *Donga ilbo,* August 3, 1926.

128. *Donga ilbo,* March 1, 1925.

129. *Donga ilbo,* January 6, 1927.

130. *Maeil sinbo,* October 22, 1928; April 24, 1929.

131. *Donga ilbo,* December 16, 1925; May 14, 1926.

132. *Donga ilbo,* June 1, 1922; August 23, 1924; February 24, 1925; June 1, 1925; July 18, 1926; December 14, 1926; July 30, 1927; May 16, 1928; June 6, 1928; May 31, 1929; November 30, 1929.

133. See, e.g., *Jung-oe ilbo,* May 23, 1927; *Donga ilbo,* November 25, 1926.

134. *Donga ilbo,* September 26, 1925.

135. *Donga ilbo,* July 25, 1926.

136. *Donga ilbo,* July 16, 1926.

137. *Donga ilbo,* March 1, 1929.

138. *Donga ilbo,* May 21, 1921; August 7, 1921; August 13, 1921; November 4, 1921; July 13, 1922; February 7, 1922; August 31, 1923; June 17, 1925; September 26, 1925; November 30, 1927; February 24, 1928; August 24, 1928; July 13, 1929.

139. *Donga ilbo,* September 15, 1924.

140. While gambling debt appeared to cause self-destructive behavior among men, cases of spouses taking their own lives because of their husbands' gambling also appeared regularly in the press. See *Donga ilbo,* February 8, 1929.

141. James Scott, *Weapons of the Weak: Everyday Forms of Peasant Resistance* (New Haven, CT: Yale University Press, 1985), 1–24.

142. *Donga ilbo,* July 13, 1934.

143. *Donga ilbo,* May 28, 1924.

144. *Donga ilbo,* March 30, 1925.

145. *Donga ilbo,* May 14, 1924.

146. *Donga ilbo,* May 19, 1922.

147. *Donga ilbo,* July 24, 1923.

148. Kim Dong-in, "Jeonjeja" [The despot], *Gaebyeok,* March 1, 1921, https://ko.wikisource.org/wiki/%EC%A0%84%EC%A0%9C%EC%9E%90.

149. *Donga ilbo,* October 7, 1926.

150. *Donga ilbo,* November 26, 1926.

151. *Donga ilbo,* January 29, 1923.

152. *Donga ilbo,* July 21, 1924.

153. *Donga ilbo,* June 23, 1926.

154. Lieberman, *Leaving You,* x.

155. *Donga ilbo,* October 2, 1921; May 25, 1922, March 2, 1923; May 12, 1924; December 12, 1924; August 29, 1925; December 9, 1926.

156. Song Hyeon-ho, *Hyeondae soseol ui haeseol* [Commentary on Korean fiction] (Seoul: Gwangdong chulpansa, 1992), 71–75.

157. Lieberman, *Leaving You*, 5.

158. *Donga ilbo*, February 4, 1923.

159. *Donga ilbo*, November 19, 1924.

160. *Donga ilbo*, August 23, 1924.

161. *Donga ilbo*, August 5, 1926. In Johan Wolfgang von Goethe's epistolary novel *The Sorrows of Young Werther*, the protagonist Werther commits suicide in a romantic manner that subsequently inspired a wave of imitative suicides.

162. Bak Jong-seong, *Sarang hada jukda*, 156–57.

163. *Joseon ilbo*, September 27–29, 1933.

164. Kim Gi-jin, "Jeolmeun isangjuuija ui jugeum" [The death of the youthful idealist], *Gaebyeok*, June-July 1925.

165. *Donga ilbo*, December 11, 1925.

166. *Donga ilbo*, June 15, 1923.

167. Hyeon Jin-geon, "Geuribeun heulgin nun" [Yearning for his scowling eyes], *Pyeheoihu*, January 1924, http://nocopyright.tistory.com/105.

168. Yi Yeong-a, "Nuga deo mullanhanga?" [Who is more promiscuous?], *Joongang ilbo*, December 8, 2011.

169. *Donga ilbo*, August 3, 1922.

170. *Donga ilbo*, April 30, 1925. Likewise, for Chang Chi-lo, a fifty-or-so-year-old former bar girl, unhappiness about her life led to despair, then mental illness, then suicide by hanging. *Donga ilbo*, January 21, 1924; April 4, 1922.

171. *Joseon ilbo*, March 29, 1928.

172. *Joseon ilbo*, August 17, 1926.

173. *Donga ilbo*, September 6, 1925.

174. *Donga ilbo*, February 13, 1922.

175. *Donga ilbo*, September 23, 1926.

176. *Donga ilbo*, November 21, 1926.

177. *Donga ilbo*, October 15, 1929.

178. *Donga ilbo*, June 30, 1925.

179. Yi Bang-hyeon, "Ilje sidae sinmun ae natanan jeongsin jilhwanja sahoe pyosang," 42–43.

180. Marsh, *Suicide*, 4.

CONCLUSION

The chapter epigraphs are from Michel Foucault, "Je suis un artificier" [interview, 1975], in *Michel Foucault, Entretiens*, ed. Roger-Pol Droit (Paris: Odile Jacobs, 2004), 95, and Ian Hacking, "The Looping Effects of Human Kinds," in *Causal Cognition*, ed. Dan Sperber, David Premack, and Ann James Premack (Oxford: Clarendon Press, 1995), 369.

1. The story discussed in this chapter is from Jeon Bong-gwan, "Jukcheomjeong dandu yua sageon" [The case of the decapitated infant in Jukcheomjeong], *Sin Donga* 544 (November 2005): 540–53; it was republished in Jeon Bong-gwan, *Gyeongseong gidam* [Strange stories from Seoul] (Seoul: Sallim, 2006), 12–47.

2. Maurice Blanchot, "Everyday Speech," trans. Susan Hanson, *Yale French Studies* 73 (1987): 12.

3. "1930 nyeondae gyeongseong georireul geotda, 'gyeongseonggidam' ui Jeon Bong-gwan gyosu" [Walking the streets of 1930s Seoul: Professor Jeon Bong-gwan's *Strange Stories from Seoul*], *Chaeneol yeseu*, accessed July 17, 2014, http://ch.yes24.com/Article/View/12947?Scode=050_002.

4. *Donga ilbo*, May 17, 1933; *Joseon ilbo*, May 18, 1933.

5. Despite the hygiene police's altruistic claims to be safeguarding public health and efforts to isolate dangerous individuals from society, there was still much skepticism toward modern medicine among Koreans, who continued to associate disturbing behavior with malignant spirits and harbingers of evil, disease, and death. Even by the late 1930s, despite numerous campaigns by the colonial state to end superstitious practices, Koreans continued to consult the *mudang* (shaman), hold a *gut* (exorcism), and carry out customary practices such as planting cockscombs, sprinkling red beans or hanging red peppers around their homes to ward off evil spirits, and hiding the afflicted in the mountains. See Choe Gyu-jin, *Geundae reul boneun chang* 20 [Twenty windows on modernity] (Seoul: Seohaemunjip), 116.

6. Jeon Bong-gwan, *Gyeongseong gidam*, 16.

7. *Donga ilbo*, March 11, 1922.

8. *Donga ilbo*, November 26, 1924.

9. Kudō Takeki, "Chōsen fujin eiji satsugai no fujin kagakuteki kōsatsu" [A scientific study of Korean women and infanticide], *Chōsen* 4 (February 1930): 27–50.

10. Newspapers used the terms *jeongsin byeongja* (mental illness), *jeonsin isang* (mental disorder), and *jeongsin jilhwan* (mental disease) interchangeably.

11. Yi Bu-yeong, "Hanguk eseo ui seoyang jeongsin uihak 100-nyeon, 1899–1999" [A hundred years of psychiatry in Korea, 1899–1999], *Uisahak* 8, no. 2 (December 1999): 160–61.

12. *Joseon ilbo*, January 17, 1926; Park Yun-jae, "Sanitizing Korea: Anti-cholera Activities of the Police in Early Colonial Korea," *Seoul Journal of Korean Studies* 23, no. 2 (2010): 151–57.

13. *Joseon ilbo*, January 17, 1926.

14. Yi Bu-yeong, "Iljeha jeongsin gwa jinryowa geu byeoncheon—joseon chongdokbu uiwon ui jeongsingwa jinryo (1913–1928) reul jungsimeuro," [Psychiatric care and its change under the Japanese government in Korea with special reference to the clinical activities at the Colonial Governmental Hospital, 1913–28], *Uisahak* 3, no. 2 (1994): 164–66.

15. In some respects, this case paralleled another sensational murder case reported in the *Donga ilbo* about ten years earlier on January 11, 1923, of a Korean resident who went on a rampage in Tokyo killing seventeen Japanese bystanders.

Although the police quickly arrested the perpetrator, he was later acquitted in a public trial on the grounds of insanity.

16. Ramon H. Myers and Mark R. Peattie, eds., *The Japanese Colonial Empire, 1895–1945* (Princeton, NJ: Princeton University Press, 1984), 222.

17. Chōsen sōtokufu, *Shisei nijūgo nenshi* [The twenty-five-year history of the administration of Korea] (Keijō, 1935), 33–35.

18. Chulwoo Lee, "Modernity, Legality, and Power," in *Colonial Modernity in Korea*, ed. Gi-Wook and Michael Robinson (Cambridge, MA: Harvard University Asian Center, 1999), 37–38.

19. Park Yun-jae, "Sanitizing Korea"; Han Ji-won, *Joseon chongdokbu uiryo minjokjireul tonghae bon wisaeng pungseup yeongu* [A study of the Government-General of Joseon's medical ethnography on hygienic customs] (Seoul: Minsokwon, 2013), 42–58.

20. C. Lee, "Modernity, Legality, and Power," 37; Park Yun-jae, "Sanitizing Korea," 164.

21. *Donga ilbo*, June 3, 1933.

22. Ibid.

23. Ibid.

24. *Joseon ilbo*, June 4, 1933.

25. Yi Bu-yeong, "Hanguk geundae cheongsin uihak ui yeoksajeok jomyeong: ilje eseo hanguk dongran ijeon kkaji" [Historical review of modern Korean psychiatry: From the colonial period up to the Korean war], symposium celebrating the tenth-year anniversary of Seoul National University Hospital, *Seoul uidae jeongsin uihak* 14, no. 1 (1989): 18–20; Yi Bu-yeong, "Hanguk eseo ui seoyang jeongsin uihak 100-nyeon, 1899–1999," 162–64.

26. Enoch Lambert, "Hacking and Human Kinds," *Aporia* 16, no. 1 (2006): 52.

27. *Donga ilbo*, June 9, 1933.

28. *Joseon ilbo*, June 8, 1933.

GLOSSARY

AKAMATSU CHIJŌ	赤松 智城
AKIBA TAKASHI	秋葉 隆
AMAE	甘え
ARIRANG	아리랑
BAK CHE-GA	朴齊家
BAK TAE-WON	朴泰遠
BAKSU	박수
BALBYEONG WONIN	發病 原因
BALGWANG	發狂
BALHWAGWANG	發火狂
BALJAK	發作
BANGNYEON	芳年
BANYEOK JOEIN	反逆罪人
BIGWAN	悲觀
BOEMIN	犯人
BONYEON JISEONG	本然之性
BOTONG SARAM	보통 사람
BUDAM	負擔
BULSSANG HAN MAEUM	불쌍한 마음
BUN	忿
BUNNO	忿怒
BYEOLGEONGON	別坤乾
BYEOLSIN GUT	別神 굿
BYEONG	病

BYEONG GUT	病 굿
BYEONSA	變死
CHAE MAN-SIK	蔡萬植
CHANGPI	猖披
CHAU YUANFANG	巢元方
CHEMYEON	體面
CHEOGA SARI	妻家살이
CHIJEONG	癡情
CHIMGUPYEON	鍼灸篇
CHIN	親
CHO MYEONG-HUI	趙明熙
CHOE HAN-GI	崔漢綺
CHOE NAM-SEON	崔南善
CHŌSEN IGAKUKAI ZASSHI	朝鮮醫學會雜誌
CHŌSEN SŌTOKUFU	朝鮮総督府
CHŌSEN SŌTOKUFU IIN	朝鮮総督府醫院
CHUKGWI	逐鬼
CHULGA OEIN	出嫁外人
CHUSEOK	秋夕
CHWIBARI	취바리
DAEDONGGANG	大同江
DAEHAN JEGUK	大韓帝國
DAEHAN UIWON	大韓醫院
DANGUN	檀君
DIAN	癲
DIANKUANG	癲狂
DONGA ILBO	東亞日報
DONGDAEMUN	東大門
DONGPALHO SIL	東八戶室
DONG-UI BOGAM	東醫寶鑑
EOGEUL	抑鬱
EUM	陰
FENG	瘋
FENGDIAN	瘋癲
FENGKUANG	瘋狂

GAEBYEOK	開闢
GAESEONG	個性
GAICHI	外地
GAJEONG GAMCHI	家庭 監置
GAMSI	監視
GANFENG	肝風
GASA	歌詞
GEUNSIM	근심
GI	氣
GIDAM	奇談
GISAENG	妓生
GOBONG GI DAE-SEUNG	高峯 奇大升
GOBU GALDEUNG	姑婦葛藤
GOJONG	高宗
GOJOSEON	古朝鮮
GONG XIA PAI	攻下派
GONGMIN WANG	恭愍王
GONGPO	恐怖
GOPURI	고풀이
GORYEO	高麗
GOSAENG	苦生
GOSU	鼓手
GUBO-SSI	丘甫氏
GUT	굿
GUGEUM	拘禁
GWANGHAE-GUN	光海君
GWANGHYEWON	廣惠院
GWANG-IN	狂人
GWANGJEUNG	狂症
GWANGJEWON	廣濟院
GWANGPOKSEONG	狂爆聲
GWANGTAE	狂態
GWONSEON JINGAK	勸善懲惡
GYEOGNI	隔離
GYEOKHWA	激化

GYEONGGI	京畿
GYEONGGUK DAEJEON	經國大典
GYEONGSEONG	京城
GYEONGSEONG JEGUK DAEHAK	京城帝國大學
GYEONGSEONG UIHAK JEONMUN HAKGYO	京城醫學專門學校
HACHEUNGMIN	下層民
HAGYEON	學緣
HAMGYEONG-DO	咸鏡道
HAN	恨
HANGANG	한강
HANJUNGNOK	閑(恨)中錄
HANPURI	恨풀이
HANSEONG SUNBO	漢城旬報]
HASOYEON	하소연
HEO GYUN	許筠
HEO JUN	許浚
HEOYAK	虛弱
HISASHI-GAMI	庇髮
HISEUTERI	히스테리
HONG GIL-DONG	洪吉同
HONG MAN-SEON	洪萬選
HONGMUNGWAN	弘文館
HUANGDI NEIJING	黃帝內經
HUCHEONJEOK	後天的
HWA	火
HWABYEONG	火病
HWAJEUNG	火症
HWANGHAE-DO	黃海道
HWANGJE NAEGYEONG	黃帝內經
HWARANG	花郎
HWATU	花鬪
HYANGYAK GUGEUPBANG	鄕藥救急方
HYANGYAK JIPSEONBANG	鄕藥集成方
HYEOL	穴
HYEORYEON	血緣

HYEON JIN-GEON	玄鎭健
HYEONJONG	顯宗
HYEONMO YANGCHEO	賢母良妻
HYO	孝
ILCHEGAM	일체감
ILLYUN	人倫
ILSANG UI GONGGAN	일상의 공간
IMJIN WAERAN	壬辰倭亂
INDARI	인다리
INHYEONG-GEUK	人形劇
INJO	仁祖
INSU DAEBI	仁粹大妃
ISANG	異常
ITAKO	イタコ
JA A	自我
JAEBAL	再發
JAKYEOL	自決
JANGCHUNGDAN GONGWON	獎忠壇公園
JANGMA	장마
JAPBYEONGPYEON	雜病篇
JAPGI	雜記
JASAL	自殺
JASALJA	自殺者
JAYEON SUNEUNG	自然順應
JEJEUNGWON	濟衆院
JEOGORI	저고리
JEOLLA	全羅
JEOM	占
JEON	錢
JEONG	情
JEONG YAK-YONG	丁若鏞
JEONGJONG	定宗
JEONGSA	情死
JEONGSANG	正常
JEONGSIN	精神

JEONGSIN BYEONG	精神病
JEONGSIN BYEONGJA	精神病者
JEONGSIN ISANG	精神異狀
JEONGSIN JILHWAN	精神疾患
JEONGSIN SORAN	精神騷亂
JEONGSINGWA	精神科
JEONGWANG	癲狂
JESAENGWON	濟生院
JEUNG	症
JEUNGSANG	症狀
JING LUO	經絡
JIRAL	지랄
JOBALSEONG CHIMAE	早發性癡呆
JOECHAEKGAM	罪責感
JOGWANGSEONG	躁狂性
JONGNO	鍾路
JOSEON	朝鮮
JOSEON ILBO	朝鮮日報
JOSEON UIBO	朝鮮醫報
JOSEON WANGJO SILLOK	朝鮮王朝
JUGWANG	酒狂
JUNG	중
JUNGJONG	中宗
JUSUL CHIRYO	呪術治療
KEIJŌ	京城
KIM CHOE-SEON	金處善
KIM DONG-IN	金東仁
KIM GI-RIM	金起林
KINNOSUKE MIURA	三浦謹之助
KUANG	狂
KUBO KIYOJI	久保喜代二
KUCHIYOSE	口寄せ
KUDŌ TAKEKI	工藤武城
KURE SHŪZŌ	呉秀三
LI	禮

LI CHAN	李梴
LI DONGYUAN	李東垣
LINSHU	靈樞
LIU WANSU	劉完素
MADANG	마당
MAEIL SINBO	每日申報
MA-EUM	마음
MANSEONG	慢性
MICHIN NOM	미친 놈
MICHIN YEOJA	미친 여자
MINMYEONEURI	민며느리
MINYO	民謠
MISIN	迷信
MISIN TAPA	迷信打破
MISU	未遂
MIUM	미움
MOJEONG	母情
MOKJONG	穆宗
MORITA SHOMA	森田正馬
MOYOK	侮辱
MURAYAMA CHIJUN	村山智順
MUDANG	巫堂
MUGIRYEOK	無氣力
MUGU	巫具
MUGWAN-NANG	武官郎
MUNHWA	文化
MUNYEO	巫女
MUSOK	巫俗
MYEONGJONG	明宗
NA	나
NA DO-HYANG	羅稻香
NA UN-GYU	羅雲奎
NAEGYEONGPYEON	內景篇
NAERIM GUT	내림굿
NAICHI	內地

NAM	남
NANCHI	難治
NINJO	人情
NOK-JIN	祿眞
NONG AK	農樂
NORYANGJIN	鷺梁津
NUNCHI	눈치
OEHYEONGPYEON	外形篇
OKCHUGYEONG	玉樞經
PAEGA MANGSIN	敗家亡身
PAESEOL	稗說
PALJA	八字
PANSORI	판소리
PI WEI LUN	脾胃論
PPURI	뿌리
PUDAKGEORI	푸닥거리
PUNGGWANG	瘋狂
PUNGJEON	瘋癲
PYEHEO	廢墟
PYEONG	坪
PYEONGAN	平安
PYEONGYANG	平壤
QI	氣
RUMPEN	룸펜
RYŪGAKU	留學
SADAEBU	士大夫
SADAHAM	斯多含
SADAN CHILJEONG	四端七情
SADO SEJA	思悼世子
SAENGHWALGO	生活苦
SAISEIIN	濟生院
SAJIK GONGWON	社稷公園
SALPURI	煞풀이
SAMCHEOLLI	三千里
SAMGUK SAGI	三國史記

SAMJONG JIDO	三從之道
SANJIAO	三焦
SASANG UIHAK	四象醫學
SEISHIN BYŌIN HO	精神病院法
SEJO	世祖
SEJONG	世宗
SEODAEMUN	西大門
SEON JIN-TAE	孫晉泰
SEONCHEONJEOK	先天的
SEONG HYEON	成俔
SEONJO	宣祖
SHANGHAN LUN	傷寒論
SHIMPA	新派
SIAGWI	施餓鬼
SIDAE ILBO	時代日報
SILHAK	實學
SILJEONG	實情
SIM	心
SIM HO-SEOP	沈浩燮
SIMJEONG	心情
SIMJIL	心疾
SIN	神
SINBYEONG	神病
SINGYEONG SOEYAK	神經衰弱
SINGYEONGJIL	神經質
SOKDAM	俗談
SOROKDO	小鹿島
SUCHI	羞恥
SUGIHARA MANJIRŌ	杉原滿次郎
SUITSU SHINJI	水津信治
SUKJONG	肅宗
SULGA	術家
SULJARI	술자리
SUNGNYEMUN	숭례문
SUWEN	素問

TALCHUM	탈춤
TANGAEKPYEON	湯液篇
TOEGYE YI HWANG	退溪李滉
TŌKANFU	統監府
TUGANG	投江
UGYE SEONG HON	牛溪成渾
UI	義
UIBANG YUCHWI	醫方類聚
UIHAKGYO	醫學校
UISIM	疑心
UIWON-IN	醫院人
UJEONG	友情
ULBYEONG	鬱病
ULHWA	鬱火
ULJEUNG	鬱症
URI	우리
U-ULHAN SIMJEONG	憂鬱한 心情
U-ULJEUNG	憂鬱症
WANKWAE	完快
WATANABE MICHIO	渡┌美智雄
WISAENG	衛生
XIAOFA	消法
YADAM	野談
YANG	陽
YANGBAN	兩班
YANGMING	陽明
YANGQI	陽氣
YANGSAENG	養生
YEOLLYEO-JEON	列女傳
YEOM SANG-SEOP	廉想涉
YEOMSEJUUI	厭世主義
YEONGJO	英祖
YEONSAN-GUN	燕山君
YI GWANG-SU	李光洙
YI GYU-GYEONG	李圭景

YI IK	李瀷
YI JE-MA	李濟馬
YI JUNG-CHEOL	李重徹
YI NEUNG-HWA	李能和
YI PIL-HWA	李苾和
YI SANG	李箱
YIN	陰
YIXUE RUMEN	醫學入門
YONGCHITANG	龍齒湯
YONGSAN	龍山
YU HUI-CHUN	柳希春
YUHAKSAENG	留學生
YUKBAEK	六百
YULGOK YI I	栗谷李珥
ZHANG CONGZHENG	張從正
ZHANG ZONGJIN	張仲景
ZHU BING YUAN HOU LUN	諸病源候論
ZHU DANXI	朱丹溪
ZHU XI	朱熹

BIBLIOGRAPHY

Ahn, D. H., and B. Y. Rhi. "Community Leaders' Reaction to Mental Disorders." *Seoul Journal of Psychiatry* 11, no. 4 (1986): 281–93.

Ahn, Kyong-Whan. "Korean Legal System and the Human Rights of Persons with Mental Disorders: Current State and Challenges." *Journal of Korean Law* 7, no. 1 (2007): 1–23.

Ahn Byung Sup. "Humor in Korean Cinema." *East-West Film Journal* 2, no. 1 (December 1989): 90–98.

Alexander, Frantz G., and Sheldon T. Selesnick. *The History of Psychiatry: An Evaluation of Psychiatric Thought and Practice from Prehistoric Times to the Present.* New York: Harper and Row, 1966.

Allen, Horace Newton. "Medical Work in Korea." *Foreign Missionary* 44, no. 11 (July 1885): 74–76.

———. *Things Korean: A Collection of Sketches and Anecdotes, Missionary and Diplomatic.* New York: F. H. Revell, 1908.

American Psychiatric Association. *Diagnostic and Statistical Manual of Mental Disorders: Fifth Edition. DSM-5.* Arlington, VA: American Psychiatric Association, 2013.

Atkins, Taylor E. *Primitive Selves: Koreana in the Japanese Colonial Gaze.* Berkeley: University of California Press, 1910.

Avison, Oliver R. *Annual Report of the Imperial Korean Hospital.* Seoul: Methodist Publishing House, 1901.

Bak Jong-seong. *Sarang hada jukda: Jeongsa ui jeongchihak* [To love, to die: The politics of love suicides]. Seoul: Ingan sarang, 2012.

Bak Tae-won. *Soseolga Gubossi ui iril* [A day in the life of Gubo the novelist]. Seoul: Munhakgwajiseongsa, 2005.

Baker, Don. "Oriental Medicine in Korea." In *Medicine across Cultures: History and Practice of Medicine in Non-Western Cultures,* edited by Helaine Selin, 133–54. New York: Kluwer Academic Publishers, 2003.

Bakhtin, Mikhail. *Rabelais and His World.* Translated by Helene Iwolsky. Bloomington: Indiana University Press, 1984.

Bartholomew, James R. *The Formation of Science in Japan: Building a Research Tradition*. New Haven, CT: Yale University Press, 1989.
Beard, George. "Neurasthenia or Nervous Exhaustion." *Boston Medical and Surgical Journal* 3, no. 13 (April 1869): 217–18.
Bernheisel, Charles F. *The Apostolic Church as Reproduced in Korea*. New York: Board of Foreign Missions of the Presbyterian Church in the United States, 1912.
Berrios, German E. *The History of Mental Symptoms: Descriptive Psychopathology since the Nineteenth Century*. Cambridge: Cambridge University Press, 1996.
Blanchot, Maurice. "Everyday Speech." Translated by Susan Hanson. *Yale French Studies* 73 (1987): 12–20.
Block, Fred, and Margaret Somers. "Beyond the Economic Fallacy: The Holistic Social Science of Karl Polanyi." In *Visions and Methods in Historical Sociology*, edited by Theda Skocpol, 47–84. Cambridge: Cambridge University Press, 1984.
Bogeon bokjibu [Ministry of Health and Welfare]. Press release, February 15, 2012.
Bruno, Antonetta. *The Gates of Words: Language in the Rituals of Korean Shamans*. Leiden: CNWS, 2002.
Burns, Susan. "Constructing the National Body: Public Health and the Nation in Nineteenth-Century Japan." In *Nation Work: Asian Elites and National Identities*, edited by Timothy Brook and Andre Schmid, 17–49. Ann Arbor: University of Michigan Press, 2000.
Chae Man-sik. "Michin ideul ui nara, dongpalho sil jamipgi isang namnyeo sasip yeoin" [The land of crazy people, my report, sneaking into the East Eight Ward, forty or so odd men and women]. *Byeolgeongon* 6, no. 4 (April 1931).
Chesler, Phyllis. *Women and Madness*. 3rd ed. New York: Four Walls Eight Windows, 1997.
Cho Myeong-hui. "Nongchon saramdeul" [Rural people]. *Hyeondae Pyeongnon*, November 1926. www.seelotus.com/gojeon/hyeon-dae/soseol/bonmun/-%EC%A1%B0%EB%AA%85%ED%9D%AC-%EB%86%8D%EC%B4%8C%EC%82%AC%EB%9E%8C%EB%93%A4.htm.
Choe, Kilsŭng. "War and Ethnology / Folklore in Colonial Korea: The Case of Akiba Takashi." In *Wartime Anthropology in Asia and the Pacific*, edited by Shimizu Akitoshi and Jan van Bremen, 169–87. Osaka: National Museum of Ethnology, 2003.
Choe Gyu-jin. *Geundae reul boneun chang 20* [Twenty windows on modernity]. Seoul: Seohaemunjip, 2007.
Choe Sang-jin and Kim Gi-beom. *Munhwa simnihak hangugin ui simni bunseok* [Cultural psychology: Analyzing the psychological state of Koreans]. Seoul: Jisiksaneopsa, 2011.
Choi, Ellie. "Introduction to 'From Tokyo to Seoul' (Tonggyŏng esŏ Kyŏngsŏng kkaji, 1917) and 'Record of Travels in the Diamond Mountains' (Kŭmgangsan yugi, 1922)." *Azalea: Journal of Korean Literature and Culture* 4 (2011): 329–36.
Choi, Sang-Chin, and Gyuseong Han. "Shimcheong Psychology: A Case of an Emotional State for Cultural Psychology." *International Journal for Dialogical Science* 3, no. 1 (Fall 2008): 205–24.

Choi, Yoon Joon. *Dialogue and Antithesis: A Philosophical Study on the Significance of Herman Dooyeweerd's Transcendental Critique*. Philadelphia: Hermit Kingdom Press, 2006.

Chōsen sōtokufu. *Chōsen jinkō genshō* [Population phenomena of Korea]. Keijō, 1926.

———. *Chōsen sōtokufu iin* [Government-General Hospital of Korea]. Vols. 1–9. Keijō, 1911–22.

———. *Chōsen sōtokufu kanpō* [The official gazette of the Government-General of Korea]. Keijō, 1910–45.

———. *Chōsen sōtokufu tōkei nenpō* [Annual statistical report of the Government-General of Korea]. Keijō, 1910–45.

———. *Shisei nijūgo nenshi* [The twenty-five-year history of the administration of Korea]. Keijō, 1935.

Chōsen sōtokufu keimu sōkanfu. *Chōsen eisei fūshūroku* [A record of Korean's hygiene customs]. Ed. and comp. Sin Jong-won and Han Ji-won. 1915. Reprint, Seoul: Miksogwon, 2013.

Chung, Christopher K., and Samson Cho. "Conceptualization of *Jeong* and Dynamics of *Hwabyung*." *Psychiatry Investigation* 3, no. 1 (2006): 46–54.

Chung, Edward Y. J. *The Neo-Confucianism of Yi T'oegye and Yi Yulgok: A Reappraisal of the "Four-Seven" Thesis and Its Practical Implications for Self-Cultivation*. Albany: State University of New York Press, 1995.

Clark, Donald N. *Living Dangerously in Korea*. Norwalk, CT: EastBridge, 2001.

Clough, Patricia Tincineto, with Jean Halley, eds. *The Affective Turn: Theorizing the Social*. Durham, NC: Duke University Press, 2007.

Compilation for the History of Korean Women. *Women of Korea: A History from Ancient Times to 1945*. Translated by Yun-Chung Kim. Seoul: Ewha Womans University Press, 1976.

Cumings, Bruce. *Korea's Place in the Sun*. New York: W. W. Norton, 1997.

Dalton, Richard J. "Korean's Refugee Status Upheld in Historic Case." *Vancouver Sun*, June 20, 2009. www.canada.com/story.html?id=82b296e4-8e87-4a3e-9760-d671e5400f84.

Dammann, Eric J. "The Myth of Mental Illness: Continuing Controversies and Their Implications for Mental Health Professionals." *Clinical Psychological Review* 17, no. 7 (1997): 733–56.

Deuchler, Martina. *The Confucian Transformation of Korea: A Study of Society and Ideology*. Cambridge, MA: Council on East Asian Studies, Harvard University, 1992.

———. "Neo-Confucianism in Action: Agnation and Ancestor Worship in Early Yi Korea." In *Religion and Ritual in Korean Society,* edited by Laurel Kendall and Griffin Dix, 26–55. Berkeley, CA: Institute of East Asian Studies, 1988.

———. "The Tradition: Women during the Yi Dynasty." In *Virtues in Conflict: Tradition and the Korean Woman Today,* edited by Sandra Mattielli, 1–48. Seoul: Royal Asiatic Society, Korea Branch, 1977.

Deutsch, Albert. *The Mentally Ill in America: A History of Their Care and Treatment from Colonial Times*. New York: Columbia University Press, 1967.
Dillon, Sarah. *The Palimpsest: Literature, Criticism, Theory*. London: Continuum, 2007.
Doi, Takeo. *The Anatomy of Dependence*. Tokyo: Kondansha, 1973.
———. *The Anatomy of Self*. Tokyo: Kondansha, 1985.
Durkheim, Emile. *The Division of Labor in Society*. Translated by W. D. Halls. New York: Free Press, 1984.
———. *On Suicide*. Translated by Robin Buss. New York: Penguin Books, 2006.
Edwards, Jason. *Eve Kosofsky Sedgwick*. New York: Routledge, 2009.
Ekman, Paul. *Emotion in the Human Face: Guide-Lines for Research and Integration of Findings*. Oxford: Pergamon Press, 1972.
Ekman, Paul, and Richard J. Davidson, eds. *The Nature of Emotion: Fundamental Questions*. London: Oxford University Press, 1994.
Eliade, Mircea. *Rites and Symbols of Initiation: The Mysteries of Birth and Rebirth*. Translated by William Trask. New York: Spring, 1998.
Em, Henry. "Yi Sang's 'Wings' Read as an Anti-colonial Allegory." *muae: a journal of transcultural production* 1 (1995): 104–11.
Engstrom, Eric J. *Clinical Psychiatry in Imperial Germany: A History of Psychiatric Practice*. Ithaca, NY: Cornell University Press, 2003.
Ernst, Waltraud. *Mad Tales from the Raj: The European Insane in British India*. London: Routledge, 1991.
Evans, Dylan. *Emotions: A Very Short Introduction*. London: Oxford University Press, 2001.
Fanon, Frantz. *Black Skin, White Masks*. Translated by Constance Farrington. New York: Grove Press, 1994.
Flam, Helen. "Emotions' Map: A Research Agenda." In *Emotions and Social Movements*, edited by Helen Flam and Debra King, 19–40. London: Routledge, 2005.
Foucault, Michel. "Je suis un artificier" [interview, 1975]. In *Michel Foucault, Entretiens*, edited by Roger-Pol Droit, 119–20. Paris: Odile Jacobs, 2004.
———. *Madness and Civilization: A History of Insanity in the Age of Reason*. Translated by Richard Howard. London: Vintage, 1988.
Geertz, Clifford. *The Interpretation of Cultures*. New York: Basic Books, 1973.
Gifford, Daniel L. *Everyday Life in Korea: A Collection of Studies and Stories*. Chicago: Fleming H. Revell, 1898.
Goeschel, Christian. *Suicide in Nazi Germany*. Oxford: Oxford University Press, 2009.
Goffman, Erving. *Asylums: Essays on the Social Situations of Mental Patients and Other Inmates*. Oxford: Doubleday, 1961.
———. *Interaction Ritual: Essays on Face-to-Face Behavior*. New York: Anchor Books, 1967.
———. "On Face-Work: An Analysis of Ritual Elements in Social Interaction." In *Language, Culture and Society: A Book of Readings*, edited by Ben G. Blount, 224–49. Cambridge: Winthrop, 1974.

———. *The Presentation of Self in Everyday Life.* New York: Pelican Books, 1990.
———. *Stigma: Notes on the Management of Spoiled Identity.* New York: Prentice-Hall, 1963.
Gomory, Tomi, David Cohen, and Stuart A. Kirk. "Madness or Mental Illness? Revisiting Historians of Psychiatry." *Current Psychology* 32 (June 2013): 119–35.
Gosling, Andrew. *Jessie's Korea: Guide to the McLaren-Human Collection in the National Library of Australia.* Canberra: National Library of Australia, 2007.
Greenfeld, Liah. *Mind, Modernity, Madness: The Impact of Culture on Human Experience.* Cambridge, MA: Harvard University Press, 2013.
Grim, John A. "*Chaesu Kut*: A Korean Shamanistic Performance." *Asian Folklore Studies* 43, no. 2 (1984): 235–59.
Haboush, Jahyun Kim. *The Memoirs of Lady Hyegyŏng: The Autobiographical Writings of a Crown Princess of Eighteenth-Century Korea.* Berkeley: University of California Press, 1996.
Hacking, Ian. "The Looping Effects of Human Kinds." In *Causal Cognition,* edited by Dan Sperber, David Premack, and Ann James Premack, 350–94. Oxford: Clarendon Press, 1995.
Han Ji-won. *Joseon chongdokbu uiryo minjokjireul tonghae bon wisaeng pungseup yeongu* [A study of the Government-General of Joseon's medical ethnography on hygienic customs]. Seoul: Minsokwon, 2013.
Harvey, Youngsook Kim. "The Korean *Mudang* as a Household Therapist." In *Culture-Bound Syndromes, Ethnopsychiatry and Alternative Therapies,* edited by Willliam P. Lebra, 189–98. Honolulu: University of Hawaii Press, 1976.
Hashimoto Akira. *Seishin byōsha to shitaku kanchi* [Mental illness and home confinement]. Tokyo: Rikka Shupan, 2011.
Heinrich, Amy Vladeck. *Fragments of Rainbows: The Life of the Poetry of Saitō Mokichi.* New York: Columbia University Press, 1983.
Heo Jun. *Wonbon Dong-ui bogam* [Treasured mirror of Eastern medicine: Original]. Seoul: Namsangdang, 1987.
Hirshbein, Laura. "Sex and Gender in Psychiatry: A View from History." *Journal of Medical Humanities* 31 (2010): 155–70.
Hochschild, Arlie R. "Emotion Work, Feeling Rules, and Social Structures." *American Journal of Sociology* 85, no. 3 (November 1979): 551–75.
———. *The Managed Heart: Commercialization of Human Feeling.* Berkeley: University of California Press, 2003.
———. "The Sociology of Emotion as a Way of Seeing." In *Emotions in Social Life: Critical Themes and Contemporary Issues,* edited by Gillian Bendelow and Simon J. Williams, 3–15. London: Routledge, 2005.
Hogarth, Hyun-key Kim. *Korean Shamanism and Cultural Nationalism.* Seoul: Jimoondang, 1999.
Honda, Yoshiharu, Hideo Suzuki, Hideharu Honda, and Satoshi Irisawa. "A Pioneer in Occupational Therapy at Mental Hospitals in Local Cities: Approaches at Shichiyama Hospital at the Beginning of Taisho Era." *Seishin shinkeigaku zasshi* 111, no. 9 (2009): 1047–54.

Hong Sun-hyang. "Hanguk yeoksa e girokdoen jeongsin jilhwan e gwanhan yeongu" [A study of mental disorders reported in Korean history]. *Singyeong jeongsin uihak* 20, no. 2 (1981): 185–94.

Horowitz, Allan. *Creating Mental Illness*. Chicago: University of Chicago Press, 2002.

Hulbert, Homer B. *The Korea Review* 2. Seoul: Methodist Publishing House, 1902.

———. *The Passing of Korea*. New York: Doubleday, Page, 1906.

Hwang, Merose. "The *Mudang*: Gendered Discourses on Shamanism in Colonial Korea." PhD diss., University of Toronto, 2009.

Hyeon Jin-geon [see also Hyŏn, Chin-gŏn]. "Bul" [Fire]. In *Unsu joeun nal*, 173–83.

———. "Geurip eun heungil nun" [Yearning for his scowling eyes]. *Pyeheoihu*, January 1924. http://nocopyright.tistory.com/105.

———. "Sarip jeongsin byeongwonjang" [The director of the private mental hospital]. In *Unsu joeun nal*.

———. *Unsu joeun nal* [A lucky day]. Hanguk munhak jeonjip 34. Seoul: Munhwa gwa jiseongsa, 2010.

Hyŏn, Chin-gŏn. "Fire." Translated by Peter Lee. In *Flowers of Fire: Twentieth-Century Stories*, edited by Peter Lee, 1–9. Honolulu: University of Hawaii Press, 1974. See also Hyeon Jin-geon.

Isen, Alice M., and Gregory Andrade Diamond. "Affect and Automaticity." In *Unintended Thoughts: Limits of Awareness, Intention, and Control*, edited by James S. Uleman and John A. Bargh, 124–49. New York: Guilford Press, 1989.

Ishida, Noboru. "Correspondence." *American Journal of Insanity* 73 (1916–17): 744–48.

Ivy, Marilyn. *Discourses of the Vanishing: Modernity, Phantasm, Japan*. Chicago: University of Chicago Press, 1995.

Jeon Bong-gwan. *Gyeongseong gidam* [Strange stories from Seoul]. Seoul: Sallim, 2006.

———. "Jukcheomjeong dandu yua sageon" [The case of the decapitated infant in Jukcheomjeong]. *Sin Dong-a* 544 (November 2005): 540–53.

Jeong Chang-gwon. *Yeoksa sok jangaein eun eotteoke sarasseulkka* [How did people with disabilities in Korean history live?]. Seoul: Geulhangari, 2011.

Jeon Gyeong-uk. *Hanguk gamyeongeuk: Geu yeoksawa wolli* [Korean masked drama: History and structural principles]. Seoul: Yeolhwadong, 1998.

Jeong Gu-seong. *Joseon ui memento mori: Joseon i beorin jadeul ui jugeum eul gieok hara* [Memento mori: Remembering the deaths of those who were discarded by the Joseon dynasty]. Seoul: Aepeulbuksu, 2010.

Jeong Gu-yeong. "Singyeong gwa chukgwi ui sangjing" [Symbolisms of enchanted lands and exorcism]. *Wolgan Joseon*, May 2007. monthly.chosun.com/client/news/viw.asp?ctod=&nNewsNumb=200705100069.

Jeong Won-yong. "Geundae seoyang jeongsinuihagui jeongaewa byeoncheongwajeong—1920-nyeondae chobuteo 8. 15 gwangbok ijeonkkaji" [The development and process of transition of modern Western psychiatry from 1920 to August 15 [1945] (preindependence)]. PhD diss., Seoul National University, 1996.

Jeong Won-yong, Yi Na-mi, and Yi Bu-yeong. "Seoyang jeongsinuihak ui doip gwa geu byeoncheon gwajeong (2): Ilje gangjeomgi ui jeongsin uihak gyoyuk, 1910–1945" [The introduction of Western psychiatry into Korea (II): Psychiatric education in Korea during the forced Japanese annexation of Korea, 1910–1945]. *Uisahak* 15 (December 2006): 157–87.

Jiang, Yonglin. *The Mandate of Heaven and the Great Ming Code*. Seattle: University of Washington Press, 2011.

Jo Hae-mun. *Na Un-gyu*. Seoul: Hangilsa, 1997.

Jo Yi-dam. *Gubossiwa deobureo gyeongseongeul gada* [Accompanying Gubo around Seoul]. Seoul: Baram Gudu, 2005.

Jones, George Heber. "The Spirit Worship of the Koreans." *Transactions of the Korea Branch of the Royal Asiatic Society* 2 (1901): 37–58.

Joseon chongdokbu [Government-General of Joseon]. *Joseon wisaeng pungseumnok* [A record of Korea's hygiene customs]. Translated from Japanese into Korean by Sin Jong-won and Han Ji-won. Seoul: Miksogwon, 2013.

Kalton, Michael C., with Oak Sook C. Kim et al. *The Four-Seven Debate: An Annotated Translation of the Most Famous Controversy in Korean Neo-Confucian Thought*. Albany: State University of New York Press, 1994.

Kanekawa Hideo. "Keijō teikoku daigaku shinkei-ka seishinka kyōshitsu no tō gakkai ni okeru gakujutsu happyō" [Academic presentation on neurology and psychiatry at the annual meeting at Keijō Imperial University]. *Seishin shinkeigaku zasshi* 114, no. 10 (2012): 1180–86.

———. *Nihon no seishin iryōshi: Meiji kara Shōwa shoki kara* [A history of medical psychiatry: From Meiji to the early period of Showa]. Tokyo: Seikyūsha, 2012.

Keller, Richard C. *Colonial Madness: Psychiatry in French North Africa*. Chicago: University of Chicago Press, 2007.

Kendall, Laurel. "Korean Shamanism: Women's Rites and a Chinese Comparison." *Senri Ethnological Studies* 11 (1984): 57–73.

Kim, Chongho. *Korean Shamanism: The Cultural Paradox*. Aldershot: Ashgate, 2003.

Kim, Daeho, and Hae-won Lee. "Post-traumatic Stress Disorder and Trauma-Related Conditions in Korean History: Literature Review of Six Cases." *Psychiatry Investigation* 2, no. 2 (2005): 18–21.

Kim, Hoi-eun. *Doctors of Empire: Medical and Cultural Encounters between Imperial Germany and Meiji Japan*. Toronto: University of Toronto Press, 2014.

Kim, Kwang-il. "*Kut* and the Treatment of Mental Disorder." In *Shamanism: The Spirit World of Korea*, edited by Richard W. I. Guisso and Chai-shin Yu, 131–61. Berkeley, CA: Asian Humanities Press, 1988.

Kim, Soonsik. *Colonial and Postcolonial Discourse in the Novels of Yom Sang-sop, Chinua Achebe, and Salman Rushdie*. New York: Peter Lang, 2004.

Kim, Uchang. "Extravagance and Authenticity: Romantic Love and the Self in Early Modern Korean Literature." *Korea Journal* 39, no. 4 (Winter 1999): 61–89.

Kim, Young-Ha. "South Korea's Struggle with Suicide." *New York Times*, April 2, 2014. www.nytimes.com/2014/04/03/opinion/south-koreas-struggle-with-suicide.html?_r=0.

Kim Dae-won. "18-segi mingan uiryo ui seongjang" [The growth of private medicine in the eighteenth century]. MA thesis, Seoul National University, 1998.

Kim Dong-in. "Jeonjeja" [The despot]. *Gaebyeok*, March 1921.

Kim Gi-jin. "Jeolmeun isangjuuija ui jugeum" [The death of the youthful idealist]. *Gaebyeok*, June-July 1925.

Kim Gi-ju. "Sorokdo jahyeuiwon nahwanja jeongchaegui seonggyeok" [The character of the leper policy of Jahye Hospital on Sorok Island]. *Yeoksahak yeongu* 44 (2011): 221–74.

Kim Gi-rim. "Hangang indogyo" [Han River Footbridge]. In *Kim Gi-rim jeonjip* [The complete works of Kim Gi-rim]. Vol. 1. Seoul: Namseoldang, 1988.

Kim Gwang-il. "Hanguk min-gan jeongsinuihak" [Folk psychiatry in Korea]. *Singyeong jeongsin uihak* 11, no. 2 (1972): 85–98.

———. "Syameonijeumui jeongsin bunseokhakjeok gochal" [A psychoanalytical consideration of shamanism]. *Singyeong jeongsin uihak* 11, no. 2 (1972): 57–65.

Kim Hui-yeong. "Murayama Jijun-i bon Jeonnam ui mugyeok sinang" [Shamanistic practices of Jeonnam seen by Murayama Chijun]. Unpublished manuscript, 2011, Jeonnam Daehakgyo Honamhak Yeonguwon.

Kim Hŭnggyu. "Chosŏn Fiction in Chinese." In *A History of Korean Literature*, edited by Peter Lee, 261–72. Cambridge: Cambridge University Press, 2003.

———. "Folk Drama." In *A History of Korean Literature*, edited by Peter Lee, 303–15. Cambridge: Cambridge University Press, 2003.

———. "Pansori." In *A History of Korean Literature*, edited by Peter Lee, 288–302. Cambridge: Cambridge University Press, 2003.

Kim Hŭnggyu, and Peter Lee. "Chosŏn Fiction in Korea." In *A History of Korean Literature*, edited by Peter Lee, 273–87. Cambridge: Cambridge University Press, 2003.

Kim Jong-u. *Jeungryero bon jeongsin hanuihak* [Records of neuropsychiatry in Oriental medicine]. Seoul: Jimmundang, 2006.

Kim Jong-won and Jeong Jung-heon. *Uri yeonghwa 100-nyeon* [100 years of Korean film]. Seoul: Hyeonamsa, 2000.

Kim Seong-gyu. *Jeong iran mueosinga* [What is this *jeong*?]. Seoul: Chekbose, 2013.

Kim Tae-hyeon. "Dong-ui bogam sinmun jeon-gan cheobang ui jeonsa e daehan yeongu" [The literature review on the process of historical changes in herb medicines in the chapter 'Sinmun jeon-gan' of *Dong-ui bogam*]. *Journal of Oriental Neuropsychiatry* 23, no. 3 (2012): 175–90.

Kim Ui-suk. *Hanguk minsok je-ui wa eumyang-ohaeng* [Korean rites and ceremonies and the yin-yang and five elements]. Seoul: Jimmundang, 1993.

Kitanaka, Junko. *Depression in Japan: Psychiatric Cures for a Society in Distress*. Princeton, NJ: Princeton University Press, 2012.

Kleinman, Arthur. *Rethinking Psychiatry: Cultural Category to Personal Experience*. New York: Free Press, 1988.

Kondo, Kyoichi. "The Origin of Morita Therapy." In *Culture-Bound Syndromes, Ethnopsychiatry and Alternate Therapies*, vol. 4 of *Mental Health Research in Asia and Pacific*, edited by William P. Lebra, 250–58. Honolulu: University Press of Hawaii, 1976.

Kraepelin, Emil, and Allen Ross Diefendorf. *Clinical Psychiatry: A Textbook for Students and Physicians*. New York: Macmillan, 1915.

Kudō Takeki. "Chōsen fujin eiji satsugai no fujin kagakuteki kōsatsu" [A scientific study of Korean women and infanticide]. *Chōsen* 4 (February 1930): 27–50.

Kushner, Howard. "Suicide, Gender and the Fear of Modernity in Nineteenth-Century Medical and Social Thought." *Journal of Social History* 26, no. 3 (1993): 461–90.

Kuzuhara, Shigeki. "History of Neurology and Education and Neurology in Japan." *KNA-JNS Joint Symposium* 3 (May 2009): 968–71.

Lah, Kyung. "South Korean Ferry Victims' Families Ask, 'How Are We Going to Live Now?'" CNN, April 20, 2014. www.cnn.com/2014/04/19/world/asia/south-korea-grieving-parents/.

Laing, R. D. *The Divided Self: An Existential Study in Sanity and Madness*. Harmondsworth: Penguin, 1960.

Lambert, Enoch. "Hacking and Human Kinds." *Aporia* 16, no. 1 (2006): 49–69.

Lambuth, David Kelly. "Korean Devils and Christian Missionaries." *Independent* 63 (July-December 1907): 287–88.

Landis, Eli Barr. "Notes on the Exorcism of Spirits in Korea." *Chinese Review* 21, no. 6 (1895): 399–404.

Lean, Eugenia. *Public Passions: The Trial of Shi Jianqiao and the Rise of Popular Sympathy in Republican China*. Berkeley: University of California Press, 2007.

Lee, Chulwoo. "Modernity, Legality, and Power." In *Colonial Modernity in Korea*, edited by Gi-Woo Shin and Michael Robinson, 21–51. Cambridge, MA: Harvard University Asian Center, 1999.

Lee, Ho Young. "Past, Present and Future of Korean Psychiatry." *Psychiatry Investigation* 1, no. 1 (2004): 13–19.

Lee, Jieun, Amy Wachholtz, and Keum-Hyeong Choi. "A Review of the Korean Cultural Syndrome *Hwa-Byung*: Suggestions for Theory and Intervention." *Asia Taepyongyang Sangdam Yeongu* 4, no. 1 (January 2014). www.ncbi.nlm.nih.gov/pmc/articles/PMC4232959/.

Lee, Peter, ed. Introduction to *Modern Korean Literature: An Anthology*, edited by Peter Lee, 1–14. Honolulu: University of Hawaii Press, 1990.

———, ed. *Modern Korean Literature: An Anthology*. Honolulu: University of Hawaii Press, 1990.

Lie, John. *Han Unbound: The Political Economy of South Korea*. Stanford, CA: Stanford University Press, 2000.

Lieberman, Lisa. *Leaving You: The Cultural Meaning of Suicide*. Chicago: Ivan R. Dee, 2003.

Lin, Keh-Ming. "Traditional Chinese Medical Beliefs and Their Relevance for Mental Illness and Psychiatry." In *Normal and Abnormal Behavior in Chinese*

Culture, edited by Arthur Kleinman and Tsung-yi Lin, 95–114. Boston: D. Reidel, 1981.

Liu Shi-yung. "An Overview of Public Health Development in Japan-Ruled Taiwan." In *Death at the Opposite Ends of the Eurasian Continent: Mortality Trends in Taiwan and the Netherlands, 1850–1945,* edited by Theo Engelen, John R. Shepherd, and Yang Wen-shan, 165–82. Amsterdam: Amsterdam University Press, 2011.

Lutz, Catherine A., and Lila Abu-Lughod, eds. *Language and the Politics of Emotions.* London: Cambridge University Press, 1990.

Lutz, Catherine A., and Geoffrey M. White. "The Anthropology of Emotions." *Annual Review of Anthropology* 15 (1986): 405–36.

Marsh, Ian. *Suicide: Foucault, History and Truth.* Cambridge: Cambridge University Press, 2010.

Matsumoto, David. *Unmasking Japan: Myths and Realities about the Emotions of the Japanese.* Stanford, CA: Stanford University Press, 1996.

Matsumura, Janice. "Mental Health as Public Peace: Kaneko Junji and the Promotion of Psychiatry in Modern Japan." *Modern Asian Studies* 38, no. 4 (October 2004): 899–930.

McDonald, Mark. "Stressed and Depressed, Koreans Avoid Therapy." *New York Times,* July 6, 2011.

McLaren, C. I. "Care of the Insane." *Korea Mission Field* 35, no. 3 (1939): 62–63.

———. "An Hypothesis Concerning the Relationship between Body and Mind." *Australasian Journal of Psychology and Philosophy* 6, no. 3 (1928): 272–82.

———. "Lessons from the Neurological Clinic." *Korea Mission Field* 21, no. 10 (1925): 214.

———. "My Beliefs." *Korean Mission Field* 28, no. 4 (1932): 75–77.

———. "The Necessary Connection between Healing of the Body and Healing of the Soul." *Korea Mission Field* 10, no. 8 (1914): 211–12.

———. "The Problem of Insanity and the Responsibility of the Church." *Korean Mission Field* 18, no. 7 (1922): 138–40.

———. "Proposed Rescue Home in Seoul." *Korea Mission Field* 22, no. 6 (1926): 133.

———. "Saturday Morning in a Hospital in Korea." *Korea Mission Field* 28, no. 3 (1932): 45–49.

———. "Things Both New and Old in Psychological Medicine." *Chinese Medical Journal* 46, no. 3 (1932): 913–26.

"Medical Work in Korea." *Foreign Missionary* 45 (October 1886): 215–16.

Micale, Mark S., and Roy Porter. *Discovering the History of Psychiatry.* New York: Oxford University Press, 1994.

Min, Sung Kil. "*Hwabyung* in Korea: Culture and Dynamic Analysis." *World Cultural Psychiatry Research Review* 4, no. 1 (2009): 12–21.

Min Seong-gil. *Hwabyeong yeongu* [The study of *hwabyeong*]. Seoul: Emel keomyunikeisyeon, 2009.

———. *Malsseumi yuksini doeeo: Maekraren gyosuui saengaewa sasang* [The Word became flesh: Dr. McLaren's life and thought]. Seoul: Yeonsedaehakgyo daehak chulpanmunhwawon, 2013.

Mizuno, Hiromi. *Science for the Empire: Scientific Nationalism in Modern Japan.* Stanford, CA: Stanford University Press, 2009.

Moose, J. Robert. *Village Life in Korea.* Nashville, TN: Publishing House of the M.E. Church, 1911.

Murayama Chijun. *Chōsen no kishin* [Ghosts of Korea]. Seoul: Chōsen Sōtokufu, 1929.

Myers, Ramon H., and Mark R. Peattie, eds. *The Japanese Colonial Empire, 1895–1945.* Princeton, NJ: Princeton University Press, 1984.

Na Do-hyang. "Mullae bang-a" [Watermill]. *Joseon mundan*, September 1925. http://snsj7537.com.ne.kr/ssol/380.htm.

Na Yeong-in. "Jasal gwa jeongsin jilhwan, geurigo joseon ui geundaehwa" [Suicide and mental illness, and Korea's modernization]. *Seoul daehak sinmun,* March 17, 2012.

Nakamura, Karen. *A Disability of the Soul: An Ethnography of Schizophrenia and Mental Illness in Contemporary Japan.* Ithaca, NY: Cornell University Press, 2013.

Nakamura, Kei. "The Formation and Development of Morita Therapy." In *Two Millennia of Psychiatry in West and East,* edited by Toshihiko Hamanaka and German E. Berrios, 125–32. Tokyo: Gakuju Shoin, 2003.

Nam, Mihee, Dae Seog Heo, Tae Yeon Jun, Min Soo Lee, Maeng Je Cho, Changsu Han, and Min Kyung Kim. "U-uljeung, jasal geurigo hanguk sahoe" [Depression, suicide, and Korean society]. *Journal of the Korean Medical Association* 54, no. 4 (April 2011): 358–61.

New, Esmond W. *A Doctor in Korea: The Story of Charles McLaren, M.D.* Sydney: Australian Presbyterian Board of Missions, 1958.

Noll, Richard. *The Encyclopedia of Schizophrenia and Other Psychotic Disorders.* 3rd ed. New York: Facts on File, 2007.

Oak, Sung Deuk. "Healing and Exorcism: American Encounters with Shamanism in Early Modern Korea." *Asian Ethnology* 69, no. 1 (2010): 95–128.

Organisation for Economic Co-operation and Development. "Korea's Increase in Suicides and Psychiatric Bed Numbers Is Worrying, Says OECD." Press release, 2011. www.oecd.org/els/health-systems/MMHC-Country-Press-Note-Korea.pdf.

Park, Yun-jae. "Sanitizing Korea: Anti-cholera Activities of the Police in Early Colonial Korea." *Seoul Journal of Korean Studies* 23, no. 2 (2010): 151–71.

Perry, Elizabeth J. "Moving the Masses: Emotional Work in the Chinese Revolution." *Mobilization: An International Journal* 7, no. 2 (2002): 111–28.

Pies, Ronald. "On Myths and Countermyths: More on Szaszian Fallacies." *Archives of General Psychiatry* 36 (1979): 139–44.

Plamper, Jan. "The History of Emotions: An Interview with William Reddy, Barbara Rosenwein, and Peter Stearns." *History and Theory* 49 (May 2010): 237–65.

Porter, Roy. *Madness: A Brief History.* New York: Oxford University Press, 2002.

Pratt, Christine. *An Encyclopedia of Shamanism.* Vol. 1. New York: Rosen Publishing Group, 2007.

Reddy, William. *The Navigation of Feeling.* Cambridge: Cambridge University Press, 2001.

Reisman, John M. *A History of Clinical Psychology.* New York: Ardent Media, 1976.

Rhi, Bou-Yong [see also Yi Bu-yeong]. "Psychological Aspects of Korean Shamanism." *Korea Journal* 10, no. 9 (1970): 15–21.

———. "Psychotherapeutic Aspects of Shamanism with Special Reference to Korean *Mudang.*" *Mental Health Research* 8 (1989): 40–55.

———. "The Roots of Korean Psychiatry and Its Development before and after World War II." In *Two Millennia of Psychiatry in East and West,* edited by Toshiko Hamanaka and German E. Berrios, 95–105. Tokyo: Gakuju Shoin, 2003.

Rosaldo, Michelle Z. "Toward an Anthropology of Self and Feeling." In *Culture Theory: Essays on Mind, Self, and Emotion,* edited by Richard A. Shweder and Robert A. LeVine, 137–57. Cambridge: Cambridge University Press, 1984.

Rosenwein, Barbara. Review of *The Navigation of Feeling,* by William M. Reddy. *American Historical Review,* 107, no. 4 (October 2002): 1181–82.

Rossi, Elisa. *Shen: Psycho-Emotional Aspects of Chinese Medicine.* Translated by Laura Caretto. London: Churchill Livingstone, 2007.

Sadowsky, Jonathan. *Imperial Bedlam: Institutions of Madness in Colonial Southwest Nigeria.* Berkeley: University of California Press, 1999.

Sass, Louis A. *Madness and Modernism: Insanity in the Light of Modern Art, Literature, and Thought.* Cambridge, MA: Harvard University Press, 1994.

Scheper-Hughes, Nancy. *Saints, Scholars, and Schizophrenics: Mental Illness in Rural Ireland.* Berkeley: University of California Press, 1979.

Schneider, Robert A., ed. "AHR Conversation: The Historical Study of Emotions." *American Historical Review* 117, no. 5 (2012): 1487–1531.

Scott, James C. *Domination and the Arts of Resistance: Hidden Transcripts.* New Haven, CT: Yale University Press, 1992.

———. *Weapons of the Weak: Everyday Forms of Peasant Resistance.* New Haven, CT: Yale University Press, 1985.

Scull, Andrew. *Madness in Civilization: A Cultural History of Insanity.* Princeton, NJ: Princeton University Press, 2015.

Sedgwick, Eve Kosofsky. *Between Men: English Literature and Male Homosocial Desire.* New York: Columbia University Press, 1985.

———. *Epistemology of the Closet.* Berkeley: University of California Press, 1990.

Seoul daehakgyo byeongwon yeoksa munhwa senteo. *Sajin gwa hamkke boneun hanguk geunhyeondae uiryo munhwasa* [A pictorial history of modern medicine in Korea]. Seoul: Ungjin jisik hangseu, 2009.

Shin, Dongwon. "How Commoners Became Consumers of Naturalistic Medicine in Korea, 1600–1800." *East Asian Science, Technology, and Society: An International Journal* 4 (2010): 275–301.

Shin, Michael D. "Interior Landscapes: Yi Kwangsu's 'The Heartless' and the Origins of Modern Literature." In *Colonial Modernity in Korea,* edited by Gi-wook Shin and Michael Robinson, 248–87. Cambridge, MA: Harvard Asia Center, 1999.

Shorter, Edward. *A History of Psychiatry: From the Era of the Asylum to the Age of Prozac.* New York: Wiley, 1997.

Sin Do-won. *Hoyeolja joseoneul seupgyeokhada* [Cholera invades Joseon]. Seoul: Yeoksa bipyeongsa, 2004.

Skultans, Vieda. "The Appropriation of Suffering: Psychiatric Practice in the Post-Soviet Clinic." *Theory, Culture and Society* 24, no. 3 (2007): 27–48.

———. *English Madness: Ideas on Insanity, 1580–1890*. Piscataway, NJ: Routledge and Kegan Paul, 1979.

Son, Annette Hye Kyung. "Modernization of the System of Traditional Korean Medicine, 1876–1990." *Health Policy* 4, no. 3 (June 1998): 261–81.

Song Hyeon-ho. *Hyeondae soseol ui haeseol* [Commentary on Korean fiction]. Seoul: Gwangdong chulpansa, 1992.

Sontag, Susan. *Illness as Metaphor and AIDS and Its Metaphors*. New York: Picador, 2001.

Staub, Michael. *Madness Is Civilization*. Chicago: University of Chicago Press, 2011.

Stearns, Peter N., and Carol Z. Stearns. "Emotionology: Clarifying the History of Emotions and Emotional Standards." *American Historical Review* 90, no. 4 (1985): 813–36.

Steinberg, Mark D., and Valeria Sobol. *Interpreting Emotions in Russia and Eastern Europe*. Dekalb: Northern Illinois University Press, 2011.

Stets, Jan E., and Jonathan H. Turner. "The Sociology of Emotions." In *Handbook of Emotions,* edited by Michael Lewis, Jeannette M. Haviland-Jones, and Lisa Feldman Barrett, 32–46. 3rd ed. London: Guilford Press, 2008.

Suh, Soyoung. "Stories to Be Told: Korean Doctors between *Hwa-byung* (Fire-Illness) and Depression, 1970–2011." *Culture, Medicine and Psychiatry* 37, no. 1 (March 2013): 81–104. www.ncbi.nlm.nih.gov/pmc/articles/PMC3585958/.

Suzuki, Akihito. "Global Theory, Local Practice: Shock Therapies in Japanese Psychiatry, 1920–1945." In *Transnational Psychiatries: Social and Cultural Histories of Psychiatry in Comparative Perspective, c. 1800–2000*, edited by Waltraud Ernst and Thomas Mueller, 116–42. Cambridge: Cambridge Scholars, 2010.

———. "Were Asylums Men's Places? Male Excess in the Asylum Population in Japan in the Early Twentieth Century." In *Psychiatric Cultures Compared: Psychiatry and Mental Health Care in the Twentieth Century,* edited by Marijke Gijswijt-Hofstra, Harry Oosterhuis, Joost Vijselaar, and Hugh Freeman, 295–311. Amsterdam: Amsterdam University Press, 2005.

Szasz, Thomas. *Coercion as Cure: A Critical History of Psychiatry*. New Brunswick, NJ: Transaction, 2009.

———. "The Myth of Mental Illness." *American Psychologist* 15 (1960): 113–18.

———. *The Myth of Mental Illness: Foundations of a Theory of Personal Conduct*. 1961. Reprint, New York: Harper and Row, 1974.

Tanaka, Stefan. *Japan's Orient: Rendering Pasts into History*. Berkeley: University of California Press, 1995.

Thiher, Allen. *Revels in Madness: Insanity in Medicine and Literature*. Ann Arbor: University of Michigan Press, 1999.

Tomes, Nancy. "Epidemic Entertainments: Disease and Popular Culture in Early-Twentieth-Century America." *American Literary History* 14, no. 4 (2002): 625–52.

Treat, John Whittier. "Introduction to Yi Kwang-su's 'Maybe Love' (Ai ka, 1909)." *Azalea: Journal of Korean Literature and Culture* 4, no. 1 (2011): 315–20.

Tu, Wei-ming. "Probing the 'Three-Bonds' and the 'Five-Relationships' in Confucian Humanism." In *Confucianism and the Family*, edited by Walter H. Slote and George A. DeVos, 121–36. New York: SUNY Press, 1998.

Underwood, Horace G. *The Call of Korea: Political—Social—Religious*. London: Fleming H. Revell, 1908.

Unschuld, Paul Ulrich. *Huang Di nei jing su wen: Nature, Knowledge, Imagery in an Ancient Chinese Medical Text*. Berkeley: University of California Press, 2003.

Unschuld, Paul Ulrich, and Herman Tessenow. *Huang Di nei jing su wen: An Annotated Translation of Huangdi's Inner Classic—Basic Questions*. Vol. 1. Berkeley: University of California Press, 2011.

VanBuskirk, J. D. "Severance." *Korean Mission Field* 21, no. 10 (1925): 203.

Veale, Jennifer. "Can Korea Protect Its Historical Sites?" *TIME*, February 13, 2008. content.time.com/time/world/article/0,8599,1712836,00.html.

Wagner, Edward W. *The Literati Purges: Political Conflict in Early Yi Korea*. Cambridge, MA: East Asian Research Center, Harvard University, 1974.

Walraven, Boudewijn. "National Pantheon, Regional Deities, Persona, Spirits? *Mushindo, Sŏngsu*, and the Nature of Korean Shamanism." *Asian Ethnology* 68, no. 1 (2009): 55–80.

———. "The Natives Next-Door: Ethnology in Colonial Korea." In *Anthropology and Colonialism in Asia and Oceania*, edited by Jan van Bremen and Akitoshi Shimizu, 214–44. Richmond, Surrey: Curzon, 1999.

———. "Our Shamanic Past: The Korean Government, Shamans and Shamanism." *Copenhagen Papers* 8, no. 93 (1993): 5–25.

———. "Shamans, the Family, and Women." In *Religions of Korea in Practice*, edited by Robert E. Buswell Jr., 306–24. Princeton, NJ: Princeton University Press, 2007.

———. *Songs of the Shaman: The Ritual Chants of the Korean Mudang*. London: Kegan Paul International, 1994.

Weiss, Kenneth. "Albert Deutsch, 1905–1961." *American Journal of Psychiatry* 168, no. 3 (2011): 252.

World Health Organization and Ministry of Health and Welfare, Republic of Korea. "WHO-AIMS Report on Mental Health System in Republic of Korea: A Report of the Assessment of the Mental Health System Using the World Health Organization- Assessment Instrument for Mental Health Systems (WHO-AIMS), Seoul, Republic of Korea, 2006." 2007. www.who.int/mental_health/evidence/korea_who_aims_report.pdf.

Yeo Hyeon-suk, Yi In-suk, Kim Seong-su, Sin Gyu-hwan, Bak Yun-hyeong, and Bak Yun-jae. *Hanguk uihaksa* [The history of medicine in Korea]. Seoul: KMA Uiryo jeongchyak yeon-guso, 2012.

Yeo In-seok. "Sebeuranseu jeongsingwa ui seollip gwajeong gwa indojuuijeok chiryo jeontong ui hyeongseong: Maekraren gwa i jungcheol ui hwaldongeul jungsimeuro" [The establishment of Severance Union Medical College's psychiatry department and the formation of a humanistic approach: Focusing on McLaren and Yi Jung-cheol]. *Uisahak* 17, no. 1 (June 2008): 57–74.

Yeom Sang-seop. *Pyobonsil ui cheong-gaeguri* [The green frog in the specimen room]. Seoul: Sodam chulpansa, 1995.

Yi Bang-hyeon. "Ilje sidae sinmun ae natanan jeongsin jilhwanja sahoe pyosang" [The social representation of people with mental disorders who appeared in newspaper articles during Japanese colonial rule]. PhD diss., Ewha Womans University, 2010.

Yi Bu-yeong [see also Yi Pu-Yong]. "Hanguk eseo ui seoyang jeongsin uihak 100-nyeon, 1899–1999" [A hundred years of psychiatry in Korea, 1899–1999]. *Uisahak*, 8, no. 2 (December 1999): 157–68.

———. "Hanguk geundae jeongsin uihak ui yeoksajeok jomyeong: Ilje eseo hanguk dongran ijeon kkaji" [Historical review of modern Korean psychiatry: From the colonial period up to the Korean War]. Symposium celebrating the tenth-year anniversary of Seoul National University Hospital. *Seoul uidae jeongsin uihak* 14, no. 1 (1989).

———. *Hanguk ui syameonijeum gwa bunseok simnihak* [Korean shamanism and analytical psychology]. Paju: Hangilsa, 2012.

———. "Iljeha jeongsin gwa jinryowa geu byeoncheon: Joseon chongdokbu uiwon ui jeongsingwa jinryo reul (1913–1928) jungsimeuro" [Psychiatric care and its change under the Japanese government in Korea with special reference to the clinical activities at the Colonial Governmental Hospital, 1913–28]. *Uisahak* 3, no. 2 (1994): 147–69.

Yi Dong-geon. *Dong-ui imsang singyeong jeongsingwa* [Eastern medicine clinical neuropsychiatry]. Seoul: Seowodang, 1994.

Yi Gwang-su. "Maybe Love" (Ai ka, 1909). Translated by John Whittier Treat. *Azalea: Journal of Korean Literature and Culture* 4, no. 1 (2011): 321–27.

———. "The Value of Literature." Translated by Jooyeon Rhee. *Azalea: Journal of Korean Literature and Culture* 4, no. 1 (2011): 287–92.

———. "What Is Literature?" Translated by Jooyeon Rhee. *Azalea: Journal of Korean Literature and Culture* 4, no. 1 (2011): 293–313.

Yi Jung-ho. *Ilje amheukgi uisa gyoyuksa* [A history of medical education during the dark period under Japanese colonial rule]. Seoul: Gukhak jaryowon, 2011.

Yi Man-yeol. *Hanguk gidokgyo uiryosa* [The history of Christian medicine work in Korea]. Seoul: Akanet, 2003.

Yi Na-mi. "Seoyang jeongsinuihagui doip gwa geu byeoncheon gwajeong: 17-segi buteo iljechogi kkaji" [The introduction of Western psychiatry and the process of change: From the seventeenth century to the early part of Japanese colonial rule]. PhD diss., Seoul National University, 1994.

Yi Neung-hwa. "Joseon musokgo" [Records of Korean shamanism]. *Gyemong* 19 (1927): 1–85.

Yi Pu-yong [see also Yi Bu-yeong]. "Illness and Healing in the Three Kingdoms Period: A Symbolic Interpretation." *Korea Journal* 21, no. 12 (1981): 4–12.

Yi Sang. "Wings." Translated by Walter K. Lew and Youngju Ryu. In *Modern Korean Fiction: An Anthology,* edited by Bruce Fulton and Youngmin Kwon, 65–84. New York: Columbia University Press, 2005.

Yi Su-yeong. *Seksyueolliti wa gwanggi* [Madness and sexuality]. Seoul: Geurinbi. 2008.

Yi Yeong-a. "1920-nyeondae soseol ui 'jasal' hyeongsanghwa yangsang yeongu" [A study on the figurative methods and meanings of 'suicide' in 1920s novels]. *Hanguk hyeondae munhak yeongu* 33 (April 2011): 207–48.

———. "Nuga deo mullanhanga?" [Who is more promiscuous?]. *Joong-ang ilbo,* December 8, 2011.

———. "Seon-gyo uisa allen (Horace N. Allen) ui uiryo hwaldonggwa joseon in ui mom e daehan insik gochal" [A study of Horace N. Allen's medicine and recognition of the Korean body]. *Uisahak* 20, no. 1 (2011): 291–326.

Yoo, Theodore Jun. *The Politics of Gender in Colonial Korea: Labor, Education, and Health, 1910–1945*. Berkeley: University of California Press, 2008.

Yu, Hyeong-sik. *Hanguk geundae uihak yeongusa* [Research on the history of modern Korean medicine]. Seoul: Hanguk uihakwon, 2011.

INDEX

abnormal behavior, 8–9, 56, 92–93, 113. *See also* deviant behavior
Abu-Lughod, Lila, 79
Acta Medicinalia in Keizo, 68
acupuncture, 25
Adams, Caroline B., 60
Adler, Alfred, 62
agoraphobia, 33
Akamatsu Chijō, 18
Akiba Takashi, 18
Alcmaeon, 42
alcoholism, 67, 93, 118, 151
Aleni, Julio, 42
Allen, Horace Newton, 51
alkaloid treatment, 67
aloha (a fundamental emotion among Hawaiians), 79
amae (dependency needs), 79. See also *jeong*
amorous passion, 125. *See also* suicide
An Jeong-il, 67
anatomy, 70
anger: and nervous disorders, 93
anomie, 93, 128
anthropological approaches: and emotions, 79
anti-social behavior, 56
Arirang, 106–107. *See also* Na Un-gyu
Associated Teaching Hospital of the Medical College of Keijō (Gyeongseong) Imperial University, 65–66. *See also* Keijō (Gyeongseong) Imperial University

asylums: admissions to, 73; pessimism about, 73–74
Atkins, E. Taylor, 18, 19
Australia Journal of Psychology and Philosophy, 68
autopsies, 69, 125, 146. *See also* cadavers; forensic science
Avison, Oliver, 52

bacteriology, 92
baekjeong (butcher), 90
Bak Je-ga, 42
Bak Je-sang, 33
Bak Tae-won, 92, 98, 118
Baek, Sin-ae, 97
Baker, Donald, 32
Bakhtin, Mikhail, 89
baksu (male shaman), 16. *See also* shamanism
balbyeong wonin (cause of disease), 112
balgwang (fit of madness), 73, 97, 101
balhwagwang (igniting-fires maniac), 113. *See also* pyromaniac
baljak (suddenly going crazy), 25, 37
balsaeng (trigger), 112
banyeok joein (enemy of the state), 121
barbiturates, 71
Bartholomew, James, 68
Beard, George, 118. *See also* neurasthenia
Bernheisel, Charles F., 53
Berrios, German, 8
Bian Que, 30

213

bigwan (feelings of despondency), 39, 128. *See also* despondency; suicide
Binswanger, Otto, 69
biological basis of mental illness, 7, 11, 70, 93, 110, 120; critics of, 7–8
bipolar disorder, 39
Blanchot, Maurice, 143
Bleuler, Eugen, 56, 68
blind, 24. *See also itako;* shamanism
bonyeon jiseong (original state), 82
botong saram (ordinary person), 112
brain: diseases of, 6; research on, 68–69
Bridge of Life, 4, 156n13. *See also* suicide
Buddhism, 20, 27; and mental illness, 37; suppression of, 90
Bumke, Oswald, 68
bun (feelings of anger), 122, 134
bune (filthy young woman), 90. *See also talchum*
bunno (rage), 1, 14, 39
bunsa (killing oneself because of indignation), 122. *See also* suicide
byeolsin gut (sacrificial harvest ritual), 19. *See also* shamanism
byeong (illness), 28. *See also jeung*
byeong gut (illness exorcism), 2. *See also* shamanism
byeongsa (silent-film narrator), 106
byeonsa (unnatural death), 124
Byzantine Empire, 17

cadavers, 69. *See also* autopsies; forensic science
carnival, 89. *See also* Bakhtin, Mikhail
Castel, Robert, 8
censorship. *See* Japanese colonialism
cerebrospinal fluid, 69
Chae Man-sik, 46–47
changpi (shame), 102
Charcot, Jean-Martin, 50
chemical bromides, 71
chemyeon (saving face), 40, 86, 101–103, 105–106
chenyeom (unwillingness to resolve the problem anymore), 40
cheoga sari (shame of living with financially strapped in-laws), 100

chijeong (crimes of passion), 125. *See also* crimes
chijeong gwan-gye (sexual liaison), 119
chimgupyeon (Acupuncture and moxibustion), 31. See also *Dong-ui bogam*
China Medical Journal, 68
chloral hydrates, 71
Cho Myeong-hui, 130
Cho, Samson, 85
Choe Han-gi, 42–44
Choe Nam-seon, 19
Choi, Ellie, 95
cholera, 20, 123
choraeng-i (servant), 90. *See also talchum*
Chōsen igakukai zasshi (*Joseon uihakhoe japji*). *See Chōsen Medical Association Journal*
Chōsen Medical Association Journal, 67
Chōsen sōtokufu (Government-General of Korea): and ethnographic surveys, 18; and Jesaengwon Act (Ordinance No. 77). 54–55; and home confinement, 47; and Korean customs and superstitions, 17–18
Chōsen sōtokufu iin (*Joseon chongdokbu uiwon*). *See* Government-General Hospital
Christianity: and demon possession, 17; and healing, 65; and mental illness, 146
chronic patients, 47, 70, 74; and admissions policies, 75. *See also manseong*
chukgi (drive away evil spirits from the body), 75. *See also gut;* shamanism
chulga oein (a married daughter is no longer part of her natal family), 135. *See also* Confucianism
Chung, Christopher, 85
chwibari (old bachelor or prodigal son), 90. See also *talchum*
cisterna magna puncture, 67
civilization: and emotions, 81; and madness, 74, 117–119, 140
climate and seasonal changes, 119
clinical psychiatry, 48, 69, 71; and bedside instruction, 70
congenital diseases, 74
Confucianism, 15; and chastity ideology, 122–123, 126; and emotions, 80–81, 84,

91; and hierarchy, 84, 90; and morality, 90–91; and patriarchy, 22, 34; and society, 34
contagious diseases, 123, 147. *See also* epidemic diseases; sanitation and hygiene
costs of institutionalization, 48, 72, 74
crime: and degeneracy, 74; and emotions, 104; and homicide, 111–116; and insanity, 182n15; and risk, 110; and social deviants, 111; and suicide, 110, 125; and women, 144
culture-bound ailments, 111
Cumings, Bruce, 84

Daehan uiwon (Daehan Hospital), 53, 54
daegan (post in the censorate), 37
dameun (lack of circulation of body fluids), 31–32
Dammann, Eric J., 7
Dangun, 19
Danxi xinfa (The essential methods of Danxi), 29. *See also* Zhu Danxi
Daoism, 25, 32
Darwin, Charles: and Social Darwinism, 111, 116–117
De Groot, Jan Jacob Maria, 23. *See also* peach tree branch
degeneration: and mental illness, 74, 76
Dejerine, Joseph, 62
dementia praecox, 56, 147. *See also* Kraepelin, Emil; schizophrenia
demographic change, 123
depression, 5. *See also* melancholy
despondency, 125, 135. *See also* *bigwan*; suicide
Deuchler, Martina, 84
Deutsch, Albert, 6
deviant behavior, 2, 111; pathologization of, 11
diagnosis: growing importance of, 48, 74; problems with classification systems, 9; routinization of, 8. *See also* nosology; labeling
Diagnostic and Statistical Manual of the American Psychiatric Association (DSM), 5, 6; criticism of, 9; inclusion of culture-bound syndromes, 11
Diamond, Gregory, 79

diankuang (madness), 28. *See also jeongwang*
dissociative disorders, 67
divorce: *See* family
Doerner, Klaus, 8
Dong-ui bogam (A treasury of Eastern medicine), 14, 30–32. *See also* Heo Jun
drug users, 70, 72, 130. *See also* opium
Dongpalho sil (East Ward Number Eight), 46, 55, 57–58, 60, 66, 70, 73, 112, 114. *See also* Keijō (Gyeongseong) Imperial University; Keijō Mental Ward
Durkheim, Èmile, 18, 109, 128
dyssomnia, 31

early marriage, 132. *See also* family; *minmyeoneuri*
Edwards, Jason, 174n75. *See also* Sedgwick, Eve Kosofsky
Ekman, Paul, 79. *See also* emotions
electro-convulsive therapy, 71. *See also* metrazol/cardiazol shock therapy, insulin coma therapy
Eliade, Mircea, 21
Em, Henry, 99
emasculation: and Korean men, 93
emotional communities, 81
emotional regimes, 78; in traditional Korea, 81–84. *See also* Reddy, William
emotional states, 12
emotional turn, 78–79
emotions: and civilization, 96; and culture, 79; history of, 78–81; in Korean fiction, 94–104; marketing of, 92–94; modern, 125;
England: and nineteenth-century asylums, 42–44
Engstrom, Eric, 69, 169n102
eogul (feelings of unfairness or victimization), 39, 88, 89, 122, 134
Eoui chwaryobang (Concise prescriptions of royal doctors), 30
epidemic diseases: and campaigns, 147. *See also* police
epilepsy, 31, 132, 144
Ernst, Waltraud, 9
Esquirol, Jean-Etienne, 124. *See also* suicide
etiology: and mental illness, 110, 147

eugenics, 116–117. *See also* Social Darwinism
Eustace, Nicole, 80, 94
everyday life, 143. *See also* Blanchot, Maurice
evil spirits, 22–24, 44; See also *gut;* shamanism
exhibitionists, 93, 145
Eysenck, Hans, 7

family: and care of the mentally ill, 139–139, 140; and divorce, 134–135; and despotic mother-in-laws, 132; and infidelity, 134; marital discord, 134; and tradition, 132–134; and tyrannical father-in-laws and husbands, 133. *See also* early marriage; *gobu galdeung, minmyeoneuri*
Fanon, Frantz, 9
feeble-minded, 74
feeling: as symptom, 92–94
fengdian (madness), 28. See also *pungjeon*
fengkuang (madness), 28. See also *punggwang*
fever treatment: *See* malaria treatment
five cardinal intents, 27. *See also* Traditional Chinese Medicine (TCM)
five vicera, 27. *See also* Traditional Chinese Medicine (TCM)
folk culture: and beliefs, 11; as emotional refuge, 89–91; *See also* emotions, *hwabyeong,* madness
forensic science, 148. *See also* autopsies, cadavers
Foucault, Michel: and abnormality, 142; and antipsychiatry, 8; biopower, 12, 123; madness and civilization, 42
Four-Seven Debate, 82; *See also* emotions
Freud, Sigmund, 62
frigid. *See* hysteria
front. *See* Goffman, Erving

Gabo Reforms, 96, 132
Gaebyeok (Dawn of History), 86
gaeseong (individualism), 82
gageum (confinement), 101
gajeong gamchi (home confinement), 74
gaksi (bride), 90. See also *talchum*
Galen, 42

gambling, 93
gamho (care and custody), 112, 139
gamsi (surveillance), 113
Ge Hong, 163n74
Geertz, Clifford, 79, 88
genetic disease and mental disorders, 93, 116, 117. *See also* hereditary disease
German medical language proficiency, 66–67
German psychiatry, 48, 71; and biological approach, 60. *See also* Kraepelin, Emil
germs, 92
ghosts and spirits, 18, 21. *See also* shamanism
gidam (bizarre stories), 142
Gilman, Charlotte Perkins, 104
gisaeng (geisha), 136
Gobong Gi Dae-seung, 82–83. *See also* Four-Seven Debate
gobu galdeung (daughter-in-law and mother-in-law conflict), 133
Goffman, Erving, 1, 7, 77, 86
Gojong (twenty-sixth king of Joseon), 33, 51
Gojoseon (Old Joseon), 19
Gong Xie Pai (Attack and Drain School), 163n74. *See also* Zhang Congzheng; Zhang Zhongjin
gongpo (fright), 39
gopuri (disentangle the grudge), 22. See also *gut*
Goryeo dynasty, 28, 30
gosaeng (hardship), 39
gosu (drummer), 89. See also *pansori*
Government-General Civil Code (Ordinance No. 13), 132
Government-General Hospital, 44, 48; and Attached Training School (*busok uihak gangseupso*), 54. *See also* Associated Teaching Hospital of the Medical College of Keijō
Great Ming Code, 35
Griesinger, Wilhelm, 7, 68
Gubo the novelist, 93, 118. *See also* Bak Taewon
gugeum (custody), 113
gut (exorcism), 19, 20–27, 137. *See also* shamanism
gwangdae (singer), 89. See also *pansori*

Gwangdong byeolgok (Song of Gwangdong), 36. *See also* Jeong Cheol
Gwanghae-gun (fifteenth king of Joseon), 38, 40
Gwanghyewon (Royal Hospital), 51. *See also* Jejungwon
gwang-in (mad person), 98, 112
gwangjeung (madness), 37
Gwangjewon (House of Extended Deliverance), 52–53
gwangpokseong (smoldering sensation of fury), 112
gwangtae (lunatic behavior), 24
gwonseon jinak (encouraging good and punishing evil), 82
gyeokwa (fire between the chest and abdomen), 40
Gyeonggi Province and shamans, 24. *See also* shamanism
Gyeongguk daejon (National Code), 34
gyeongni (isolation), 112
Gyeongseong (Keijō), 91, 93; and Industrial Exhibition (Gyeonseong gongjin hoe), 173n66
Gyeongseong uihak jeonmun hakgyo. *See* Keijō Imperial University

Haboush, Jahyun, 39
hacheungmin (underclass), 149
Hacking, Ian, 142
hagyeon (ties to school and learning), 84
han (resentment), 12, 15, 40, 44, 78, 87–89, 105–106, 107–108
Han River Footbridge, 93, 126
hanafuda (flower card game), 46. *See also hwatu*
hanpuri (expressing one's *han*), 22. *See also han*
Hara Shinsho, 67
Harvey, William, 42
hasoyeon (appealing for sympathy), 86, 88, 100
Hattori Rokuburo, 67
Heo Gyun, 90
Heo Jun, 14, 31–32. *See also Dong-ui Bogam*
heoyak (mentally feeble), 100, 147
hereditary disease, 74, 116; and insanity, 92
hidden scripts, 94

Hikari Shingo, 67
Hippocrates, 42
history: and emotions, 79–80. *See also* emotions
Hochschild, Arlie R., 77, 106
hōigakubu (medical jurisprudence division), 148
Hokkaidō: and mental illness, 73
homosexuality, 93
Hong Man-seon, 23
Hong Sun-hyang, 33
Hongmungwan (Office of the special counselors), 37
Horowitz, Allan, 8
hospitalization costs, 146. *See also* institutionalization
hucheonjeok (acquired or external), 117
Hunter, S. A., 68
hwa (anger), 12, 39
hwabyeong (fire illness), 1, 2, 11, 15, 39, 40, 89
hwajeon (fire ritual), 21. *See also gut;* shamanism
hwajeung (fire-rage), 40
Hwangdi Neijing (Inner Canon of the Yellow Emperor), 14, 28, 29, 31, 32. *See also Hwangje naegyeong*
Hwangje naegyeong. See Hwangdi Neijing
hwapuri (an aggressive burst of anger), 40.
hwarang, 33
hwatu. See hanafuda
Hyangyak gugeupbang (First aid prescriptions using native ingredients), 30
Hyangyak jipseonbang (Great collection of native Korean prescriptions), 302
Hyegyeong, Lady (widow of Prince Sado), 39–41
Hyeon Jin-geon, 77, 98, 99–103, 104–105, 136, 170n2
Hyeondeok (forty-first king of the Silla dynasty), 33
Hyeongsa panryejip simnirok (Criminal case studies, trial documents for the king), 122
Hyeonjong (eighteenth king of the Joseon dynasty), 34
hyeonmo yancheo (wise mother, good wife), 22. *See also* Confucianism
hyeoryeon (blood-kinship ties), 84

hyo (filial piety), 36. *See also* Confucianism
hypochondriac, 52
hysteria, 12, 52, 67, 111, 119–120

i (will), 81
illyun (moral imperatives), 34. *See also* Confucianism
ilsang ui gonggan (everyday spaces), 92
imae (village idiot), 90. *See also talchum*
imbeciles, 116–117. *See also* Social Darwinism
Imjin waeran (Japanese invasions of Korea), 38
impulsive behavior, 93
indari (human bridge), 20. *See also* shamanism
Infectious Disease Prevention Act, 149, 173n66. *See also* sanitation and hygiene
inhyeong-guk (puppet shows), 89. *See also* folk culture
Injo (sixteenth king of the Joseon dynasty), 35, 36
inpatient treatment, 57, 70, 147. *See also* outpatient treatment
insanity: and global statistics, 112
insomnia, 31
institutionalization, 48, 72, 93, 112; and family consent, 147
insulin coma therapy, 71. *See also* electroconvulsive therapy, metrazol/cardiazol shock therapy
intellectuals: and madness, 94–99, 128. *See also* Japanese colonialism
Ireland, 9
isang (abnormal): *See* abnormal behavior
Isen, Alice, 79
itako (Japanese blind shaman), 24. *See also* blind; shamanism

jaebal (relapse), 115
jagyeol (individual suicide), 121. *See also* suicide
jahye uiwon (provincial charity hospital), 72
Jangchundan Park: and suicide, 93
jangma (monsoon season): and madness, 118
Japan: and mental illness, 112; Mental Hospital Act, 50; Mental Patients' Custody Act, 49, 50; Penal Code, 49

Japan Society of Neurology and Psychiatry, 50, 68
Japanese colonialism, 91, 94, 110, 143; and collective emotional suffering, 106–197
Japanese psychiatry: in Korea, 54–59; German-style biological approach, 60
Japbyeong pyeon (miscellaneous diseases), 31. *See also Dong-ui bogam*
japgi (literary miscellany), 36
Jaspers, Karl, 68
jayeon suneung (relationship with nature), 28
Jejungwon (House of Universal Relief), 51
jeom (fortune teller reading), 21. *See also* shamanism
Jeon Bong-gwan, 142–143
jeong (emotional attachment), 12, 40, 78, 81–82, 84–85, 92, 100–101, 103, 105–106, 108, 172n37. *See also* emotions
Jeong Chang-gwon, 10
Jeong Cheol, 36
Jeong Yak-yong, 42
Jeongjo (twenty-second king of the Joseon dynasty), 122
jeongsa (amorous love suicide), 135
jeongsang (normal), 116
jeongsin (spirit/vitality), 28. *See also jingshen*
jeongsin byeong (mental illness), 100, 115, 145, 151
jeongsin isang (mental disorders), 46, 113, 143
jeongsin jilhwan (mental disease), 145
jeongsin soran (mental disturbance) 126
jeongwang (madness), 28. 31–32. *See also diankuang*
jeonjil (madness), 36
Jesaengwon (Social welfare institute), 54, 55. *See also* Saiseiin
jeung (illness), 29. *See also byeong*
jeungsang (symptoms), 223
ji (knowledge), 81
jinglo (meridians), 27. *See also* Traditional Chinese Medicine
jingshen (spirit/vitality), 28. *See also jeongsin*
jiral (insane fit), 101
jiyeon (regional and hometown ties), 84
Jo Maeng-je, 3

jobal chimae (early dementia praecox), 46. See also dementia praecox
joechaekgam (feelings of guilt), 39
jogwangseong (mania), 74
Jones, George Herber, 19
Joseon dynasty, 28, 37; and madness, 15
Joseon wangjo sillok (Annals of the Joseon Kings, The), 22
Joseon uibo (*Korean Medical Journal, The*), 68
Journal of Medical College in Keijō, The, 68
jugwang (alcohol crazy). See also alcoholic
jung (monk), 90. See also *talchum*
Jungjong (eleventh king of the Joseon dynasty), 37
jusuljeol chiryo (charm away the illness), 22. See also *gut;* shamanism

Karenina, Anna, 95
Karufuto (Sakhalin): and mental illness, 73
Keijō (Gyeongseong) Imperial University, 18; and Medical College and Hospital, 46–47, 48, 50, 65–71, 73, 76, 119–120, 127, 135, 138, 145, 148, 151, 152
Keijō (Gyeongseong) Mental Ward, 66. See also Dongpalho sil; Keijō Imperial University
Keio University, 96
Keizo Journal of Medicine, The, 68
Keller, Richard, 9
Kennogwan, 71, 92. See also medicine; placebo pills, pharmacology, psychotropic drug
Kim Dong-in, 133
Kim Gi-jin, 136
Kim Gi-rim, 109, 126
Kim Gwang-il, 10, 22, 158n44
Kim, Hoi-eun, 168n77
Kim, Hŭng-gyu, 89, 90, 91
Kim, Soonsik, 96
Kim, Young-Ha, 4–5
Kinnosuke Miura, 50
Kitamura Yojin, 67
Kitanaka, Junko, 123
Kleinman, Arthur, 9–10
kleptomania, 93, 145
klinik (clinic), 66, 69
Koch, Robert, 92

Korea Mission Field, The, 68
Korean Traditional Medicine, 30–32
Kraepelin, Emil, 7, 14; and clinical method of diagnosis, 50; and nosology, 70, 76
kuang (madness), 28–29. See *Hwangdi Neijing*
Kubo Kiyoshi, 66, 67, 68
kuchiyose (spirit talk), 24
Kudō Takeki, 144. See also crime
Kultur (civilization and culture), 93
Kure Shūzō, 50, 55, 68
kymographion, 69

labeling: and madness, 6, 8, 12, 110, 147. See also nosology
laboratory research, 48
Laing, R. D., 7
Landis, Eli Bar, 19, 161n34
Lean, Eugenia, 80
Lee, Ho Young, 67
Lee, Peter, 90
Lehman, Heintz, 7
leprosy (Hansen's disease), 51, 55, 132, 144, 150, 176n34; and asylums, 8, 47, 71
li (principle), 82. See also Confucianism
Li Chan, 29. See also *Yixue rumen*
Li Dongyuan, 29. See also *Piwei lun*
Li Gao, 31
Lie, John, 173n54
liget (a fundamental emotion among the Ilongot tribe), 79
Linshu (spiritual pivot), 28. See also *Huangdi neijing*
literature: and emotions, 81–82
Liu Wansu, 31, 163n75
longitudinal study, 70. See also Kraepelin, Emil
Longobardi, Nicole, 42
looping effect, 142, 151. See also Hacking, Ian
lumbar puncture, 70
luminal (barbiturates), 67
lunatics, 73
Lutz, Catherine, 79

madang theater, 89. See also folk culture
madness: history of, 6–10; as a social epidemic, 109–141; during the Joseon

madness *(continued)*
　　period, 145–156; and modernization, 13; as a palimpsest, 10–11; and the supernatural, 145. *See also* mental illness
ma-eum (state of mind), 84–85, 86, 89, 102, 105
malaria treatment, 67, 71
Malinowski, Bronislaw, 18
mania. *See jogwangseong*
Manjirō Sugihara, 67, 68
Man-sen no ikai (Manchuria-Korea Medical World, The), 68
manseong (chronicity), 58, 131, 147. *See also* chronic patients
March First Movement, 97, 128; and print culture, 110
marriage and suicide, 121. *See also* family; suicide
Marsh, Ian, 140–141
Matsumoto, David, 87
Matsuzawa Hospital, 56. *See also* Kure Shūzō; Tokyo Metropolitan Sugamo Hospital
Maudsley, Henry, 68
Mauss, Marcel, 18
McLaren, Charles Inglis, 10, 42, 59–65, 68, 75–76; and spiritual treatment, 61
medical chemistry, 70
medical gaze, 123
medicine. *See* pharmaceuticals; placebo pills, psychotropic drugs
melancholy, 119. *See also* depression; *senchimental*
Mencius, 83. *See also* Confucianism
menopause, 120
mental health care: public perceptions, 137–139, 140
mental illness: and absence of legislation, 3; and care, 111; and children, 118; and climate/seasonal change, 118; and coercive treatments, 8; and confinement, 8, 11, 111; and criminalization, 111, 115; and culture-bound syndromes, 10; and demedicalization, 7; as a disease of civilization, 73; and diagnosis of, 110–111; explanations of, 116–121; and homicide, 111–113; and immorality, 119; and Mental Health Act, 2–3; and Mental Practice Act, 2; as a national problem, 3; and nerves, 92; and sexuality, 119–120; and social contexts, 9; and somatization, 10, 11, 15, 30; South Korean concern with, 2–6; and statistics, 72, 73; and symptoms, 110–111; and workplace discrimination, 3. *See also* labeling; madness
mental hospital: as a therapeutic or custodial institution, 71–75
metrazol/cardiazol shock therapy, 8, 71. *See also* electro-convulsive therapy; insulin coma therapy
michin nom (crazy man), 101
michin yeoja (crazy woman), 110, 113, 146
microbiology, 70
Min Seong-gil, 10, 158n44
mind doctors: *See* psychiatrists
minmyeoneuri, 132. *See also* early marriage; family
minyo (folk songs), 89. *See also* folk culture
misin tapa (eradicating superstition), 148
Mitchell, Silas Weir, 69
Mitsukoshi Department Store, 99
Mitteilungen aus der Medizinischen Akademie zu Keijo (Messages from the medical academy to Keijō), 68
mium (hate), 39
miyalhalmi (old widow), 90. See also *talchum*
modernity: and civilization, 94, 140; and suicide, 121
Mohirarin (mozarin), 71
mojeong (mother-infant *jeong*), 85. See also *jeong*
morbid heredity, 117. *See also* Social Darwinism
Morita (Masatake) Shoma, 68. *See also* Morita therapy method
mortality and morbidity, 93
moyok (feeling insulted), 39
mudang (shaman). *See* shamanism
mugiryeok (helplessness), 39
mugu (shaman's tool), 23. *See also* shamanism
Mugwannang, 33
mujeong (heartless), 85, 95
munyeo (female shaman). *See* shamanism

Murayama Chijun, 14, 18, 22–26
musok (shamanism): *See* shamanism

Na Do-hyang, 130, 136
Na Un-gyu, 106. See also *Arirang*
Naegyeongpyeon (Internal landscape of the human body), 31. See also *Dong-ui bogam*
naerim gut (initiation rite), 21. See *gut*, shamanism
naichi (metropole), 95. See also *gaichi*
Nakamura, Karen, 9, 157n35
nam (other/out-groups), 85
Namdaemun (Gate of the Exalted Ceremonies): *See* Sungnyemun
nanchi (incurable illness), 132
Nanyang: and mental illness, 73
narcissism, 93
neurasthenia, 58, 62, 64, 67, 75, 75, 110, 118, 120; as an urban scourge, 122. See also Beard, George
neurological disorder, 121
neurology, 66
neuropsychiatry, 66
neurosis, 93
neurotic, 12, 62
New, Esmond W., 61, 65. See also McLaren, Charles Inglis
Nissl, Franz, 50
Nok-jin, 33
nongak (traditional farmers' music), 89. See also folk culture
normalization. *See* labeling
North Chungcheon Province: and shamans, 23. See also shamanism
North Gyeongsang Province: and shamans, 25. See also shamanism
North Pyeongan Province: and shamans, 25. See also shamanism
nosology. *See* labeling, Kraepelin, Emil
nunchi (tact), 12, 40, 78, 86–87, 101–103, 106

Oak, Sung Deuk, 19–20, 26, 53–54
Oehyeongpyeon (External appearances), 31. See also *Dong-ui bogam*
Oh, Mi-sook, 2
Okchugyeong (Daoist text), 25

ondol (heated-floor), 23
opium. *See* drug users
organ theft, 147
Organisation for Economic Co-operation and Development (OECD): and mental health, 2, 3; and hospitalization, 3
Outpatient treatment, 57, 147. See also inpatient treatment

paega mangsin (damaging the reputation of the family), 88
paeseol (scribblings), 36
palja (fate), 87
pansori (epic song), 89–90, 123. See also folk culture
Pantoja, Diego, 42
paranoia, 33, 110
Pasteur, Louis, 92
pathology, 71
patients: and privacy laws, 112
peach tree branch, 14, 23, 25. See also shamanism
pedagogy research, 49, 70. See also Keijō (Gyeongseong) Imperial University
peritraumatic distress, 33
pharmacology, 71: and advertisement, 147. See also *Kennogwan,* medicine; placebo pills, psychotropic drugs
physiology, 70
Pies, Ronald, 157n35
Piwei lun (Treatise on the spleen and stomach), 29. See also Li Dongyuan
placebo pills, 71. See also *Kennogwan,* medicine, pharmacology, psychotropic drugs
Plamper, Jan, 80
police, 18, 107, 111, 118, 123, 126, 137, 140, 143–153, 182n5; and epidemic prevention campaigns, 92; and hygiene, 149; and sanitation, 26;
Polyani, Karl, 129–130
postpartum depression: and mental illness, 120–121
Post-Traumatic Stress Disorder (PTSD), 39
poverty, 93: and suicide, 123, 131
ppuri (hereditary transmission), 20. See also shamanism
premature ejaculation, 31

press: and sensational yellow journalism, 178n89
preventive medicine, 71
professional psychiatric journals, 48
psychiatrists, 93
psychiatry: American, 9, 70; British, 9, 70; and colonialism, 9; continental, 9; and discrimination, 51; and mental disorders, 110–111; and mental hygiene, 93; and university medical curriculum, 65
psychopath, 145
psychopathology, 9, 39
psychotherapy, 33
psychotic disorder, 33
public health, 93, 149, 182n5
pudakgeori (scapegoat concept), 22. See also *gut*, shamanism
punggwang (madness), 28. See also *fengkuang*
pungjeon (madness), 28. See also *fengdian*
Pyeheo (Ruins), 96
Pyeongan Province: and shamans, 24
Pyeongyang, 118
pyromania, 113, 145

qi (vital energy), 15, 27, 83
Qi Bo, 28. See also *Hwangdi neijing*
quantification projects, 48
quarantine and vaccination campaigns, 149. See also epidemic diseases, police
Quetelet, Adolphe, 124

Radcliffe-Brown, Alfred, 18
recidivism, 116
Reddy, William, 78, 80, 87, 89. See also emotional regimes
rehabilitation: and mental illness, 48, 93
Rhi, Bou-Yong. See Yi Bu-yeong
Ricci, Matteo, 42
Ringer's solution, 67
Rosaldo, Michelle Z., 79
Rosenwein, Barbara, 80
Rothman, David, 8
rumpen (unemployed intellectuals), 128
rural-urban migration, 92; and industrialization, 128. See also Japanese colonialism

ryūgaku (study abroad), 67, 68, 95, 168n77. See also *yuhak*

sadaebu (literati), 38
Sadaham, 33
Sado (prince, heir of King Yeongjo), 38, 40–41
Sadowsky, Jonathan, 9
saenghwalgo (hardship of life), 105, 123, 128
Saiseiin. See Jesaengwon
Sajik Park: and suicides, 93
Salpêtrière, 10
salpuri (acts to drive out or strike out an evil spirit), 21, 40. See also shamanism
Sambiaso, Francesco, 42
Samguk sagi (History of the Three Kingdoms), 27, 33
samjong jido (three rules for women), 22. See also Confucianism
sanitation and hygiene: department of, 74, 123, 148–149, 182n5. See also epidemic diseases; police
sanjiao (body cavities), 27. See also Traditional Chinese Medicine
sashiko (makeshift cages), 49
Schall von Bell, Johann Adam, 42
Scheper-Hughes, Nancy, 9. See also Ireland
schizophrenia, 39, 67. See also dementia praecox; Kraepelin, Emil
scopolamine, 67
Scull, Andrew, 8, 17
Sedwick, Eve Kosofsky: and male homosocial desire, 174n76
Sejo (seventh king of the Joseon dynasty), 36
senchimental (sentimental), 119. See also melancholy
Seodaemun Prison, 47
Seon Jin-tae, 19
seonbi (scholar), 90. See also *talchum*
seoncheonjeok (innate), 116
Seong Hyeon, 24, 36. See also *Yongjae chonghwa*
Seonjo (fourteenth king of the Joseon dynasty), 30
Seonjong (ninth king of the Joseon dynasty), 24
Severance, Louis H., 53

Severance Union Medical College and Hospital, 10, 11, 48, 53, 59–66. *See also* McLaren, Charles Inglis

sexual freedom and desires: and suicide, 35. *See also* Werther effect

shamanism: and Christianity, 17, 19–20, 26; and Confucianism, 15–17, 21–22; and exorcism, 58, 75, 137; Japanese ethnographers, 17–19; and mental disorders, 23; and *mudang*, 16, 17, 21, 26, 146, 150; and *munyeo*, 25; and spirit possession, 16, 20, 26, 182n5; and the supernatural, 145. *See also* Akamatsu Chijō; Akiba Takashi; Murayama Chijun; *musok*

shame, 2, 99, 145

Shang Han Lun (On cold damage), 29. *See also* Zhang Zhongjin

shengui (spirits), 29

shimpa (melodrama), 106

Shorter, Edward, 7

siagwi (Buddhist rite offering food to hungry ghosts), 126

sijong (post in the Censorate), 37

silhak (practical studies), 23, 42

siljeong (depression from losing one's wealth), 31

Silla dynasty, 33

Sim Ho-seop, 55, 67

simdeukjil (illness of the heart), 40

simjeong (heart and feelings), 85–86, 88, 100, 101, 106–107

simjil (anxiety), 38

sin (ethereal spirit), 31. See also *Dong-ui bogam*

sinbyeong (initiation sickness), 17, 20, 41, 42, 146. *See also* shamanism

sin-gyeong (nerves), 142

sin-gyeongjil (nervousness), 39

sin-gyeongsoeyak (neurasthenia). *See* neurasthania

six atmospheric forces, 27. *See also* Traditional Chinese Medicine

six fu organs, 27. *See also* Traditional Chinese Medicine

smallpox, 116. *See also* epidemic diseases

Smallside, London, 43

Snow, John, 92

social constructivists. *See* emotions

social face: *See* Goffman, Erving

social misfits, 116

social pathology, 92–93

social prophylaxis, 74, 169n102. *See also* Engstrom, Eric

society: and well-being, 123, 140; and security, 123

sociology: mental illness, 8–9; and emotions, 79

sodium hydroxide: and suicide, 125

soft therapeutic programs, 56

Sontag, Susan, 1

Sorok-do sanitarium. *See* leprosy

South Jeolla Province: and shamans, 19

sphygmograph, 69

Spitzer, Robert, 7

Starwell, Richard, 59. *See also* McLaren, Charles Inglis

Statistics: and insanity, 93, 112; and suicide, 121, 123–124, 135

Staub, Michael, 118

Stearns, Carol Z., 80

Stearns, Peter N., 80

Stigma, 1, 2, 48, 93; and hospitalization, 139

St. Vitrus Dance (chorea minor), 63, 67

suchi (shame), 12

suicide, 93, 114, 121–137, 141; copycat, 135; and social stressors, 12; as a social phenomenon, 124; in contemporary South Korea, 3–5; in traditional Korea, 121–123. *See also* Werther effect

Suitsu Shinji, 50, 55

Sukjong (nineteenth king of the Joseon dynasty), 35, 40

sulfuric acid treatment, 67–68

sulga (conjurer), 24. *See also* shamanism

suljari (drinking party), 85, 100

Sun Simiao, 163n75

Sungnyemun, 1. *See* Namdaemun

superstition, 17, 26. See also *misin tapa*

Suwen (Basic Questions), 14, 28. See also *Hwangdi Neijing*

Suzuki, Akihito, 50

syphilis, 51, 74, 118, 119, 147; treatments for, 69

Szasz, Thomas, 7–8, 157n35

taedium vitae, 93, 125. See also *yeomsejuui*

Taiwan: and mental illness, 73
talchum (mask dance), 89–90, 123. *See also* folk culture
Tangaekpyeon (Herbal concoctions), 31. *See also Dong-ui bogam*
taryeong (depression caused by demotion), 31
Three Kingdoms Period, 27
Toegye Yi Hwang, 82–83. *See also* Four-Seven Debate
Tōkanfu (Residency-General), 53
Tokyo Imperial University, 118
Tokyo Metropolitan Sugamo Hospital. *See* Matsuzawa Hospital
Tolstoy, Leo: and realism, 81–82
Tomes, Nancy, 92
torticollis, 67
Traditional Chinese Medicine (TCM), 10–11, 15, 27–30, 75, 146
trepanation, 16
Tu Wei-ming, 84
tuberculosis, 92, 132, 147. *See also* Infectious Disease Prevention Act; sanitation and hygiene; urban scourges
typhoid fever, 199. *See also* Infectious Disease Prevention Act; sanitation and hygiene

ubuntu (human kindness), 84
Ugye Seong Hon, 82. *See also* Four-Seven Debate
uisim (suspicion), 39
uiwon-in (doctors), 25
ujeong (friend's attachment), 100
ulhwa (accumulated stress in social life), 122
Underwood, Horace G., 19
unemployment, 93
unrequited love: and suicide, 125
urban scourges, 92, 147. *See also* Infectious Disease Prevention Act; sanitation and hygiene; tuberculosis
uri (we) 40, 84, 85–86, 92, 103. *See also* emotions
u-ulhan simjeong (depressed state of mind), 97

vagabonds, 93
vagrancy, 118

VanBuskirk, J. D., 59, 64
venereal disease. *See* syphilis
vernacular fiction, 89–90. *See also* folk culture
verschamte manie, 67
Vesalius, Andreas, 42

Wagner-Jauregg, Julius, 62
Walraven, Boudewijn, 20
wankwae (never get fully healed), 117
Wasserman reaction, 67
weapons of the weak, 104, 132
Weimar Republic: and suicides, 124
Werther effect, 135, 181n161
Willis, Thomas, 42
women and madness: in literature, 103–106
World Health Organization: and mental health, 2

xiaofa (purgative therapies), 29. *See also* Shan Han Lun; Zhang Zongjin

yadam (unofficial histories), 89–90. *See also* folk culture
yang, 23
Yang Yonghe, 163n74
yangban (literati class), 19, 34, 90
yangming (yang brilliance), 29
yangqi (yang inversion), 28
yangsaeng (nurturing life), 32. *See also* Daoism
yeollyeo-jeon (state canonization of widows who committed suicide), 122
Yeom Sang-seop, 96–99, 130–131, 136
yeomsejuui (taedium vitae). *See* taedium vitae
Yeongjo (twenty-first king of the Joseon dynasty), 38, 40
Yeonsan-gun (tenth king of the Joseon dynasty), 38–40
Yi Bu-yeong, 10, 22, 33, 54, 66, 71, 158n44. *See also* Rhi, Bou-Yong
Yi Gwang-su, 81–83, 94–95, 98
Yi Gyu-gyeong, 42
Yi Ik, 42
Yi Jema, 164n111
Yi Jung-cheol, 63, 67
Yi Jung-ho, 70

Yi Neung-hwa, 19
Yi Pil-hwa, 54
Yi Sang, 98–99
Yi Su-yeong, 10
Yi Tae-jun, 98
Yi Teuk, 5
Yi Wan-yong, 107
yin, 24
Yixue rumen (Introduction to medical learning), 29. *See also* Li Chan
yongchitang (dragon-teeth broth), 33
Yongjae chonghwa (Associated writings of Yongjae). *See* Seong Hyeon

Yu Hui-chun, 16
yuchijang (detention house), 149. *See also* police
yuhak. See *ryūgaku*
Yulgok Yi I, 82. *See also* Four-Seven Debate

Zhang Congzheng, 14, 31, 163n74
Zhang Jinyue, 163n74
Zhang Zhongjin, 29, 163n74. See also *Shan Han Lun*
Zhu Danxi, 29. See also *Danxi xinfa*
Zhu Xi, 82. *See also* Confucianism
Zhu Zhenheng, 31